SO FAR,
SO GOOD

SO FAR,
SO GOOD

A Memoir

BURGESS MEREDITH

LITTLE, BROWN AND COMPANY

BOSTON   NEW YORK   TORONTO   LONDON

First Edition

Quotations on pages 205–206: Copyright © 1962, 1990
by James Thurber Literary Estate. From *A Thurber
Carnival*, published by Samuel French, Inc.

Excerpt from "September Song" by Maxwell Anderson
and Kurt Weill. Copyright © 1938 (Renewed 1966) by
Tro-Hampshire House Publishing Corp. and Chappell and
Co. By permission of Warner/Chappell Music, Inc.

Library of Congress Cataloging-in-Publication Data

Meredith, Burgess
    So far, so good / by Burgess Meredith. — 1st ed.
        p.   cm.
    Includes index.
    ISBN 0-316-56717-5
    1. Meredith, Burgess, 1909–   . 2. Actors — United States —
Biography.   3. Theatrical producers and directors — United States —
Biography. I. Title.
PN2287.M615A3   1993
792'.028'092 — dc20
[B]   93-5314

10 9 8 7 6 5 4 3 2 1

MV-NY

*Published simultaneously in Canada
by Little, Brown and Company (Canada) Limited*

Printed in the United States of America

To Kaja, for meeting me at the crossroads,
and for bringing me Jonathon and Tala

Contents

SO FAR,
SO GOOD

First Night
1935

W HY WAS I so ungodly nervous on that afternoon over a half century ago? To be precise, it was September 25, 1935, in my apartment on Manhattan's East Side. I was roused from a restless nap as a series of volcanic colors exploded inside my head.

Lord knows, I shouldn't have been this much on edge. An awful lot of Impressively Serious People were announcing that I was an honest-to-God star. At twenty-four! Two years before, my very first leading role on the Broadway stage had brought me the kind of notices that are most often just the stuff of a young actor's dreams. Critic Ben Washer had written, "Burgess Meredith, in reality a Broadway newcomer, has walked onto the stage in the principal role in *Little Ol' Boy* and stood his amazingly difficult ground with . . . a performance that for canniness of characterization and the sheerest nth degree of perfection, is astounding!"

The *New Yorker* critic, Robert Benchley, noted, "I had to consult the back of the program to find out who Burgess Meredith was although I do not expect to forget him again."

Even that Broadway colossus Walter Winchell pontificated: "The role of Red Barry [in *Little Ol' Boy*] skillfully performed by Burgess Meredith is typically James Cagney. Perhaps Cagney will be seen in the same role one day when it comes from the Hollywood studios, but Meredith needs no tutoring from Cagney and it will be a crime to assign that part to anyone but Meredith."

And, to add the finishing touch to the dreams of any actor — young or old — my performance in that 1933 play was singled out in the Associated Press poll of New York drama critics as among the year's best. O. O. McIntyre wrote, "[*Little Ol' Boy*] reveals Burgess Meredith as the most thrilling young actor of his day."

So why did I feel that someone was jumping up and down on my chest?

I fought my way out of bed and fell on the floor. I heard singing — a man singing. From far off. The door opened and there stood my friend and roommate, the seventy-year-old veteran actor Richard Bennett.

"Awake and sing!" roared Dick. "The hour has come! *Winterset* opens tonight!"

"Oh Lord," I whispered. "What time is it?"

"Get up, goddammit!" said Dick.

To my credit, I did get up. It is to the credit of all actors who get up on such occasions. I sat on the edge of my bed and rolled my head into place. I stood up and stretched — there was a crackling noise.

I tried to talk; I was as hoarse as a cricket.

I made testing noises and hummed a few tuneless notes. My voice sounded like the crumpling of cellophane. This was the end — the final stab. My voice had deserted me!

"Move your ass!" shouted Dick. "Let's get going!"

I wiped my face, started to dress, and in a grunting voice recited lines of the play — a line for a shirt, a line for a sock, lines for a tie, shoes, pants, and so on.

I looked at the clock. Half past six! In one hour and thirty minutes I would be on the block at the Martin Beck Theatre before twelve hundred executioners.

"I'm nervous," I said.

"If you're nervous," Dick answered, "forget it — you'll feel worse at seventy."

"Thanks," I said. "I'll remember that."

When we got down to the street, I grabbed Bennett's arm. "Dick, don't drive! Let's take a cab — will you? Don't drive! Will you please? Not drive! In this traffic? Will you not?"

Said Bennett, "My boy, why spend seventy-five cents when we have a car?"

"I'll pay it, Dick! I'll pay it ten times."

"It takes my mind off this damn play to drive."

And we were off, rushing at a mighty Bennett pace. We passed cars at peculiar angles, accompanied always by Bennett's unending blasphemy. His language was fine gargantuan stuff, and it frightened men and angels, but it didn't move a small, city-owned emergency trailer, which we sideswiped and dragged twenty feet to the corner of Seventh Avenue near 53rd Street. I am not exaggerating; those are the facts.

The damage to our car was negligible — a door and a fender — but I think Mayor La Guardia, wherever he is, must still be looking for that trailer.

The effect on me was curious. I began to cough. I closed my eyes and missed much of the race that followed.

"Evening, Mr. Bennett," said the stage doorman, "Your car's in bad shape, ain't it?" I paused and made a wish — an actor grabs at superstitions like a drowning man grabs at a spar — that things would go better than they had so far that day.

"Here you are, Mr. Meredith." I was handed a fistful of telegrams. To myself I thought: *More than last time, kid, more than last time.*

I went through the various processes — making up, sniffing smelling salts, getting into costume, getting into character. By the time "First Act" was called, I had collected a large part of my senses.

Vague faces rushed by me. I wished them good luck. I kissed Margo, my leading lady, who played my love. I prayed, shivered, tuned myself up. I walked down to Bennett's room and shook his hand silently . . . and the curtain rose!

In the infinite darkness offstage I waited for my entrance cue. I reached down to touch the floor without bending my knees. I couldn't.

Stagehands pushed me aside and the scenes changed. And changed again. Then, at the proper cue, I walked on stage and began to be someone else.

In my small shelter under the bridge I spoke blank-verse love to Margo.

". . . *if I owned a dream — yes, half a dream — we'd share it."*

A chill settled on my supposedly hot words and afflicted the audience with bronchitis. It became a race between me and a kind of mass whooping cough. My shoulders began to ache, my mouth was parched, a curious alienation settled on me. Despite being center stage, I couldn't focus. My mind wandered to a thousand lands. Why had we driven over? Why was I not inspired? All the while I pumped out lines that had once seemed so full in rehearsal and now seemed so empty. The coughing and wheezing in the audience increased. I stopped and looked helplessly out front. Like white crosses on an ancient battlefield, the audience stared back.

I managed a few more lines . . . and then Margo spoke.

Her voice was clear, her eyes fiery. I was ashamed of myself. Reaching deep down inside me, I started to function.

". . . *take defeat, implacable and defiant, die unsubmitting."* This quotation is on the flyleaf of my copy of *Winterset,* in the handwriting of its playwright, Maxwell Anderson. I am grateful, because I know what terrors I must have given him during those opening moments of the first night.

Things got better as the evening went on. When I made my entrance in the second act to face Dick, I felt triumphant . . . until he began to speak. He sounded low and tentative. I heated up my feelings, my lines. His fingers fumbled in front of his mouth, there was perspiration on his forehead. But then he found the pace, the rhythm, the center of meaning. In one giddy moment he stopped again and we were stretched on the rack of a long, unused pause. But he went on. Each word stronger, calmer, more certain . . . until we found a reality we had never found before. We lost ourselves in the excitement, the discovery. It was a redemptive moment, and that doesn't happen often.

Before the final curtain, the old rabbi spoke final words over my body. I tried not to move, to breathe, to exist.

> "*. . . yet is my mind my own,*
> *yet is my heart a cry toward something dim*
> *in distance, . . ."*

and the curtain fell.

Shrieking audience, bravos, twenty curtain calls are very nearly a matter of form at Broadway opcnings. But that opening was special; or so I have come to believe.

Then came dressing room scenes, ecstatic, moving, noisy! Judith Anderson, Guthrie McClintic, Maxwell Anderson, Margalo Gillmore, Jo Mielziner, a hundred celebrities all rushing in. Some crying, all smiling. We were a success, they said. Someone opened a bottle of champagne and we all drank.

Hours later only the night watchman, my sister, her husband, and I were left in the theater. The show was over, the bottles were empty, and all the lights were out — except for one lonely work-bulb hanging over the orchestra pit.

Then I wandered by myself into the empty streets of Broadway. A happy, misty condition settled on me, which lasted until the morning papers came at about 2:00 A.M. I bought one, read it, and went home to bed.

As I drifted asleep, my subconscious sneaked out and taunted me:

"You weren't even mentioned . . . in the *New York Times!*"

"God help me," I said in my dreams.

The next day brought happy news. *Winterset* was a hit, and I played each performance with joy on Broadway and on tour for over a year. No question about it — the *Winterset* opening was a pure triumph. Robert Garland wrote in the *New York World Tele-gram*, "*Winterset* goes on. It should go on. If this department wore a hat at this season of the year, it would once more doff it in honor of Guthrie McClintic, the producer, to Jo Mielziner, the scene designer, and to Burgess Meredith, the most gifted young actor in America."

These and the other kind words that came my way served to catapult me into a professional and social whirl.

Wolcott Gibbs, legendary critic and writer for *The New Yorker*, profiled me in that august publication. The attention was flattering and his whimsical evaluation was fairly accurate:

> The "young man of remarkable genius" is twenty-eight, five feet seven inches tall, weighs a hundred and thirty-five pounds, and his pointed face might more reasonably belong to a jockey. His clothes, especially his hats, have a crumpled, offhand air, and at the moment it has seemed to him suitable to let his ginger-colored hair grow long on top, so that in dimmer lights he looks rather like a chrysanthemum. His friends call him Buzz, or Bugs, and either of these in some vague way seems descriptive. . . . In any case, Meredith's extraordinary success on stage has practically nothing to do with what he looks like.

This article marked the beginning of a warm and rewarding friendship that was to last for years. It also served to introduce me to Gibbs's colleagues — Robert Benchley, James Thurber, Dorothy Parker, Harold Ross, St. Clair McKelway — who in turn would enliven and enrich my life, personally and professionally.

But, even more important to me than Wolcott's praise, the success of the play allowed me to meet attractive women, which was mainly what I was searching for in those hot days. And the woman who most brightly lit the New York scene when I appeared in *Winterset* in 1935–1936 was Tallulah Bankhead. Her character, antics, the strength and color of her personality equaled the splendor of her performances on stage and had made her both famous and notorious.

Tallulah sent word I had aroused her interest. Traditionally, Tallulah was a fiery man-eating goddess who swooped from the skies and picked off young men (and, occasionally, women) as they appeared, one by one. She was associated with a variety of bachelor playboys who were the elite of café society. Jock Whitney was the most famous. In my fantasies, it was therefore inevitable that I would be tapped to meet her. Otherwise my success would not have been complete.

She wired me to come to the Gotham Hotel, where she camped for a long time — and *camped* is the right word for it. I realized it was fruitless to resist the siren's beckoning, so after the theater on the appointed evening I arrived at her famous suite. I could hear cheerful noises inside as I rang the bell. The door flew open and there she was, stark naked, with the rest of the people in the background chatting, exchanging witticisms, playing cards, drinking, paying no attention to her.

She sang her hoarse greeting — "Dahling!" — and pulled me into the room, threw her arms around me, and put her tongue in my mouth. It was a bit sudden, but the most remarkable aspect of the scene was the casualness with which the dozen or more people around us carried on their cardplaying, their conversation, their drinking.

Tallulah always kept her figure pretty trim, though how she managed it is a mystery. She took no exercise, and never dieted. She drank what she wanted and ate what she wanted and slept seldom. Her working hours were the night hours, and what sleep she got was in the din of the day. But there you are.

Tallulah was riding a quadruple reputation of lesbianism, small-boyism, socialism, and theatricalism. She bestrode various parts of the social scene, made a lot of splash, and had endless vitality.

That same evening I was introduced to a custom she had of passing cocaine around. She would give a sniff of it to you on the edge of a nail file or something of the sort, and you were supposed to feel that helped matters. She also enjoyed getting people "mated" — people she thought would synchronize, so to speak. She insisted I meet every person present, and as I was introduced, she described how she and I were going to make the town hum about our upcoming affair. Everyone took the news in stride, but, of course, I was not consulted in the matter. It was assumed I would accept the coronation and, come to think of it, I did.

Everybody was getting high as the evening progressed. Tallulah circulated, still nude, and still no one paid attention. When she'd finished her duties as hostess, she got around to me and explained we'd better go to bed because she was dying of the Grand Desire. We went into her bedroom.

By this time I was wondering whether I could live up to her expectations. After all, I had some pretty important men to follow.

So we made it to her bedroom and turned the lock. Now comes the moment which best describes her antic spirit. We piled into bed and went to it. The moaning and the groaning were operatic. She was a fulsome lady and I was captivated. However, just before the consummation, she pushed me aside and said, "For God's sake, don't come *inside* me! I'm engaged to Jock Whitney!"

But if I had committed half the excesses that friends such as Wolcott Gibbs reported in his *New Yorker* profile of me, I offer in my defense that I was young, just twenty-four, amazingly successful and spurred on by an unquenchable enthusiasm for all the things a great city offers without charge to her most favored residents.

But, although I did not recognize it at the time, this and all the other approvals never glowed quite as brightly as they might have, and it has taken me many years to recognize the tiny empty core that lay at the center of it all. It's instinctive to share your success with your family but, by then, my mother was dead and there had never been a bridge to my father.

I'd always been a boy who lived within myself and even after that dizzying trip to the bright lights — and all the years since then — that loneliness has never been filled.

Let me tell you why.

Cathedral Choir School

ALL MY LIFE, to this day, the memory of my childhood remains grim and incoherent.

If I close my eyes and think back, I see little except violence and fear. My mother was in constant despair and my father, a doctor manqué, drank heavily. His violent quarrels with my mother were so threatening to a young boy that I find myself thankful for the curtain that time has placed between then and now.

In those early years I somehow came to understand I would have to draw from within myself whatever emotional resources I needed to go wherever I was headed. As a result, for years I became a boy who lived almost totally within himself.

I say "almost," because I am still warmed by the memories of my older sister, Virginia Louise Meredith. I loved her, and that love still shadows my reminiscences. She raised me, fed me, encouraged me as best she could.

When I was very young, about seven or eight, Virginia married a struggling engineer, Arthur Whiteside, who was equally close.

I recall that Art and my sister lived at one time on Central Park West. Every time I see the building, I remember when the Whitesides were living there and I was singing as a boy soprano in the great choir at the Cathedral of St. John the Divine nearby on 110th Street and Amsterdam Avenue.

I came from Lakewood, Ohio, a suburb of Cleveland. There I was more or less pushed into the career of singing, in spite of my asthma, which was clearly a detriment to anybody trying to sing! A teacher by the name of Professor Harry Mansville trained me. He tried to teach me to sing in what he called a "chest tone"; but of course my voice was soprano. I could not have been more than eight or nine, but I remember that the professor's favorite vocal exercise was for me to sing one phrase on a single note. The phrase was "Ah, now I see, do you?" Then he would say: "Of course you see! Now try it a note higher!" I think he felt that the phrase "Ah, now I see, do you?" had enough vowels in it to cover all emergencies.

I was so young that I scarcely knew what was happening. Apparently my mother scraped up the money to pay Professor Mansville, and if the man did nothing for my singing, he did persuade the family to enter me in a nationwide audition for the Paulist Choristers Boy Choir of New York. This was about 1920. I have a vivid recollection of that audition. There was a Father Finn who greeted a great crowd of us in St. Mary's Church in Cleveland and accompanied us when we sang. I recall he was kind and helped me sing the scales and a sacred hymn. He put his hand on my shoulder and said, "You have a good voice and you'll hear from us."

My victory — for a victory it turned out to be — was announced in the press, and a newsreel was taken of me singing. I remember this particularly, because the newsreel was shown at a double-decked theater — the same program ran upstairs and downstairs. My mother and I watched me several times by going upstairs to see one newsreel and then going downstairs to see the same thing repeated. It took several hours to watch myself three or four times. There was no sound, of course; just subtitles and me silently singing and being congratulated by the jovial

Father Finn. It was exhilarating to see myself in the movies — a heady experience because, up to then, my life had been drab.

After notifying me that I had won, the Paulist Fathers moved on . . . to choose other prize-winning sopranos in other cities. They sent me official letters informing me where to report in New York the following spring.

In my life I don't believe there has ever been anything as exciting as my first trip to New York. From the dark forests of Cleveland suburbs to the celestial surroundings of Manhattan . . . it was another planet. No subsequent trip to Paris or London or Rome would ever give me the same excitement. I remember talking to people we knew and finding only one fellow who had actually been to New York — a journey to Paradise.

Strangely, although I recall the excitement of leaving, I don't remember any details of the trip; it must have been an overnight run on the train. Either my mother or my sister must have gone with me.

About this time, my sister and my brother-in-law moved to New York. There they began to have second thoughts about my attending a Roman Catholic choir school! My mother's family was very poor and very Protestant; they came from Northern Ireland. I never met my paternal grandfather, but my maternal grandfather was the Reverend Oliver Olymphus Burgess, an invalided, retired Methodist minister in Cleveland. He sent word that before I descended into dark Catholic influences I should try out for a decent Protestant choir somewhere.

So before we reported to Father Finn's church, my sister arranged another audition for me, at the Protestant Cathedral of St. John the Divine — the largest church in America, still under construction . . . a vast, unfinished stone edifice on twelve acres of ground. The leader of the choir in those days was Dr. Miles Farrow, who explained that if he liked my voice I could become one of forty boys who made up the soprano section in that vast cathedral; in return for singing five days a week and two services on Sunday, the church would provide schooling, board, and lodging.

Dr. Farrow and his colleagues were intrigued to meet the

prize-winner of the rival Paulist choir; the lad who would turn down Father Finn's offer. They auditioned me and accepted me and I remember they said a strange thing: "Well, you are a little old for a soprano. We like them a year younger, but you have an opening here if you want it."

So at the ripe old age of ten I joined the Cathedral of St. John the Divine choir — I hope my mother or my sister properly notified the good Father Finn — and my life changed. I came into a different culture, a new way of life, new friends. At first it was painful. I had only attended public school for a couple of years; when I was ill with asthma, my mother had let me stay home. At the cathedral they were startled to learn that there were many basic subjects, particularly arithmetic, which I knew absolutely nothing about. I could read and had read a lot — *Jungle Book*s, Horatio Alger and so on. But now I was faced with the challenge of schooling myself twice as fast as anybody there.

The Choir School had a Dickensian flavor to it. We wore stiff Eton collars, uncomfortable coats, and long pants. I fear to dig much deeper in my memory of those four years; it is too much like analysis, that uncovering of forgotten fears and pleasures.

Clothes were important in that school. On Sundays we wore white cottas and purple cassocks with stiff white collars and shiny boots. If I close my eyes, I can smell the incense . . . and hear the endless hours of Sunday services, singing Palestrina and Bach and all the great composers of sacred music. We could feel the deep vibrations of the organ, which seemed to come from below us. And when we sang, our voices were lost in the echoes.

The school required that a good portion of our time was spent inside the church, dressed appropriately. Every day we attended services and sang. Also there were regular singing classes in a small, paneled rehearsal room. The dormitories were meticulously laid out. Now it seems to me that we were always in some kind of stylistic dress, even when we went to play games. We played baseball and soccer in the shadow of great stone buttresses. There were mild contests between the Sharps and the Flats, the rival athletic teams, chosen by lot. Our food was simple and good, but we were not allowed to eat nuts — they might stick in our throats!

The Cathedral Choir School gave me a fair amount of classical schooling. The teachers were good and I had the desire to learn. From an anxious, insecure boy I developed into something of a leader. Apparently I was able to put my fears aside because I became head prefect — the boy who policed other students' behavior.

My asthma diminished and the memory of my mother and father's quarrels receded. I was still very insecure, but I began to be able to confront my problems one by one. My confidence had increased to the point where I tried out for, and won, the lead in the school production of *Peter Pan*.

I can still remember the shock, the astonishment I felt when that small audience cheered. The memory remains with me.

I was friendly with my fellow students but I established no lasting relationships. One of the "masters," as the teachers were called, interested me in history and, at that young age, we were taught Latin and some foreign languages. But no one — then or now — has ever been able to breed in me even a rude skill in arithmetic.

We had to leave the Choir School when our voices changed, since we could no longer keep up our side of the arrangement. As Dr. Farrow, only half in jest, once observed, "The only fellas admitted here are those who can warble."

We were supposed to return home during vacations, so it was then that I had to face the unpleasant truth that there was no home for me to return to. My father had retreated to Canada and my mother was living as best she could, sometimes with an aunt, sometimes with friends. Once in a while I would stay with my sister and her husband at their small apartment.

When I could not go to my sister, I would accept invitations to visit with the families of some of the students, particularly the Edward S. Hewitts, who owned an estate at Lake George and a large house in town. It was through their son, Andy Hewitt, that, at the age of twelve, I caught my first glimpse of high society.

My holiday vacations with the Hewitts were pleasant. I was nervous in that society but I admired the security those people had, if not always in their character, in their economic lives. I have never ceased to love beautiful homes since those formative days.

My four years in the Choir School were strict and disciplined — we were never allowed out of sight. We were too young to have freedom. We could not leave the cathedral grounds without guidance.

The headmaster, Wilson MacDonald, a slight man with thick glasses and a thick black beard, was a fine influence. He understood my insecurity and was concerned for me. He knew I was alone, except for an occasional visit from my sister. He was a very disciplined minister of the high Episcopalian faith. He was also an Amherst graduate and later helped me go to that college. He came from where they grow the Concord grapes in upper New York State. I remember he told me he had stock in Welch's grape juice business. He was not rich, but he quit his job as headmaster in order to become a missionary in the Philippine Islands. He was killed in a military ambush, the details of which I never learned. By that time I had moved on to Amherst College and learned that the good man had left me five hundred dollars in his will. It came in very handy, and I spent it very fast.

The sad fact is that my voice, which started out so sensationally, never developed. I became an occasional soloist, but not the lead. Although I had the vocal endowment, my nerves were not dependable. My mind did not permit my voice to flow. I have been complimented for the quality of my speaking voice, but relatively few people know that I sing, although I have recorded several albums. One of them, *Songs and Stories from the Gold Rush*, was a best-seller and was recently reissued as a compact disk. However, to this day, when fatigue sets in, my voice dries, becomes constricted.

In time the asthma and the allergies would come under control, but for the next fifteen years I suffered attacks. They always seemed to happen in times of crisis, when I faced problems. Time has been a healer and the years have brought security. It could not have happened at a better hour — as the sun goes down, I feel healthier now than I did in my childhood.

Sometimes I look back on the four years at the Choir School

through a cloud of curious melancholy. I do not always remember those early days with joy; and that may be a pathological condition, since I had no sense of being slighted nor any reason to feel inferior. There was no reason why I should not have been happy. Particularly in contrast to what my life had been. Today, I am grateful for the way life treated me but, still, the memory is sad.

To what better place could I have gone? I escaped the incessant illnesses and the poverty of our living conditions back in Ohio, where we were financially dependent on distant members of the family. One nearby relative, my uncle Oliver, perpetually came to our house drunk — a distracted, totally deaf man. Those memories are dim but they are there. I still relive the sight of my father and my mother shouting in rage at each other. I replay in my mind the fear I felt of my brother, who was ten years older than I — a talented man, driven by a rampant temper. I have never been able to shake off those early fears engendered by the melancholy environment I knew before the Choir School.

Only my sister Virginia and her husband gave me help and perspective. When they could find the time.

The Cathedral Choir School was a healing experience, but it gave me dim comfort, probably because I rejected its basic purpose. I rejected it because I was overwhelmed by it: the cathedral and the rituals. But I always hoped for some mystical experience, believing it would come to pass. And perhaps it might. We hope for that till the end of our lives, all of us.

The exotic part of the Choir School episode came in the form of a teacher named Elmendorf Lester Carr. Mr. Carr was an impressive character. He was a large man with an elegant social background and a dominating mother who looked a little like Franklin D. Roosevelt's famous mother. Carr was the assistant headmaster. He taught French and Latin, and was, I suspect, a repressed homosexual. Mr. Carr liked to beat us on the bottom with a large board, a breadboard with a handle. It was a constant habit of his to whack you on the ass with this board when you were out of order. Then, as an honor of being hit by him, a small service stripe was put next to your name on the board!

We realized that if we endured this whap, Mr. Carr would not officially record it. Nor would you suffer further punishment. In other words, the whap was full payment. In place of official demerits you could take the breadboard treatment.

Looking back, there were several of these antic teachers around, or so it seems to me now. There was a young fellow who was a head prefect. He was a tall, intellectual chap, who seemed to be plagued by inner problems; and he, also, liked to whack you on the bottom! After I left I saw very few people from the school, but I did run into this man. He had become a Roman Catholic priest. We discussed the past and he admitted he had gay drives in those days and had been fighting them ever since. He was a decent, troubled soul who managed to solve his problems by helping other people.

Also, at the school, was a student named Lanny Ross. Perhaps people have forgotten Lanny, but he went on to become a star athlete at Yale, and a singing star on radio. Lanny used to bring a rich uncle to the Choir School. That uncle took six or seven of us lads for vacations at the Château Frontenac in Quebec. He was a big guy, too, but of course everybody looked big to us at that age. He got me into bed and made very definite gropes. I remember that the size of his cock was terrifying and I yelled for help. He got furious and told me to get the hell out of his bedroom and stop bothering him! I left.

That event gets interesting when I go deeper into my memory bank. After leaving the lecherous uncle's bedroom, I fell on my head while trying to ice skate and woke up hours later, asking the assembled crowd around me, "Where am I?" and getting the curious answer: "Meredith, if you ask us that question once more, we'll really pound you on the head."

I finally learned I had fallen backward on the ice and suffered a minor concussion. It was startling to me then, and remains so today. The amnesia lasted several days. The lecherous uncle, the fall on the ice, and the amnesia were interconnected.

The fact is that I did develop a peculiar sexual quirk for a lady who taught gymnastics at the school. Primarily she taught mathematics, but on the side she taught calisthenics and she was proud of her athletic prowess. A friend of the headmaster's, she looked old-maidish, wore thick glasses, and as I look back, seemed a fine person. But I developed a letch of wanting to wrestle with her and I could, at will, achieve an erection on her behalf. I tried to think of ways of luring her into the gym alone, but didn't get anywhere. I had no luck in the sexual field and remained wary of the homosexual advances that sometimes surrounded us.

Young choirboys seemed to attract homosexuals in those days, and I suppose there is no reason why it shouldn't be true today . . . the ethereal voices, white robes, purity, and so forth. And lacking the protection of a family may have made me particularly vulnerable. I think my inability to cope with all of this, my distrust of it, combined with a curious yearning for muscularity in women, was enough to confuse anyone.

Shades of Sigmund Freud and Oscar Wilde!

The one Dickensian aspect of the Cathedral Choir School I remember are the elaborate church services. The Good Friday service lasted three hours, during which we had to stay in our seats looking straight ahead. Stark upright — a kind of Daumier scene. Very often some of the younger choirboys fainted from the stifling atmosphere, the hard wooden seats, the drone of the organ, the discipline. I remember many times we would become nauseated. When that happened, the only thing to do was vomit up the sleeve of our purple cassocks. We would hold our sleeves and stagger out under the glare of the visiting bishops and deans. I had my share of those dizzy spells. I don't believe I ever fainted, but I vomited regularly during the four years.

That practice of attending church each day of my life during the school year was continued when I went to Hoosac, another church school. When I finished that stint of seven years — four in the Cathedral Choir School and three at Hoosac — I was ready to skip church services for a while. I had had it, eucharistically speaking. I found the experience elusive and incomprehensible. I received no solace in that garden. I would not have made a good monk.

Hoosac School

WITH RECOMMENDATIONS from the Cathedral Choir School, and with financial help from my mother's only well-to-do brother, Howard Burgess, I enrolled at Hoosac School.

It was run by the rector, a man by the name of Dr. Edward Dudley Tibbits. It had been founded as some sort of imitation of an English school — a poor man's Eton . . . with a High Church background and extensive religious training. Reverend Tibbits was an Episcopal minister. The chapel belonged to the school, but villagers were welcomed to the services. I read the literature that comes occasionally from Hoosac. The chapel is still there, but the school has moved into a large mansion on a nearby property.

In my day that mansion belonged to Tibbits's cranky older brother, a terrifying ogre who would thunder and yell at us . . . but you sensed he was proud of his younger brother, our rector. The two brothers were in their middle sixties when I got there. They were opposite sides of the same coin . . . one was very religious and the other very vituperative.

Looking back, those three years seem melancholy, a bit sad in remembrance. I don't know why I wasn't happier. Apparently most fellows who went to Hoosac were contented. It is in the Berkshires, near Bennington, where the leaves turn brilliant colors in the fall and the winter snow is dry and sparkling. The surrounding fields and villages are pristine and attractive. Architecturally, the school resembled a cigar box; only the chapel had character. Also the main dining room was large and friendly. It was constructed like an old English hall at Eton or Oxford. The tables were carved oak — long, rugged refectory tables. There I sat, but found nothing that touched me intellectually or spiritually. Perhaps I had not overcome my childhood terrors.

Again, there were shadows of homosexuality; I remember one time I was hugged by Father Tibbits himself . . . and while that was proceeding, a young priest walked in, who afterward kept asking me, "What was going on?" I played the game up to a point, because I had no money except an occasional handout from a reluctant uncle. When that money gave out, and it did frequently, good Father Tibbits would dig up a scholarship for me and I'd be able to get through another semester, eating and learning and sorrowing.

Hoosac did not expose us to much literature, poetry, or theater. The teaching was not inspiring, but there was a master we all liked. His name was Julian G. Hillhouse, and we considered him an intellectual. He was quiet, and always sighed when he smiled — a trait that kept us guessing. I have tried to find a role like that ever since — so far, no luck.

Because I had no home, my vacations were spent at haphazard places, including Nantucket, where I worked at a yacht club for bed and board and tips. On one vacation I worked for a student's family. Best of all, I went on a scholarship to Camp Dudley on Lake Champlain. There I won a singular honor: I was voted the "top new boy of the year." I got it because I had started to entertain people. My voice was changing, but I croaked out a few ditties, with undeserved success.

In retrospect, Hoosac was a dulling experience; but I did learn

to enjoy esteem there. I received a medal at the end of one year
for recitation. I remember doing a scene from *A Midsummer Night's
Dream* and recently found a faded photograph of that event.

I became editor of the school paper, *The Owl*, which I quickly
put into debt. Wolcott Gibbs said in his *New Yorker* profile of me,
"Under his casual regime it ran so far into debt that for several
years after he had gone it survived only haggardly. So anemic
were these subsequent issues that the embarrassed editors
changed its name to the 'Owlet.' "

Hoosac had an annual Yule log celebration that brought it
minor fame. I played the court jester, the leading role in that
festivity. I also won a couple of writing prizes, one on the curious
theme of "The Benefit to Christian Civilization from a Complete
Understanding and Friendly Relationship between the United
States of America and Great Britain." It was called the Brooks
Cup. I won it two times.

But the achievement that pleased me above all others was that
I passed the State College Entrance Examination — a difficult
across-the-board written test . . . ancient language, modern language, math, geography, history, and so on. I did so well I was
admitted to Amherst College on a scholarship.

All this while my family was scattered and unhappy. My sister
and her husband were the only ones I could contact. And they
were struggling on their own. I was haunted by fears, financial
and personal. I had no money whatsoever. My greatest sorrow
was the lack of warmth, lack of family. I developed no great
ambition and no goal. Nothing stirred me deeply, nothing lighted
my mind. I was strangely depressed by the school's religiosity,
which I rejected with, I think, some guilt.

As a postscript, I visited Hoosac in 1989. The current students
enjoy it more than I did. The school seems better organized. We
didn't ski as they do now. We skated occasionally when there
was ice — now they have a good hockey team. We played rugby
and that's all. I remember the first day I tried out for the team I
broke a bone in my shoulder while trying to tackle somebody.
My asthma was recurrent. Though I fish wide and far and throw
my bait about, I haven't yet caught the essence of how I felt about

Hoosac School when I was there. My hunch is that Hoosac, for me, had a kind of *Oliver Twist* atmosphere. Yet I should be grateful that I was fed and watered and a little hay was thrown into my stall; but that's all I am grateful for.

The kindliest light that came out of the Hoosac experience was a passing flicker in my mind that I liked theater. I had never seen a play, but I could act better than anybody in the school. They even asked me to return a year after graduation to play the court jester again. Of course there was no competition.

Amherst
1927–1929

AMHERST, BRAVE AMHERST — a name known to fame in the days of yore-ore-ore!" or however the song goes. It reminds me of many years ago at Amherst when two undergraduate pals and I combined as a trio to sing our way at commencement time into the various alumni gatherings — there to warble gloriously and be rewarded, by plump and beaming alumni, with tumblers of grapefruit juice and gin! We sang to the classes of '25, '22, '18, and on up; and so pleased was I with my company and my fine voice that I finally sank — joyous and smiling — onto the dewy grass near the Lord Jeffrey Inn, there to sleep until morning.

I entered Amherst in 1926 on a scholarship. Uncle Howard had helped put me through Hoosac, but he went broke, so at Amherst I was on my own.

I arrived there with maybe ten dollars; no more. However, the scholarship provided a room in one of the dormitories. I had a roommate named Tracy. But no money, and there were no jobs.

I went in a bewildered way to classes, without books. I borrowed some of Tracy's. He was kind about it. At the end of three weeks I went to Dean Esty. I said, "I have been starving. I have no books, no money. What shall I do?"

He was amazed. He, who must have met many students with difficult problems, was amazed. He thought for a few seconds. Then he said:

"You had better leave college, work for a year, and get a little money together. Your problems are too heavy. There are boys here without any money — but very few; and they made preparations for part-time jobs and so on earlier, much earlier. You had better work for a year." I agreed with him.

"What," he asked, "have you been using for food?" I said, "A kind boardinghouse lady let me eat on credit the first week. Then the president of the Amherst Bank advanced me twenty-five dollars."

"He did what?" asked the dean.

"Well," I said, "I went to him and showed him a will which left me five hundred dollars, but which wouldn't be settled for a year, and would the bank advance me twenty-five dollars? He laughed and wrote out a personal check and said to repay it when I could. I bought a sweater, several books, and spent the rest eating. It's gone now."

The dean said, "I will give you a letter of recommendation that might help you get a job. You leave college for a year — then come back. Make your plans early, though, for jobs and such. And save your money."

He dictated a letter to this effect: "To whom it may concern . . . ambitious boy . . . deserves a chance . . . want him back. (Signed) Dean Esty of Amherst College, Amherst, Massachusetts."

In one month I was a reporter on the *Stamford Advocate*, in Stamford, Connecticut. I had an aunt there, sort of a David Copperfield's Aunt Betsy, who fed me for a while until I got that job reporting. It was an episode I smile at now, but it racked me at the time.

My assignment was to write obituaries. One day I handed my old-fashioned editor a scoop about a murder, to which I had been an eyewitness. My story included all of the details — except the name of the victim.

The editor studied me a moment and remarked that I was in the wrong profession. I agreed. He said, "Well, you needn't quit yet," but I said, "No, I'll leave today. I'm on a bad roll and I better move on."

I quit and made my way to my brother's store in Cleveland, Ohio. It occurred to me, of course, that I was completing a dark circle: Cleveland was where I had started a few years before.

My brother was as hapless as I — he was always trying new ventures and always failing. He was like e. e. cummings's famous uncle, who kept raising chickens which the skunks would eat. The uncle failed at everything until he died and started a successful worm factory.

My brother's name was George Howard Meredith. He was talented musically and the high point of his life was when he briefly became a jazz drummer with the Benson Orchestra of Chicago. He was good at beginning a project but had no mind how to make it work. And when it didn't work, he drank.

Most recently George had started a haberdashery in Cleveland. He immediately ordered more merchandise than he could ever pay for. George was on the brink of bankruptcy before he began! The creditors showed up on the first day.

Instead of salary I wore the new clothes and tried to sneak them back on the racks. To calm myself I made some progress with a girl named Geraldine, but she dropped me before I got around to enjoy it.

The final moment came when Meredith, Inc. was legally foreclosed and my haberdashery days were history.

It was almost Amherst time again. Two months more. I uncrumpled my letter from the dean again and I got a temporary job cub-reporting on the *Cleveland Plain Dealer* — just until it was school time.

In the meantime I philosophized:

"I am gaining experience. I have earned an honest dollar. I have not saved much money — how could I? The most I made was eighteen dollars a week and I had to live; but I am eager for knowledge and

somewhat prepared. Also I'm more worldly — no longer a cloistered
prep-school pupil, no longer a virgin."

I put through my newspaper copy early during those last few
weeks. I was drinking a bit, you know, toughening myself up;
and anxious to see my friend Dean Esty, and Tracy, and the kind
president of the bank. (Strange I can't remember his name. Especially since when I wrote him to tell him I was leaving Amherst
and to thank him, he sent me fifteen dollars more, saying, "I
know how hard your struggle will be. Accept this small gift to
help you on your way.")

I said good-bye to my brother and to my mother, whom I was
to see only once more, and set sail in my small tumbly car — a
Star, which I had bought for fifty dollars — to ride toward the
Tents of the Wise Men.

The journey was an eager one, a bouncing, bounding journey.
Sleepless, with intermittent blowouts. And at least fifty dollars —
fifty honest smackers. But most important, I was in plenty of
time for rushing, for jobs, for victory.

My Star and I rolled into Amherst early one September morning. I forget the exact day and date. I remember that it was about
5:00 A.M. I pulled up by the big square in the center of town,
turned off the motor, and leaned back in my seat.

The vision was lovely; the leaves would soon turn. It was
intensely quiet. No one was about. I felt thrilled. I felt confident.
The bugle in my heart was blowing — the walls of Jericho would
surely fall!

I clambered out of the car. The sun was rising red and lusty
and the trees were green and wet. I stretched out my arms — a
bit dramatically — and gave thanks.

Then I looked at my poor Star. It was tired and frazzled. I
patted it. I looked at the buildings. They were wreathed in smiles.

"Well, boys! Remember me?"

I daydreamed they answered: "Hello, Meredith, better luck
this time!"

I drove to the Perry Inn, and took a bath.

The next three days I looked for a place to stay. "Pardon me,"
I would say, "but I am a new student and I need living quarters.

Could I perhaps tend your furnace for a modest guest-room suite?''

Finally I rang the doorbell of a large, handsome house. A maid answered and advised, ''The Madame is in the garden.'' She pointed the way and I went.

There I found a striking-looking middle-aged woman, pruning rosebushes. She was wearing gauntlets to protect her hands from the thorns.

She listened to my story, studied me for several seconds, then threw down her gauntlets and said, ''Come in and have tea.''

For some reason I knew she would help me. During tea she asked:

''Do you know my name?''

''No,'' I confessed.

''I am Madame Bianchi. This is Emily Dickinson's house. I am her grandniece.''

I caught my teacup, which had slid away.

''This is Emily Dickinson's . . . house?''

There was silence again for a space.

''There are no rooms here to spare, but I know what we can do.'' She left me abruptly and I could hear her talking on the phone. Finally she came back.

''You will go to a Mrs. Thompson's. She is the most beautiful character in this world. She is eighty-seven years old. She wears black for her husband, who died when she was twenty-one. She is sublime and lovely and kind. No one but you could work for her; she never has had anyone work for her. I will furnish your room with things I have here. Good-bye.''

I walked out, grateful and happy.

Mrs. Thompson . . . Mrs. Esther Thompson! Other students have degrees and book-learning — but they never knew Mrs. Thompson when they were at Amherst.

Her luminous, lovely face and the memory of that meeting is as clear as yesterday. She talked to me and said, ''Come back at seven.'' It was about five. At 6:30 I returned. She said:

''I wanted you at seven.''

''I know — I was anxious . . .''

"Come in."

"This is your room," she said, smiling. "You will just tend my stove; that's all. And make your bed."

I soon learned why she had wanted me at seven, not earlier. She had wanted time to pray.

The fine, ample Mrs. Perry gave me a job at her hotel, the Perry Inn, as a dishwasher. Two meals a day. Each meal took an hour and fifteen minutes. There were no automatic dishwashers in those days, so it was a greasy, endless job. I emanated smells like an old frying pan, but the food problem was solved.

Then the fraternity rushing season began.

I went from house to house. They looked at me. They talked to me. The Psi Upsilons bought my car for forty dollars — cash. What a wealthy crew that was!

I did not receive a single bid.

Neither did the black students. Or the Jewish students — none of us did. It depressed me, but I had my beautiful room with some of Emily Dickinson's furniture.

So the year began.

I doubt if any of the students remember me. I knew only a few of them. A faculty member, Mr. Dyer, and his wife were friendly to me, a lonely boy in college.

But an oppressive despair came over me. I was deeply affected by the social barriers set up by the fraternity system — by the rejection of the well-dressed and the handsome. I discovered that, curiously, I had no sense of defiance, no outrage, and my self-image became as greasy as the pots I washed. At the end of two months I was seriously depressed, a state that hit me like an illness. My boyhood alienation became deeper and colder.

Sundays I went to the Reverend Kinsolving's vesper teas, where I sang in his choir for four dollars. But afterward I went alone to my room or to the Perry kitchen in despair.

Then I began to drink. I found some companions — I remember one was named Cleaves and another Fox. I would flee from the pots and the pans of the Perry, and make for Northampton, where there was a speakeasy that sold alcohol cheap. In ginger ale. I fell in love with an attractive Smith girl whose first name was Mary. (I've heard from her since; she's married and has grandchildren.) The little money I had went for trolley fares and alcohol.

I sought these respites frantically and then, sobered, I would walk into the classroom and present half-prepared lessons. My marks went down like a stock market crash — worse and worse, week after week. I am not proud of the way I was.

One day an exponent of the Oxford religious movement came into town. A "Buchmanite." A Rhodes scholar. He spoke at Kinsolving's tea. He was impressed, he said, by my understanding, and would like to talk to me sometime. I agreed.

The next morning we met at the appointed room where he was staying. I remember I was suffering from a great hangover. He declared I was a "chosen one" — he was going to designate me as leader in a religious movement in the college.

Me? Lead? Not even a fraternity man — no such thing in God's Mansion.

Lead! Me! — of poverty and pans, the great unknown. He said, "Tell me your sins."

I said, "I've sinned in every way possible . . ."

He said, "Have you sinned with your roommate?"

"I have no roommate."

"Well — with another man?"

"No, Jesus Christ, no!" I answered.

"Don't swear," he admonished.

The man seemed doubtful and I felt miserable and lost.

The hangover was getting bad by now; his interest, and my mindless emotion, and him thinking . . .

Finally I began to hiccup and cry.

"*Now,*" he said triumphantly, "you are ready for God."

Well, I was a sorry mess for anybody, much less Jehovah.

"What can I do?"

"God will reveal," he advised.

My next thought was to ask whether God would get me into a fraternity to meet a few friends; and this struck me so funny — with me on my knees, confessing what must have been mild iniquities to an Oxford man — that I started to laugh and ran out of the room. An hour later I found myself near the agricultural school still running and sobbing.

That particular experience with God saddened me. I was ashamed of the whole maudlin business. I tried to concentrate on my studies, but I was hopelessly far behind.

One day the mail brought me a check for seven dollars. It was from my Buchmanite confessor, who wanted me to journey to Boston to attend a religious meeting of some sort. After studying the check carefully, I rushed to the proper office and with that check I bought my first prom ticket.

That night I danced; white shirt-fronts, melodies from muffled trumpets, warm cheeks, warm hearts; and then the music stopped and she and I walked out into the night where I looked at the stars and hoped to God I was forgiven.

Professor Curtis Canfield issued the orders for theatrical tryouts. Faustus! That fitted my mood and so I applied. At the proper hour I went into a room where sat, among others, two prominent seniors — Alan Scott and Arthur Wilmurt. I declaimed and I was chosen at once.

That could have been my triumph and my change of heart, but the dean's office declared me ineligible for all extracurricular activities until my studies improved. Those were the rules and regulations, and I knew they were right. But I wondered why I had fought so hard to arrive nowhere.

However, it turned out that I had gained two friends: Alan Scott, the first Rhodes scholar to come out of Amherst, and Art Wilmurt, who became a successful Broadway playwright.

It is interesting to note that four years later, Alan and I were rooming together in Greenwich Village when he wrote his immensely successful play *Goodbye Again,* and a few years after that, I coproduced Wilmurt's beautiful translation of *Noah,* which appeared on Broadway and repeated its success in London with Charles Laughton in the lead. I later starred in it in Chicago and other cities.

. . . and on that sad, sad day in Amherst if we could have looked forward . . . we would have discovered that the Lord works in mysterious ways, his wonders to achieve.

Technically, the end of Amherst for me came when Dean Esty learned I had gone to Northampton to play, of all things, Sir Toby Belch in *Twelfth Night* with the Smith College Dramatic Club. He ordered me to his office.

"I have a mind to expel you," said the dean. "We don't allow you to act in our own dramatics, because your studies are poor, so you travel ten miles to Northampton. Why?"

I answered, "I am sorry." And indeed I was; it was dull and unsuccessful, the whole procedure.

And that was the end of the year, and the end of Amherst and me.

There are a few good memories of those dismal months: an English teacher from Hobart, a sardonic man, who got me to read *The Education of Henry Adams,* which I have never forgotten. Also there was Professor Packard, a dynamic history teacher, to whom I confessed I had cheated once and he laughed, congratulated me for telling him, and gave me my only A. Then there was Miss Kennedy, the coach's daughter, a good friend of mine, who never stopped trying to raise my courage. But above all there was the continuous blundering sadness of my life during that period.

Then came the stinging realization of defeat. Not only had I hit bottom, but I had no money to leave town.

Debts and defeat.

No carfare.

"How can I get out of here?" I asked over and over again.

Then Cleaves, my friend Cleaves, told me about the Kellogg declamation prize of fifty dollars, for which anyone was eligible, regardless of scholastic standing.

Fifty dollars would do it! Only two days to prepare, though. I rushed to the library and extracted Rostand's *Cyrano de Bergerac.* I learned the last scene — the death scene: *"And you, too, Folly, you; I know that you will lay me low at last . . . I will fall fighting . . . my white plume."*

I won that money easily. I roared my lines at the judges until they succumbed and announced me winner.

"Amherst, brave Amherst," I hummed as I left that small, elegant New England college — left riding in a Pullman car and thinking, "Maybe someday, who knows, Amherst may ask me how I liked it. Who knows?"

In 1939, Amherst College gave me an honorary degree. I was very grateful and it was far more than I deserved.

New York

W HEN I WALKED AWAY from Amherst, bad times followed me. I had a series of failures.

My first job in New York, a temporary one, was as a
Wall Street runner at twenty-five dollars a week. After sickening
of that assignment, I worked a few weeks selling ties at Macy's
and then joined up as a cadet seaman on the Munson Steamship
Line sailing to South America.

In Venezuela I went ashore with two Scandinavian mates, got
foolishly drunk, and arrived late back on the ship — to be thrown
in the brig. The captain canceled all leaves for the rest of the trip.
Cadet seamen were not treated as criminals, but we could be
confined to quarters for proper cause. The captain of this ship
suggested that in the future I should stay away from nautical work
of any sort. "Don't go near a ship," he said, earmarking another
profession I was told to avoid.

Incidentally, the ship was infested with monstrous fleas, or at
least my sleeping quarters were. To protect myself, I put the legs

of my cot in cans of kerosene. It did the trick, but the smell was awful.

Back in New York, I hung around living from hand to mouth, renting a room from a family in Brooklyn who dealt in what was then regarded as pornographic literature, particularly the works of Frank Harris.

My finest moment came while I was working at the complaint desk in the fur department of Saks Fifth Avenue. That job ended when I told a customer that karakul was expensive because it had been a cold winter, and the little bastards had retired shyly under the ice. Another bungled profession.

Then, one lucky evening, I went to a party given by Aruziag Costigan, a charming Armenian lady, a semi-invalid who taught piano at my old Choir School and who had tried to teach me to play. I didn't learn much piano, but we had become friends. She told me about a theater group run by Eva Le Gallienne, where they took in apprentices. Now there are many places to study acting, but in the 1930s this was the only good one. It was called the Civic Repertory Theatre and was located in Greenwich Village on 14th Street and Sixth Avenue.

So Madame Costigan arranged a meeting with the famous and beautiful Eva Le Gallienne. Eva sat down and talked with me for twenty minutes and said, "Yes, you come along. I'm sure you'll be fine." It happened that quickly and that simply — and it salvaged my life.

In my apprenticeship group were John Garfield, Howard da Silva, Robert Lewis, and others who became successful. We acted in small apprentice shows and we were coached and directed by a remarkable lady from Dublin — Ria Mooney. Ria had been an actress in that fair city before she came to join Le Gallienne. She later returned to Ireland and was appointed director-in-chief of the famous Abbey Theatre — a position she held until her death in 1973.

In the apprentice section Ria directed me in *Playboy of the Western World,* and after that play good things started to happen.

At first I was nervous and disoriented — I overslept and arrived late for a student performance of *Outward Bound*. Late for my first major part! Also, I had begun to lead a rampant Greenwich Village life.

Yet, after a few months I attracted the notice of the older members of the company, especially Edward Bromberg, and Robert Ross, who was later associated with Laurence Olivier. Whatever energy I didn't dissipate in Greenwich Village parties, I used effectively in the acting classes.

I should mention two extracurricular activities. The first was making enough money to live on. For this I washed dishes, scrubbed floors, delivered groceries.

The second activity was a series of wild rent parties that Robert Ross and I organized in an apartment we shared. For a while those parties became a fad in the old Village and celebrities dropped by on weekend nights — Carl Van Doren, the then-famous black singer Spivy, John O'Hara, and Jock Whitney are some who come to mind.

For three dollars we would entertain the customers and serve them bathtub gin. In that way we paid the rent for our apartment over a plumbing shop at 629 Hudson Street. Our rent parties became an off-Broadway hit.

I put what was left of my energies into the apprentice theater. Eva told me she worried about me; she said I was "spitting in God's face" — a phrase I never forgot. I tried to moderate myself, but I could not resist a good celebration. Celebrating was a part of me, and only the passage of time has begun to subdue that problem.

Eventually I earned Miss Le Gallienne's respect, and she gave me minor roles to play in her regular productions. She also paid me my first professional income — something like forty dollars a week. It made a sea-change in my life.

The first professional role I played was the servant of the Nurse in *Romeo and Juliet*. In that part I got slapped in the face every night and got my first laugh!

As the photographer in *Liliom*, I had one line: "The lady looks at the gentleman, and the gentleman looks straight into the camera." Years later I played the lead, Liliom himself, opposite Ingrid Bergman.

The last acting assignment I had with Le Gallienne's company was in *Alice in Wonderland*. I played three parts: the Duck, the Dormouse, and Tweedledum. As the Duck I had roller skates strapped to my knees, as the Dormouse I hiccuped, and as Tweedledum I sang a duet with Tweedledee. In each role I wore a full mask — my own face was never visible.

Then came the tap on the shoulder and two Broadway plays were offered to me. Though I didn't know how I could bring it off, I accepted both.

My doing two plays at the same time brought me publicity — the first press I ever had. My sister wrote me, "You are becoming a news item, little brother. Now, buckle up!" The two plays were *Little Ol' Boy* and *Threepenny Opera* — the lead in one, a minor part in the other.

Little Ol' Boy was written by Albert Bein, who had lost his right leg riding a freight train. The play he wrote took place in a reform school. It was my first Broadway appearance and I was blessed with my first good notices — years went by before I did any better.

The play closed quickly, but I was on my way — the gates to the Promised Land were starting to open.

Albert Bein lived in a small rented room on the Lower West Side. He was a great talker and a fine writer, a young man of twenty-three or twenty-four. Joe Losey discovered the play, decided to direct it on Broadway, and contacted a friend of his, John Hammond, Jr., to put up the money. They found me in the Village and offered me the leading role, a redheaded, teenage killer called "Little Ol' Boy."

I think back on that experience with wonder. Joe Losey became an internationally famous movie director, John Hammond, Jr., became one of the top recording impresarios of the world for over three decades, and I became . . . whatever I am.

Bein's story was sad from the beginning. He was brought up in a reform school and was fifteen when he lost his leg. He told me he was inspired by a dream to write *Little Ol' Boy*.

He was so sure of its success that he had persuaded his landlady, to whom he owed many months of rent, not to worry, because the play would bring them fame and fortune. On opening night the director, Losey, and I got fine notices, but the critics said the play was worthless.

They were wrong, but that's what they wrote. After the show, Albert Bein went back to his rooming house to discover that he had been locked out. He phoned me and said he had no place to stay. I got a cot ready and he slept at my place for two weeks.

The rest of us were offered jobs and praise but Albert was given no recognition. This was unfair, because without his special language we would have been nothing. Proof of that was that *Little Ol' Boy* still plays around the country in college and amateur productions.

Bein married a friend of mine, Mary George, and did have a couple of his later plays produced, but now his work is largely forgotten.

My role of the reform-school killer fascinated the New York critics. The last time they had seen me was as Tweedledum, the Dormouse, and the quacking Duck! So now, as a savage killer, I gave them a jolt.

It was a time of happy success for me and for President Franklin D. Roosevelt. His show went even better than mine. It was the beginning of a New Deal for both of us.

The Straw Hat Theater
1930

BEFORE I GOT my first Broadway job, I learned much of my craft in that hardest of drama schools: summer stock.

In the spring of 1930, a young man named Walter Tupper Jones raised a lot of enthusiasm, slightly less money, and converted a long low barn out in Mount Kisco, New York, into a theater. Mr. Jones was stage manager for Eva Le Gallienne and had enormous vitality. He threw out the hay, the long-abandoned automobiles, and the manure; he rigged up some chairs and a stage, and opened the box office for advance ticket sales. It was as hectic a beginning as any summer theatrical enterprise and one of the first. It clings in my memory because I was only a few months an actor, knew very little about the theater, and nothing about this frenzied species.

Eva Le Gallienne had pride in her young manager and, being a generous soul, agreed to open his season with the balcony scene from *Romeo and Juliet*, the one-act play *One Sunday Morning*, and something else, providing Mr. Jones reproduced her 14th Street scenery. I was a friend of Tupper's — so I traveled up with him during the four weeks in which the theater was conceived, built, and publicized.

I happened to be staring at the operation on the Friday before the opening Monday, wondering vaguely whether we could get the stage finished, the toilets in, and the scenery in place, when I glanced over into an adjoining field to discover that a rival activity was under way — the Westchester Dog Show. Crates, caravans, kennels were suddenly in the process of erection. Tweed-stricken matrons were climbing over the horizon, and before long — before I could completely comprehend the situation, before I could sense the inevitable conflict between canine and human exhibitionism — some of the beasts themselves began to appear. I remember distinctly a group of them, blue-blooded spaniels, disdainfully sniffing a few mongrel actors who were sitting alongside the road, studying their lines.

Tupper was inside, had been there all day streaking a midnight cyclorama, and when I told him the news he looked up from his paint cans with an agony that only a world war or a summer theater can bring about, and whispered: "What dog show?"

Of course the dogs wouldn't move, and the actors couldn't. The only consolation was that the Westchester Dog Show opened on Sunday, while the Westchester Playhouse opened the following night — there could be no great problem for the critics.

But as the dogs kept coming, the hysteria mounted.

At our dress rehearsal, the elegantly dressed dog fanciers strolled over to watch the actors — whose points were knobby and whose tails were dragging on the floor.

Only Le Gallienne could send the intruders to their kennels. She would lash them away with a few words and then go on with her lines: "Wherefore art thou Romeo? Deny thy father . . ."

A real Diana, that lady; she kept her pack together, and we worshipped her.

Monday afternoon, another dog show — Monday night, Shakespeare. Just in time the curtains were hung, the lights set, the balcony nailed together. Inside, pretty Westchester ushers with orchids and long evening dresses puzzled over the unnumbered rows; outside, Boy Scouts directed limousines and station wagons onto outraged velvet lawns. In the box office the ticket racks were scrambled and the reservations thrown in a heap; backstage — O Hecuba! The water would not run, so plumbers and managers and actors and greasepaint were stirred round and round until the wigs hung like willows and perspiration fell like rain.

I was not in the opening bill, so I ran back and about, borrowing lipstick and bringing pails of water and words of comfort to the cast and crew until, suddenly, it was nine o'clock — and the gongs of death announced, First Act . . .

The theater is a place of miracles; but I had never realized it so strongly as when, that opening night at Mount Kisco, standing at the back of a rickety old barnyard house, I saw the wagon-wheel of lights on the ceiling dim down, the footlights begin to glow against the dark. Then the breathless hush, the expectant, throbbing quiet, as the curtains parted slowly . . . and there, in the moonlight, was the immortal symbol of young love: Juliet's balcony . . . the wall . . . the soft, blue night . . . the melancholy ritual of young love. First Romeo — does he come first? — finding no one. Finally, the lovely Juliet, alone, speaking to the night. Centuries of young dreams and aching desires began to unfold . . . and I remember, just as the world gave way to unreality, just as the magic became complete — those goddamn dogs began to howl.

The curs should have been asleep, probably had been; but the intense and consecrated stillness awoke their miserable souls and they bayed and whinnied and yowled like a demented orchestra sitting in a pit of thumbtacks.

Eva had withstood years of hardships, had battled unthinkable odds. She was high priestess in a temple flung about with elevated trains and continuous Communist parades lurching past the gates. Her 14th Street edifice did not have a radiator but which sang like a tree toad, nor was there a board in the floor so young, nor a chair so secure, that did not groan rheumatically when you touched it. But, bless her intrepid soul, she never had to contend with two hundred neurotic, overbred, foam-flecked hounds of hell. And, as she finished the scene in a burst of pantomime, I think she whispered to her God that she had met her match.

I got onstage the second week. It was in a play called *Wedding Bells* — or did *The Guardsman* come next? Whichever, it was the beginning of five years of playing in stock, unceasing and tumultuous. Looking back it is hard to distinguish one summer from another, one barn from the next. Arden and Millbrook and Newport and Falmouth and Buffalo and Nantucket and Cape May and Chicago and Philadelphia and Locust Valley, Red Bank, Easthampton, Westport. I went to every one and more. Fifty dollars a week if I was lucky — plus room and board and transportation; one hundred and fifty dollars at Newport; doughnuts at Red Bank; asthma at Locust Valley; and I was married at Cape May.

In retrospect, those days are glamorous and highlighted with remembrances of white beaches and black nights; parties in slacks, and long onerous hours of study; with only one positive, conclusive observation possible — that never, not *once*, did any week or any day or any hour have a moment of calm.

I recall doing Marchbanks at Mount Kisco with three days of preparation. (That was after the dogs had left and the creditors had set in.) I can see the director throw down a script of *Lady Windermere's Fan* or something like it and moan: "Here it is Thursday and you crack-heads should conclude you can't do this English comedy. It is insane and brutal, and if you open, the Westchester people will vote to turn this barn back to the horses."

He churned about the room; the actors' faces were drawn and we stared drearily at our scripts. We expected this to blow over, so we could resume. But no. "Get Jones!" said the director. "Get Jones!" One of the actors, who was squatting, lay back and covered his face with his hat. None of the rest moved until Tupper came running in. He had received a legal summons from an unpaid contractor an hour before and he looked punch-drunk.

"Jones!" said the director. "We will do *Candida*. Pedro de Cordoba lives near here and he will do Morell; and Hotcake here — Meredith — will do Marchbanks."

I probably have the details mixed, but these are more or less the facts. That's the way I got my first big role.

The telephone hadn't been cut off, so Jones called New York

and in a few hours twelve copies of the Shavian classic arrived. We read the play, and set about to learn the lines.

I see a white bed and a funny floor lamp, which fades as the morning sun comes through the window; and I can hear myself saying the words again and again — trying to pound them into my brain —

"Morell . . . you think I'm afraid of you? I'm not afraid of you — it's you who are afraid of me!" And on and on, Saturday, Sunday . . . Monday.

It's difficult to tell about past emotions. Actors have to parade theirs all the time, and consequently we keep a few secrets just to make ourselves feel complete. Ezra Pound called someone a "bundle of broken mirrors." That describes an actor.

Nevertheless, I will tell you that on that night, with the foot-lights on the blinding side, I tasted what I have difficulty in tasting again — the tears that fall when a performance is finished and the audience cheers and the curtain closes and opens and opens and closes and you know you haven't missed a bloody line . . . by very much.

Cape May was a rickety place — an old converted casino. In the space where we built the scenery there used to be a carousel. Some of the horses and camels with red noses were still heaped in the corner. When actors made up in those days, we sometimes put red in the corners of our eyes to dazzle the audience, and this always made me think of those merry-go-round animals at Cape May, with their painted red eyes and lips, fixed up like actors.

At Cape May, Alfred de Liagre, Otis Chatfield Taylor, Robert Ross, and I ran the enterprise jointly, and I can still recall a thousand frenzies. One week we tried out a new mystery melodrama; and on opening night, at the end of the first act, the heroine duly fainted in my arms when she heard a noise in the supposedly deserted house. The trapdoor behind me opened slowly on sched-ule, and the audience gasped with horror. I fanned the heroine and waited for the curtain to descend — the audience must not know who was sneaking in via the trapdoor until the last act! But the curtain stayed up. I fanned some more, and de Liagre (the villain) closed the trap and started to open it again. The curtain remained up, my arms ached from fanning, and de Liagre, in a fitful mood, began to open and close the trapdoor furiously, making noises like a bass drum. The audience had a tolerant nature, but was glad to hear me announce I would go to the kitchen for some water.

As I raged into the wings, I saw the stage manager sitting beside the curtain ropes reading next week's script.

"Take the curtain down, you bog-bottom!" I said.

"Take your time," said Otis Chatfield Taylor as he set aside his book and lowered the rag.

Very few people returned for the next act because Cape May is a summer resort, the drinks outside are good, and people are easily perplexed.

It was at Cape May, too, that one Saturday morning rehearsals were postponed, the doors opened, and a hundred friends and patrons filed in — free of charge. The stage was banked with flowers and there were six little flower girls, daughters of friends and neighbors, dressed in white. The mayor of Cape May walked across the boards, his hands shaking with nerves. He read a tremulous wedding ceremony over two of us. It was my first marriage, to Helen Derby of Montclair, New Jersey. Afterward there was champagne; and that night I played the juvenile lead. No time for a honeymoon in those hot, summer-stock days.

Champagne always reminds me of Millbrook, where Edith Barrett played Candida marvelously. She managed to improve my acting while being tormented by arthritis, which frequently made her cry with pain. But the audiences never knew. Most actresses are saints. They work and suffer and sometimes they make acting a gallant profession. Edith was one of the saintlier artists.

Getting back to champagne: there was a wealthy weekender at Millbrook who had once been kicked by a horse, it having had no other ill effect upon him except to make him benevolent to actors and actresses. He had a swimming pool and gardens and a beautiful home, and in every cranny, under every hedge, in baskets, trays, and in butlers' arms, were champagnes of rare vintage. Just for us. We poured it into our scrambled eggs and rubbed it into our hair. We floated in his swimming pool with spindle glasses balanced on our chests and we went to our beds nestling our hot cheeks against cool unopened bottles of Ayala '21. That was a wondrous man — he gave us poor devils a taste of luxury that predated the hoopla of Mt. Olympus . . .

On I hurtled to Newport, where I played *Man in the Zoo*, which was the first new play ever essayed in that luxurious summer theater. Opening-night tickets there were $6.60. We had never heard of such prices. I received a rustic's thrill when the elegant Mrs. Moses Taylor and one of the young Vanderbilts came to witness our dress rehearsal of a zoo scene.

The plot of the play was intricate and had something to do with exhibiting a human being behind bars so the public could study Homo sapiens as it studies other species in close confinement. The animal imitators were jumping around throwing hay in the air as I walked onstage, and when I started to speak, the inside of my nose tickled. Because I was allergic to straw and hay and weeds, I sneezed twenty-two times by count. I sneezed so long and violently that I melted like a candle on a stove.

I was scraped up and sent home, where I was given doses of ephedrine. Mrs. Taylor ordered the straw on the stage wetted down and said she herself would play in the mob scene for our opening the next night — to rescue me if I needed it.

This, as it turned out, was nearly a fatal decision on her part because, with my eyes red with pollen, my heart leaping from first-night excitement, I rattled the cage door so mightily that the hinges flew off and a length of chain screamed through the air, kissed Mrs. T's cheek, and knocked over a small girl standing in the wings.

Nothing came of it — the play never went to Broadway — but the notices were kind and the audience were all millionaires and very generous with their applause.

Summer theaters still go on, though they are removed from

me now, but the glow stays in my heart and the gleam is in my eye — I shall do it again! I envy the boys and girls on the cowshed circuit. It is more exciting than Broadway or Hollywood; younger and more romantic. All kinds of roles, all hours of rehearsals, all sorts of vacation-mooded excitement. It reminds me of Robert Louis Stevenson's lines: "In summer, quite the other way, / I have to go to bed by day."

So they went, those summer-theater days and nights. It all seems now like a sweet dream of wild boyhood.

The secret attraction of summer stock was — and I hope still is — the wondrous rapport that exists between actors and audiences. There is nothing stiff or formidable between actor and audience; no strain, no challenge. It starts and ends with a smile — at every performance.

Katharine Cornell

WHEN I CAME to New York in the mid-1930s, I believed, like most other young actors, that the royalty of the American theater consisted of four women and one man. The women were Katharine Cornell, Helen Hayes, Eva Le Gallienne, and Lynn Fontanne, and the man was Alfred Lunt. There were others, but these were the tops; hardworking, enormously successful superstars in a thriving theater. To have a role in one of their plays was more than a privilege, it was a kind of knighthood. The title of "First Lady" was handed back and forth among the gals, but generally Katharine Cornell wore the crown because she had the largest following, the greatest succession of hits, and probably the most prestige.

I never worked with Lunt or Fontanne, but I apprenticed with Le Gallienne, lived next door to Helen Hayes, and, in the longest and closest theatrical association of my life, I did seven plays with Katharine — we called her Kit — Cornell and her husband, the director Guthrie McClintic, from 1934 to the end of World War II. After that, I saw the McClintics only occasionally. Yet every memory of those earlier days is vivid. Kit and Guthrie were a colorful, glamorous, and somewhat secretive couple, and those of us who worked with them liked them enormously and owed them a great deal.

I remember the "first call" I had from their office in Rockefeller Center in 1934. I arrived nervous and excited. Kit was sitting there looking beautiful; a gentle-mannered lady, very quiet. Incidentally, this sense of repose, this lack of temperament, is a quality I've never seen in any other star, at least to such an extent.

Guthrie, on the other hand, was talkative, nervous, and witty. I recall at that first meeting he launched into an abrasive discussion of the Group Theater and the Method actors who were looming on the horizon and whom he did not like. I felt Kit watching me and smiling and finally she touched her husband's hand and interrupted him. "Guthrie, I must go. Persuade this boy to come into *Barretts* next week so we can get acquainted before we rehearse the Van Druten play."

Guthrie, though a little miffed at not being allowed to finish his tirade, said, "Fine."

When Kit left, he confided, surprisingly, "She's a marvelous woman. You've no idea." Afterward I was to hear him say that many times. I finally figured out he was simply a fan of hers; that is, despite being her husband, he had a curiously detached admiration of her gifts, a kind of stage-door crush on the lady.

Thus, in a few minutes I was offered two roles, a small one in the third revival of *The Barretts of Wimpole Street* and a larger role, opposite Miss Cornell, in John Van Druten's *Flowers of the Forest*.

The *Barretts* revival went smoothly enough. But just before the opening of *Forest* I noticed Kit seemed nervous, apprehensive. We talked, and she confessed that she always suffered this kind of stage fright. She said, "I wonder sometimes why I keep acting."

I was amazed. Here she was, the most successful, the most beloved actress in the American theater, at the peak of her career, and yet apparently suffering from nerves underneath that outward display of serenity and success.

However, on occasion, stage fright is justified.

On opening night, a few moments after the curtain went up
and just as I started my first speech, a woman in the second row
of the audience had an epileptic seizure. She started to scream
and snort as though possessed. The ushers raced down the aisle,
and the audience and I were traumatized. Only Kit Cornell, so
apprehensive an hour before, became calm. As calm as Mother
Earth. She took me by the shoulders and began to ad lib. "You're
not well . . . lie down and let me rub your forehead." I lay down
on a sofa as if I were hypnotized. Kit, still talking, put a pillow
underneath my head and comforted and cajoled me and miraculously rubbed my head with cologne she had conjured up from
somewhere onstage.

By and by the ushers carried the now catatonic lady up the
aisle and out of the theater and the audience resettled itself, probably wondering if it were all part of the plot. Kit, still in character,
said to me, "Now, Gerald [or whatever my stage name was],
you're fine now, your color's back, now tell us that lovely poem
again."

My motor started, and I was off and running. As to the play,
the critics didn't think too much of it, but as usual they adored
Miss Cornell, though not half as much as I did.

In 1942 I played Marchbanks to Miss Cornell's Candida. Kit
had played the role many times, had in fact made it her own in
this country. I had played it in stock, but never with Kit. This
was at the start of World War II, and General George Marshall,
a friend of Kit's, asked her to do the play as a benefit for the Army
Navy Relief Fund. She agreed, and she and Guthrie started to
assemble an all-star cast. They decided on me for Marchbanks. I,
however, was a three-month draftee private at the Santa Ana
Army Air Force Base in California.

Somehow Kit and Gertrude Macy, her general manager, got
me on the phone and asked me to play the part. "I'd love to, but
I'm in the army air force cleaning latrines at the moment," I said.
Kit laughed; "Sit tight. Don't move."

Within two hours, my commanding officer summoned me to
his headquarters. He looked shocked and was staring at a telegram

on his desk. He said, "Private Meredith, I'm ordered to fly you to New York at once to act in some goddamn play! Some goddamn war, eh, Private Meredith?"

In ten hours I was in New York rehearsing with Kit and Guthrie, Dudley Digges, Raymond Massey, Mildred Natwick, and the others. Kit explained we would play a brief run of benefit performances to raise money for the Fund. I'm not sure of the exact figures, but tickets were something on the order of $50 or $100 apiece, very high prices in those days. At any rate, the production was sold out before we opened, and both the critics and the army were ecstatic. Richard Watts wrote for years about the production. It ran for six weeks in New York and two weeks in Washington and earned a fortune for the Fund.

But Raymond Massey's favorite story was the surprise Kit gave me on opening night in Washington, D.C., after the curtain. There was a pounding on my dressing room door and a martial voice hollered, "Private Meredith — open up!"

"Who is it?" I yelled.

"General Marshall — open up, Private Meredith."

There, in truth, stood the great man himself all covered with ribbons and beside him was Katharine Cornell, still in the long brown dress of Candida. They were both laughing, and, after a moment, so was I.

Of course, when the show closed I had to go back to camp and, so help me God, pick up the mop where I had left it. But those weeks with Kit Cornell were a wonderful reprieve. All during the war, I carried the picture of the two of us doing that fireplace scene together. I still have it.

A Marriage, a Musical, and Maxwell Anderson

BUT EVEN BEFORE the war, life had begun in earnest. The first of my four wives was Helen Derby, a vivacious, attractive girl of twenty-three from Montclair, New Jersey. Her father, Harry Derby, was president of American Cyanamide. She was a divorcée and the mother of a three-year-old daughter. We met at an after-theater party in Montclair. I was fascinated by her volatile nature, so quickly changing, so close to the surface. Her spirits continuously jumped from high to low, from sad to ecstatic in dazzling sequences. I think I was the first actor Helen had ever met, and she was the first psychosomatic I had come across. We caught fire quickly and it was quickly over.

But not before we were married, during my first hectic excursion toward the Broadway theater, as I moved from the cool safety of Eva Le Gallienne's small repertory theater through summer stock into the blaze of Broadway. That change was radical and fast. The thirties and early forties were roaring times — Franklin Delano Roosevelt was president and the fuse of World War II was smoldering.

We rented a small apartment in Manhattan at 27 West 10th. I recall it vividly, every inch of it. It was the first "home" I'd ever had.

Our marriage was physically wild. I am ashamed to remember the violent scenes we had. She had a temper and a habit of hitting me — until I broke her jaw! We were appalled and ashamed of our actions, both of us.

It all ended when I raided Helen's apartment with detectives and caught her in flagrante delicto. I brought the evidence to her father and laid it on his desk. He accepted it as only a good businessman can, and said he was sorry I had to go through all that nonsense. We shook hands, signed new papers, and that forlorn love affair, that tag-end of a fateful marriage, was dissolved forever. I was confused but I was legally free and unencumbered.

Two years later I married again, to Margaret Perry, the daughter of Antoinette ("Tony") Perry, the Broadway director after whom the Tony Awards are named.

In the first month of our marriage the phone rang — it was the *New York Times*. They called to tell me Helen had committed suicide. They said she had asphyxiated herself in the kitchenette of her Washington Square apartment — the same apartment I had raided with detectives. I remember now that Lionel Stander, the actor, a radical and amusing fellow, helped me through that episode. It seems, from this distance, there was a continuum of suicides in those sad days.

As a postscript, I became friends with Helen's father. After the funeral, we would meet and talk occasionally. Though our lives were widely separated, we enjoyed talking with each other — we were both trying to find our way, the millionaire and the ham actor. The man had lost not only his daughter, Helen, but, some time after, his son and then his wife. He lived on bravely with only his granddaughter remaining, Helen's daughter. He has gone now, but his granddaughter is grown and has a family. We exchange cards on the holidays, but we have never seen each other since she was a child.

So despite early success, my arrival on the Broadway scene came with attendant problems, emotional and financial. Immediately following *Little Ol' Boy* I went into a Broadway show called *She Loves Me Not,* a musical comedy about Princeton University undergraduates.

The plot? One of the students smuggles a beautiful chorus girl into his dormitory room. That was then considered a naughty concept. Polly Walters played the girl and John Beal was the boy. I, by luck, got the part of a young undergraduate, called Buzz, which was my own nickname.

Buzz was a fast-talking chap who distinguished himself by being able to tap dance, eat an apple, and do homework at the same time. It was a hilarious part and the play was an instant hit; the first I had ever been in. I think my salary was $400 a week, very good pay in those days. My friends, who were poor, and my brother, who was intoxicated, would line up outside my dressing room on payday and help me get rid of any excess cash.

A sad note: during rehearsals of this comedy I flew to Canada where I held my mother in my arms as she died. She had retreated there a few weeks before to join my father. The saddest aspect of her death was that for the first time I could have helped her financially.

When I got back to the theater, the director, Howard Lindsay, asked me about my mother. "She died," I said. Moved by my numb distress, Howard said quietly, "Let's take the rest of the day off — we'll continue tomorrow."

Not content with being in a Broadway hit, I also accepted the leading role in a radio show called *Red Davis,* about an all-American boy of about sixteen, who always got into trouble because he was mischievous and luckless. The problem was that we had to play the show "live"; there was no such thing as taping then. We broadcast early for the East Coast and later for the West Coast.

I undertook the radio job to keep my mind busy and increase my income. I was greedy. I had moved into an East Side apartment in the same block where I was to visit my psychoanalyst twenty years later. I acquired an English valet named Wood, a darling guy with a wicked Cockney tongue. So I had double incomes and double duties.

I broadcast my radio shows first at 7:00 to 7:30 P.M. and then at 11:00 to 11:30 P.M., and in between — from 8:00 to 10:00 P.M. — I performed in the theater. I had moved on from *She Loves Me Not* to *Flowers of the Forest* with Katharine Cornell at the Martin Beck. The timing of these events was so critical that I hired an ambulance to run me across town. This ambulance would pick me up at the stage door of the Martin Beck, and clang me across town to the NBC Studios in time to leap before the microphone and say, "Hello, Mom," or whatever my first line happened to be. This ambulance routine was noised around the city, and I started to crawl into the lower strata of fame.

Then came a catastrophe. One night I missed the repeat radio program completely! They had changed the time of the broadcast and though I was informed, I forgot and wandered in late.

You can imagine the confusion and perhaps dismay of the listening audience when the poor director, whatever his name was, had to step in and try to imitate me on the spot. People wrote to NBC by the thousands, demanding to know what had happened to poor Red Davis. The Beechnut sponsors were furious and couldn't wait to fire me.

My missing the broadcast was fatal. Beechnut pulled the program off the air as soon as possible. As compensation, Katharine Cornell and Guthrie McClintic invited me to become a permanent member of their company. This began our association of seven plays in as many years.

But it was a long time before I tried radio again! When I did, I gave it my full attention.

My association with the Cornell office came simultaneously with Maxwell Anderson's coming backstage and saying, "I have written a play I hope will interest you." I told Guthrie about the play and he bought it. The name of the play was *Winterset* — the first of three plays that Max wrote, Guthrie directed, and I performed.

It was a lucky decade for me — long runs, many awards, and a motion picture version of *Winterset*.

Winterset was a fiery epistle for the time. After we opened, they put my name above the title — which meant I had formally become a star! Becoming a star was a significant matter in those days, so on my twenty-eighth birthday I borrowed a camera and took a picture of my name in lights.

Both professionally and personally, my life was changing fast. The lovely redheaded Margaret "Maggie" Perry became my second wife in a simple ceremony at Sneden's Landing, which was a small stop-off across the Hudson from upper Manhattan in Rockland County. She was quite a girl, Maggie was. Wealthy in her own right, a delicate beauty, she was a young Dietrich. Unfortunately, our union didn't last. But I was fond and foolish about her then and we bought a farm together near Maxwell Anderson's home.

Max lived in Rockland County, New York, and owned a considerable amount of property on South Mountain Road near New City. His home was a long drive from New York City, but the countryside was lovely.

When he first invited me there, we sat in his little red house and he read *Winterset* to me. It was written in iambic pentameter — but using colloquial language. It had a gangster setting, and its impact on me was stunning.

I spent several days with him and expressed my enthusiasm and gratitude for being given the leading role. I was in awe of him. He was a large, lumbering man who wore glasses and spoke quietly and eloquently. It seemed to me he knew everything there was to know. No subject eluded him — he had that kind of omniscience, which he lightened with a sly sense of humor.

Maxwell Anderson was the fatherly influence I never had known before. Perhaps he came along too late to change me, but he quietly did his best, particularly in the beginning. He raised my sights. I did not agree with many of his political ideas — he was extremely antigovernment — but we became close friends.

At the end of my marriage to Maggie Perry and after my marriage to Paulette Goddard, I pursued some great and lovely ladies — Ingrid Bergman, Marlene Dietrich, Hedy Lamarr, and others. It was a frolicsome period and it took up a good stretch of my time and energy. Max worried about me, as he well should have, and we saw less and less of each other as the years went by, but he tried gently to slow me down.

Above all, he helped me find a spot of land where I could get away from the city.

The property he found was sixty acres, next to a village called Mount Ivy. As soon as I could, I bought this land and lived there until a few years ago. A park was named for me there in 1991. I attended the opening ceremony and spoke as clearly as my emotions allowed.

My close relationship with Max lasted through three plays: *Winterset, High Tor,* and *The Star Wagon.*

High Tor takes its title from the name of a small mountain on the Hudson River, the highest point of the Palisades, in an area originally settled by the Dutch. There is now an airplane warning beacon at the top.

After *Winterset,* Anderson was anxious to start *High Tor,* but first I was scheduled to make the film of *Winterset.* After I returned from California, we took long walks around the countryside and discussed our hopes and plans for the future. A couple of days before the play opened, Max and I walked to the top of High Tor, near the beacon, and solemnly shook hands and promised that if the play was a success, the two of us would buy the entire mountain. At that time High Tor was for sale for some reasonable amount, about twenty-five thousand dollars. Today you couldn't buy it for twenty-five million.

The play opened, and it was a success, but we did *not* buy High Tor. We broke our promise — unfortunately for both of us, I guess.

But *High Tor* almost failed. Anderson wanted Mab, his wife, to play the heroine. However, in the opinion of Guthrie McClintic, she was not right for the role. I liked Mab very much, but I agreed with Guthrie and he got her to resign. All this happened during the road tour, before coming into New York, and I recall that during this turmoil I suggested that my own wife, Maggie Perry, replace Mab.

At that point McClintic exploded; he said that the situation was getting manic. He yelled, "I want no more wives! Let's get some fucking talent in this show!"

The actress who replaced Mab was Peggy Ashcroft, who salvaged the play.

After *Tor*, Max conjured up the third play for me, *The Star Wagon*. In it I played opposite Lillian Gish, who returned to the stage after many a year. And that, too, was a hit. Luck stayed by our side.

Max was at the height of his power. He wrote *Wingless Victory* for Miss Cornell, *Elizabeth the Queen* for Helen Hayes, and, when I introduced him to Ingrid Bergman, who was staying at my house when we did *Liliom* together, Max wrote a play for her too. It was the story of Joan of Arc. Anderson was unsurpassed at custom-writing plays for actors and actresses; and he wrote to order with dispatch and, generally, with success.

In those days Maxwell Anderson was both an important playwright and a strong influence. Now his plays are seldom produced. *Winterset* is rarely revived, but in its time it was considered "wildly radical." Today, it has little resonance, yet it is beautifully written.

Max, together with Kurt Weill, wrote a fourth play for me, *Knickerbocker Holiday*. But in the final version the older man's role — ultimately played by Walter Huston — dominated the story line. It was his show, from start to finish, and when I withdrew from the play to work with Orson Welles, it was a decision that hurt Max and surprised Kurt.

On a personal level, Anderson was disturbed by my frequent changes of wives and girlfriends; then, years later, suddenly — he, too, left his wife!

It was a shock to everyone when it happened; I equated it to Moses changing his religion. Anderson's love had been steadfast until that very moment.

The shocking ending of that separation was suicide. In the spring of 1953, Mab came to visit us one evening, composed and quiet. Later that same night, after she got home she locked herself in the garage, turned on the engine, and died of carbon monoxide poisoning.

After Mab's suicide, Anderson remarried and moved away from Rockland County and away from his children. I would never have guessed that such a quiet, scholarly man would develop such explosive marriage problems.

He died in 1959 in a Nyack, New York, hospital. Alan, his son, told me the details of his death. Max had a habit of looking at his watch while he was talking with you. He was a great watch-gazer. He valued time and he was not frivolous about the passing of hours. In the hospital he lay in his bed, looking thin and wan, but he roused himself from a coma and asked for his eyeglasses and his watch.

Alan perched his glasses on the bridge of his father's nose and handed him his wristwatch. Max glanced at the hour, closed his eyes, and died.

I missed him greatly and still miss him. It was a relationship I should have treasured even more than I did.

Kurt Weill and Lotte Lenya

THE STORY of my friendship with Kurt Weill is a tale of unfulfilled plans and missed opportunities. We were friends but, in retrospect, our failures appear more interesting than our fulfillments.

My relationship with that gifted man began three years before he came to this country and continued until his death in 1950, a stretch of about seventeen years. And, although he has gone, our relationship still continues, stronger than ever, until this present day — a total of more than half a century.

We had our share of failures, Kurt and I, but we enjoyed the experiences even if we accomplished less than we dreamed.

Although we were friends, I doubt if Kurt Weill was as much interested in my thoughts as I was in his.

The same with Lotte Lenya. When I was trying out a new production of *Johnny Johnson* in Aspen a few summers ago, I telephoned Lenya every week and she never once mentioned the frustrations of the past — she talked about the future. She was enthusiastic about our experiments out there in Aspen and made

no remarks like "I hope to God this one works out, Burgess."
But let me start at the beginning:

I was less than twenty years old when I quit Eva Le Gallienne's
apprentice group to play my first real part in a Broadway show.
The show was Bertolt Brecht and Weill's *Threepenny Opera*, directed by Francesca von Mendelssohn and produced by John
Krimsky. That 1933 presentation was the first Brecht/Weill play
ever staged in this country — and Weill was still in Germany.

I was hired to play the small role of "Crooked Finger Jack." I
had only a few lines; but this engagement began the first of a
series of what I choose to call my "Kurt Weill Coitus Interruptus."
No sex intended. Purely metaphoric.

Although I had no songs to sing, I fell in love with Weill's
music, which seemed to me unworldly and wonderful. Its uncanny effect haunts me to this day.

The lyrics and the book — I forget who did the adaptation —
were clumsy, with verses like:

> For soldiers holsters
> Must be their bolsters
> From sea to shining sea . . .

But I was happy to be in my first Broadway show, and to hear
Weill's abrasive music.

Then, as I've previously related, a funny thing happened on
my way to the theater. During the second week of rehearsal, I
was approached by Joe Losey and John Hammond, Jr., to play
the leading role in a show they were producing, *Little Ol' Boy*. I
was happy about this sweet turn of events, but I told Losey and
Hammond I was in rehearsal with *Threepenny Opera*.

They said they knew about that, "But you should read our
play. There are ways to work these things out." It was the first
time I heard that phrase. I was to hear it again many times in my
life.

So I read their play and was bowled over by the towering star
part. I couldn't resist it! I would do it, I said, if they could arrange
with Actors' Equity to get me out of *Threepenny*. They arranged
it the following day.

Equity ruled I could make the change but I had to play *Three-penny Opera* for two weeks before I could leave. Those were the rules then and are the same today. It is called "giving your notice."

So I gave my notice; I would play *Threepenny* in Philadelphia, rush back at midnight to New York to rehearse *Little Ol' Boy* the next day, and then return to Philly to play again. Quite a jog.

Both plays opened within three weeks of each other in New York and both plays were instant failures. *Threepenny Opera* was a failure the first time out and so was *Little Ol' Boy* its first and only time out. But despite the box-office failure of both shows, I received a gift from each of them.

From *Little Ol' Boy* I received a set of notices that made me a star, and from *Threepenny Opera* I received the gift of Kurt Weill's music — and a desire to play in a Weill musical before my life was over.

To this day I have never acted in one of his musicals. I came close, but it never worked out.

In September 1935 Kurt came to the United States, and in 1936 he wrote the music for *Johnny Johnson,* with a book by Paul Green and direction by Lee Strasberg. It was a play I tried out for, but was turned down by the Group Theater.

At that moment in time the Group Theater decided I was an upstart — ignorant of what they called the Stanislavsky "Method." They told me that in spite of my early success, I wasn't "ready" for them.

I decided there was nothing I could do but find a way to contact Weill personally, which I did. We hit it off immediately and be-came close friends.

In December 1937, Kurt Weill, Charles Allen, and I formed a corporation that we called the Ballad Theatre. Our purpose was to produce plays in which a new musical form would be used. A chorus of singers, like a musical Greek chorus, would sing the story line, and the actors would go into action only when the mood was prescribed by the chorus.

The chorus would be large and varied and, most important, would replace the orchestra. In other terms, the voices would perform the harmonies and functions of the orchestra, provide the narrative and exposition, and accompany the lead singers.

I forget where Kurt said the idea came from. Either he had experimented with it in the past or had dreamed it up, I don't remember. Of course, the idea derives essentially from the Greeks, but not in musical form.

The story Kurt suggested we do first was "Davy Crockett." It would work like this:

When, for instance, Davy Crockett's girl found a letter from Davy, she would pick it up and start to read it. But instead of the girl saying the words, she would look at the letter; and the chorus, a cappella, would sing the words she was silently reading and describe the thoughts she was thinking until it was time for her solo. Then, when she began to sing, she would be accompanied, not by an orchestra, but by the same chorus. If any musical instrument was used, it had to be a part of the action — like a flute, a guitar, a harp, a drum, and so on. In short, it was to be a "Ballad Theatre."

Of course, according to our habit, we never got any further in this endeavor than filing the papers!

I never heard if Kurt carried out this Ballad Theatre idea elsewhere. There was a whiff of it in *Down in the Valley*, but there they used an orchestra. I am still fascinated with the notion. I remember something akin to the idea was used later by a friend of mine, John La Touche, in his opera *Ballad of Baby Doe* and in *Ballet Ballads*, both hits.

Kurt, Maxwell Anderson, and I tried a version of it in the cantata "Magna Carta," where it worked well, but it was a radio broadcast and never performed on stage.

Our next coitus interruptus went better for Kurt than it did for me. I am speaking about *Knickerbocker Holiday*.

One day, Max Anderson asked me what I'd like to do after *The Star Wagon*, and I told him I wanted to do a musical with Kurt Weill if he would write the book.

Anderson liked the idea, so I brought Kurt to the country to meet him. It was a momentous meeting. They got along instantly and began a friendship that lasted for the rest of their lives.

I remember the afternoon we three were strolling in the woods and Max brought up the idea of adapting Washington Irving's *Knickerbocker History of New York*. He said he admired Irving and was fascinated by the old Dutch settlers who lived in the very countryside where we were walking. It was during that walk that the idea of *Knickerbocker Holiday* was born.

The next day Kurt and I hurried to buy copies of Washington Irving's works and were intrigued. As the play developed over the months, important changes took place. As I've mentioned, my role, young Brom Broek, became less interesting, while the part of old Peter Stuyvesant grew bigger and better. I was beginning to feel a chill come over me.

Guthrie McClintic withdrew as director for the same reason: he didn't like the way it was heading.

Just at this point, Orson Welles and John Houseman, then at the peak of their glory, asked me to join them to play Prince Hal / Henry V to Orson's Falstaff in a forthcoming Theatre Guild production of five Shakespeare plays. I accepted their offer.

So, once again, I deserted a Kurt Weill musical, and once again a dream was broken or deferred.

Under Josh Logan's direction *Knickerbocker Holiday* went on to become a hit. The big role, however, was Walter Huston's — the part meant for me was insignificant and seldom mentioned.

My six-year professional association with Maxwell Anderson was broken and never mended.

On the other hand, Orson, Houseman, and I never came into New York with our production of *Five Kings*. We struck out before we started.

Houseman has written about *Five Kings* in his autobiography. I will give you my version later, but now I will detail the forlorn and continuing story of my coitus interruptus with Kurt Weill.

One of Weill's biographers, Ronald Sanders, in his book *The Days Grow Short*, wrote that in 1938, "There was a possibility that Walter Wanger, a well known Hollywood producer, would do a film of 'Johnny Johnson' with Burgess Meredith in the title role." Unfortunately, Mr. Wanger lost interest and I suffered my second divorce and took off for Europe.

That same biographer went on to say, ". . . Weill moved up to

Rockland County to live in close proximity to Maxwell Anderson, Henry Varnum Poor and actor Burgess Meredith. . . ."

The only thing I can add to that is that there was a rift in our relations after I quit *Knickerbocker*. In time, Kurt and Max forgave me — after all, they fared better than Orson and I did and they had Walter Huston to console them — but the air was chilly for a year or so.

Eventually we three resumed our friendship, especially after I married Paulette Goddard, whom they liked, and Kurt and I proceeded to our next failed efforts.

In 1940, Norman Corwin produced a successful Sunday afternoon radio show called *The Pursuit of Happiness*, in which I acted as moderator, guide, and host. The most famous of our productions was a musical number called "Ballad for Americans," written by John La Touche and Earl Robinson and sung gloriously by Paul Robeson. We initiated readings from the Bible by Charles Laughton and the first appearance of a talented young fellow named Danny Kaye.

Those were heady times on radio, and I was determined to get Weill and Anderson involved. I sold Corwin on the idea, and the result was a cantata called "The Ballad of the Magna Carta," with me speaking the chorus. Anderson said, "I hope the part is big enough for Burgess this time!"

I said to Kurt, "Well, we finally did a radio show — now let's get something on the stage!"

Kurt smiled and said: "We will, we will in time," but it never happened.

However, something else happened later — a film called *Salute to France*.

The year was 1944, and World War II was blazing.

Four months before the Allied invasion of France, I was taken off active duty as an army air force officer in England and sent to the United States to make an indoctrination film about France. The purpose of the film was to explain to the Allied troops what the French people were like — after having been locked up in Hitler's prison. Eisenhower wanted our troops to understand the French before we stormed the Channel.

Instinctively — almost from habit — I asked Kurt Weill to write the score. Kurt wasn't exactly French (!), but I figured he had written many beautiful French songs, so he was the composer I wanted.

I also enlisted Jean Renoir to direct the French version, and Garson Kanin to help me with the American version. Also recruited were members of the French underground as advisers. I produced and acted in the film. It is still an effective film, and it did its job.

After we finished, I turned the film over to the Office of War Information to be circulated, but some of the boys in the back room got hold of the negative and, for reasons known only to the devil, cut out the beautiful theme song Kurt wrote and Paul Robeson sang!

I wish I knew where that song went. The army would never say — they played innocent. There seems to be no copy of it in Kurt Weill's files, or they haven't found it if there is. Interruptus again!

Our collaborative efforts had failed thus far — but we still had a way to go: a revival of *Threepenny*, which the Actors Studio West put on a few years ago in Los Angeles and from which I withdrew because I was appalled at the direction.

And so it went . . . on and on . . . *"But the days grow short as you reach September — and the autumn weather turns the leaves to flame — and I haven't got time for the waiting game."*

Eventually Kurt and Lenya settled down, and were happy — a complete change. When I first knew them I didn't consider they had a serious marriage, any more than the two or three marriages I had gone through were serious.

But it came to pass that the Weills settled down more than any of us. They lived in Rockland County surrounded by American antiques, a brook flowing by, and they assumed, little by little, the conservative stance of Maxwell Anderson. As an example, Weill and Anderson worked on a musical version of *Huckleberry Finn*, which is 180 degrees different from the revolutionary, fist-clenching style Kurt had developed in Europe with Brecht. I am not stating this as a criticism — I ran a quaint antique shop for a while!

There are other memories. For instance, Kurt was playing on my tennis court in Mount Ivy when he collapsed and was taken to the hospital. He appeared to make a good recovery and I was not alarmed when less than a year later he had an attack of flu. But his health deteriorated rapidly.

One day I called Weill's home to find out how he was. The maid answered the phone and said, "Oh, Mr. Meredith, you're coming to the funeral, aren't you?" And that is how I learned Kurt Weill had died.

I answered, "Oh yes, I called — I just called to see when the funeral would be." And she said, "This afternoon, in an hour."

It was sudden and terrible. The funeral was at a local church and a nearby cemetery. But I could not get to the funeral because I was in the middle of the final dress rehearsal of *Our Town* in New York City, with Robert Montgomery directing, who let me out as soon as he could. I telephoned the maid again to tell her that I was rehearsing and couldn't get to the funeral. Would she explain to Lenya that I would be there as soon as I could.

I drove to Weill's house that night, and we had a gentle wake. Only a few people were there — Lotte Lenya, Mrs. Walter Huston, who was a good friend of Lenya's, and one or two other close friends and myself. We sat there laughing and crying and drinking to Kurt, the way you do, and when it was time to go to bed Lotte Lenya said to me, "Would you sleep in Kurt's bed tonight? Just stay there, you know, so it won't be lonely in the house tonight? Nan Huston is sleeping here and the Caniffs will stay, and a couple of other people . . . I don't want to be alone."

So I went to sleep in Kurt's bed, and at about four in the morning I was shaken awake by Lotte Lenya, who asked, "Can you drive Mrs. Huston in to New York? Walter Huston is dying, and she must go to him."

I was tired and in despair from the wake and the shock of

Kurt's sudden going, but I pulled myself together and drove Nan Huston to New York. She sat there quietly and asked me not to talk. So we drove silently and had gone as far as the George Washington Bridge before she said, "All right, it's all right. Thank you." And I drove on into the city to play in *Our Town* that evening on live television.

Later I realized that it was during the time we were driving from New City to the bridge that Walter Huston died. Exactly to the hour.

It was a time of sadness and loss, but I treasure many tranquil, happy memories.

Years before, Kurt and I sat on his porch on South Mountain Road, chatting away, and I said to him that my life was being pulled apart while his seemed to be settling down. He said yes and he was glad about himself because he knew, given time, he would have Lotte all to himself. And, in fact, so he did.

In another conversation, Kurt said to me, "I know I can never be Bach, but I'm as good as Richard Strauss." That remark made us both laugh because Kurt had told me that years before, Brecht got angry at Weill and said he was "a would-be Richard Strauss."

Tallulah Again

SHORTLY AFTER Margaret Perry and I were married, the two of us visited Tallulah. The evening started in a curious way. Tallulah had a secretary, a stocky girl who adored her. She seemed to me to be a kind of bodyguard, as well as a secretary and general confidante. During the evening as Tallulah and I began to reminisce, the secretary started to make advances to Margaret. Margaret was generally broad-minded, but this time she slammed out of the place and I followed.

When I caught up to her, she explained that what really irked her was what she called the "stratification" of the situation. She felt she had been relegated to the lower class, as it were. It wasn't so much the lesbianism as it was the fact she had been the target of a hireling!

Margaret's life with me was not an easy one. The same week she had been targeted by Tallulah's stalwart assistant, I brought a hive of bees to our home in the country. They were supposed to be put outside the windowsill, so we could watch them from inside as they flew to the fields and back again. Being a little unsteady, however, I installed the hive backward, so the bees swarmed inside and into the grand piano. Not long after that, Margaret got around to divorcing me.

Eventually Tallulah got married. She chose John Emery, or Ted as he was known to his friends. A braver man there never was, to marry that formidable lady. I must say he made it last longer than anybody thought possible. But the fact it lasted at all, or that it happened at all, astonished many people. It certainly did me.

Ted and Tallulah took up residence in the Elysee Hotel. This was soon to become known as the Bankhead hotel. Every place she lived became known as Tallulah's place: hotels, country homes, whatever. As an example, some time before I met her, Tallulah had bought a splendid house in Rockland County. She ordered the architect Rollo Peters, a scenic designer and Broadway actor, to make various changes. He fell asleep in the house the night he finished work, and when he woke the house was on fire. Peters saved his own life by leaping out of a second-floor window, but the house was gone. Only the great brick walls and blackened fireplaces were left.

For years those ruins were known as the "Tallulah Bankhead house." Whatever Tallulah touched, her flag flew over it.

Later I bought the property as an investment and fixed it up. I soon sold it, and, when she has a spare moment, I expect Tallulah haunts it from time to time. To this day it is still referred to as the Tallulah Bankhead property.

Some girls have a way of taking over. Paulette Goddard had a similar knack. At the time she and I were married, we lived in my country house for a year or two, and of course it became known as Paulette's place. One's ego gets bruised, if one dwells on it long enough.

Tallulah and Ted's new home in the Elysee also became known as the "Easy Lay Hotel." They were soon surrounded by the same people who always surrounded Tallulah, wherever she moved: a colorful, pleasure-oriented group who played at night and slept through the day.

From time to time I would stay in town when I had an early call at the theater in the morning. One evening after the show I thought I would drop in at the Bankhead/Emery establishment, to see what was happening. As usual, a party was in progress, with many beautiful people. I was tired and wanted a good sleep before the next day's matinee, so I asked Tallulah if she had a sleeping pill. Tallulah had exactly the right prescription, a large purple number, and popped it into my mouth. Before long I could feel its soporific effect and started for the door. But fate decided otherwise.

Into Tallulah's apartment came a beautiful, raven-haired girl. Even in my slumbrous condition I responded. Tallulah introduced us and said she knew the girl and I were destined for each other. I had my hat and coat on, but I sat down to reconsider. I realized I was fighting Morpheus for the gift of this dark angel. Tallulah came by and saw my problem. She went to her medicine cabinet and found a bright red pill, which she gave me with a dash of water and a scoop of brandy, and told me it would do the trick. "It will overtake the sleeping pill," said she.

In five minutes I leaped from the lower depths. It was a super benzedrine pep-capsule, and it flung me to the ceiling and beyond. The girl and I got together under Tallulah's ministrations and, although I didn't shine at the matinee the next day, the night was spent in glory.

Tallulah's proclivity for dispensing cocaine was famous. Bea Lilly quoted Tallulah as saying, "Dahling, I tell you it is *not* habit forming. I've taken it every night for years!"

Bea Lilly also told the story about herself and Tallulah coming in to Claridge's in London late one night. Bea was also Lady Peel, wife of Sir Robert Peel. The two ladies weaved into that elegant hotel and Tallulah asked the desk clerk for "Lady Keel's pee"! The baffled clerk said, "I don't know what you want, madame." Bea, loyally supporting her friend, said, "She wants what she asked for. She wants Lady Keel's pee! But if you have mislaid it, we'll take Lady Peel's key."

*   *   *

One of Tallulah's last plays was *Midgie Purvis*. It was written by Mary Chase and produced by Robert Whitehead, and I directed it in 1961.

I still think *Midgie Purvis*, which was about a woman who refused to grow old, was potentially one of the best properties I have ever had anything to do with. Mary Chase, who wrote the hit play *Harvey*, had a sharp wit and offbeat imagination.

When Bob Whitehead and I decided to stage the play, it was his idea to use Tallulah. I was dubious about it because I knew Tallulah wasn't in the best of health. She had been ill and hadn't worked for a while. We went to see her at her town house and sat beside her. Tallulah was in dishabille as usual, and her voice was as fierce as the screech of a bluejay. She had read the play and said, "Of course I'm going to do it, when do we start?"

She had a cold but her mood was electric. She threw out sparks. She was witty, profane, and ready to bite before she was bitten.

Afterward I expressed concern to Robert Whitehead. He said, "No, we should go with her. She's got a good one in her and another one after that. She'll fool you." Well, she did all of that. The making of that play was a bizarre experience from beginning to end.

There were basic problems. At first the play didn't work, because while individual scenes were fine, they didn't add up. It was a tricky problem to solve. Mary Chase was one of the most prolific writers in the world. When she sat down at a typewriter, words poured out. Whitehead and I would tell her what we thought didn't work, and she would create not a new sentence, not a new paragraph, but a whole new scene. Overnight.

This was as startling a problem as not having enough. It is difficult and confusing for actors to have to learn new lines and then go on the same night and play them. The difficulties didn't show until we got an audience. We had a long run out of town. This was during the Kennedy inauguration and we were in Washington.

The second problem was Tallulah. I knew it arose from her illness; it engendered a loss of confidence in herself. She became critical, and unfriendly to the cast, which included a number of children. The kids, with whom she had many scenes, were terrified of her. Everyone's performance suffered, and it was difficult to develop any esprit de corps.

I recall one incident, a week before opening. A little boy, a darling child of nine or ten, was crying in his father's arms in the dressing room. He was afraid to go onstage with Tallulah. The father was remarkable. He said, "You'll do it; just think how proud you'll feel when you pull it off. You'll go out there and give a fine performance and you'll be proud of yourself and we'll be proud of you." The kind of talk they gave Daniel before sending him into the lion's den; and even though this child faced similar odds, he too pulled it off.

One of the child actresses in *Midgie Purvis* became a singing star and now has two beautiful children about the same age as she was then. Her name is Pia Zadora! She was, and is, an outstanding performer and recording artist, but I know her best now as my neighbor in Malibu.

I was compassionate about Tallulah because I came to realize how insecure she had become in those twilight years. We weren't geared to think of her as frightened, but she was. Frightened and ill . . . and yet still brave. Brave as a young warrior.

In one of our war counsels the financial backers wondered if we could get rid of her; she seemed to be pulling the play apart. Her fright didn't show, only her defensive temper. They suggested we get Maureen Stapleton to come in and replace her. We said it was unthinkable to fire Tallulah — morally and contractually impossible.

I argued that the play wasn't working yet, but it was getting there. Our problem was that we weren't concentrating on the play; we had become off-balance because of Tallulah's panic, although the children and older members of the wonderful cast accepted the new scenes and the endless rewrites. We were getting near New York, three weeks from the opening. I claimed, and the producers backed me, that light was beginning to show. We had changed the play drastically and Tallulah had a whole new set of costumes. She played a young woman in the opening scene — which she had not done in the original version — and then became older and older as the plot proceeded.

The play opened in New York with a miraculous first-night performance on everybody's part. The next day the notices were mixed. I left for England to start a film. In one week I received a wire from Whitehead. He said a general strike of stagehands had erupted, followed by the worst blizzard in memory. The gods were against us. All elements combined to shorten our Broadway run. The losses were staggering and we were forced to close. The weather, the strike, and age did us in.

Tallulah never completely regained her health, but in my memory she remains blessed with talent, spirit, and beauty.

Franchot Tone

THE FIRST TIME I met Franchot, he had the lead in a Maxwell Anderson play called *Night over Taos,* produced by the Group Theater. He was tall and handsome, had an oriental valet, and was very rich. I was what was called a "walk-on," with no lines at all, but it was my first Broadway appearance.

Later, during the run of *Winterset,* we had our first important meeting. He sent word to me that he and his new bride, Joan Crawford, were coming to see the play. The Joan Crawford–Franchot Tone marriage had the kind of impact later accorded to the marriage of Richard Burton and Elizabeth Taylor. Joan was the principal leading lady of MGM and he was the emergent playboy Broadway star, just moving into Hollywood and about to take over. The public interest in their union was phenomenal, and on the night they came to see *Winterset* the streets outside the theater were jammed with thousands of swerving and milling fans. Backstage, we could hear the buzz of the audience through the curtain as Joan and Franchot took their seats.

After the play they both came backstage, with policemen helping them make their way through the crowds and into my dressing room.

I changed into street wear and we made our way back through the crowds. We got into a long, black, chauffeured limousine, again with mounted police clearing the way. We went to a famous ex-speakeasy called Tony's, the rage of New York, on 52nd Street. The excitement when we arrived was no less than when we left the theater. We burst through the doors and were ushered the length of the long, narrow restaurant to a seat at the rear.

Joan had been beaming and laughing during the trip, but when we sat down I noticed she hung her head in strange dejection. Franchot, always a fashionable fellow, was ordering drinks and calling hellos and acting his roles as a bon vivant, newlywed, and movie star.

Finally he said to Joan, "Why are you unhappy?"

She said, "I was just terribly snubbed."

I didn't think I had heard her right. How could she be snubbed with thousands of people cheering us on our way?

But she repeated, "Yes, I was snubbed by Joe Schwartz," a familiar figure around town — an agent and producer.

"By Joe Schwartz?" I said. "When in the name of God did that happen?"

She said, "Didn't you see him snubbing me when we came into this restaurant?"

I couldn't figure how she had had time to notice anything when we came in, with the cheers of the crowd ringing in her ears. At the time I guessed it was her eccentric way of starting a conversation; certainly more interesting than talking about the weather.

I got to know Joan over the years and she made a good life for herself. I would say she accomplished 90 percent of her full capabilities, maybe 95 percent. I think the average person is lucky to do half that well.

But the night I met her it intrigued me to find her so vulnerable. Aside from being snubbed, she talked about other difficulties in her life. Her main problem was how close-ups were shot in the movies. They were not to her satisfaction and she explained why.

Evidently she prepared her parts thoroughly, and when ready to give her all, she wanted it to happen then, at once. But movie directors had a "habit," she explained, which was harmful to well-prepared actors. This "habit" was to take the long and medium shots before the close-ups. "By the time they get to the close-ups," she said, "the actor and actress have used up their energy on long shots, which don't show the full emotional capability of the artist." She said she was tired by the time the close-ups came. She asked me what she should do about it — it made her very upset.

Well, as I had never made a movie, I was flattered — as I am sure she realized — to think this great star would ask my advice about close-ups and long shots.

After Franchot ordered, he settled down to tell his impressions of *Winterset* (he liked it very much), and the rest of the evening went on in blazing spirits. Dozens of people joined the table till the late hours. Everyone toasted the newlyweds. It was Franchot's first marriage — later he went on to quite a few more. He liked getting married.

They were high times, champagne times. The glamour of the moment meant a lot to us in those days. From this distance I find it hard to understand why, but it certainly was true then.

I don't know how good Franchot's influence was on me or mine on him. Aside from *The Man on the Eiffel Tower*, a movie we made together in Paris, most of our coventures were in pursuit of pleasure. We shared many a bottle and many a girl, both in New York and Hollywood, in our bachelor days. There were also some quiet times in Canada at his hunting lodge.

One New York incident comes to mind. Tone asked me to pick up a girl he wanted me to meet. When I got to her apartment, she turned out to be a lady wrestler! She had huge muscles and rabid passions. I was lucky to get out alive. Looking back, it was more interesting than a quiet dinner at "21," but as a working actor, director, and writer, once was enough for me.

All of us talked about wild times — we skirted the edges —

but in all honesty we talked more than we dissipated. Discipline was essential, and so, I learned, was concentration.

Tone had a secret side to him. It was his love of the Canadian woods. He was a fine woodsman. Most people knew him only as a playboy, a friend of Howard Hughes and De Cicco and all the other high rollers. He was the chief charge-account customer at "21" and Ciro's and the Stork Club. Every place he went he was the chosen playboy — elegantly dressed, handsome, towing an array of lovely women. His career never reached the height his ex-wife's did, because, I think, he seemed to have had too much given to him. Wealth, for example. His father was the president of the Carborundum Company. Brains. Phi Beta Kappa from Cornell. Talent. A superstar. Problems. Lack of discipline. But he enjoyed life to the end, loving and being loved by an army of fans and friends.

When I went to Hollywood to make the film version of *Winterset,* I visited Franchot and Joan at their beautiful home, where he told me the definitive story about his marriage to Joan Crawford. He explained that being married to a superstar had its puzzling moments.

"It's something like this," he said. "I come home and want to make love. But Joan has to be careful because of her complex schedule. For example, she must get her homework done, her lines learned every day. She has continuous meetings with the producer or the director or somebody else equally important each evening. She has to get up at 4:00 or 4:30 in the morning, in order to get to the hairdresser and on to the set. She needs a massage at night before she can sleep for a few hours. She has to eat sparingly and exercise constantly.

"When I kiss her, I am told, 'Tomorrow. Tomorrow, darling, tomorrow.' And tomorrow comes and another series of problems arises and I'm set aside with that same whisper: 'Tomorrow, tomorrow, tomorrow.' Or 'George Cukor is coming' or 'I mustn't be disturbed — I have an early-morning call.'

"This goes on and has been going on; and when Saturday

comes and I expect it's finally my turn, I'm disappointed again. Other duties, other priorities arise. Conferences about the next script. Talks about dancing lessons. Discussions about yoga, tennis, and swimming lessons and so on. I'm kept off balance.

"Now the other day, I'd gone to bed early, tired of waiting around, and the maid came in and whispered, 'Miss Crawford will see you now, Mr. Tone.' And you know, I was so eager, so nervous, I couldn't get the job done!"

I also remember Franchot's mother, who was a character in her own right. Franchot had some of his biggest problems with his mom. She was always walking into nightclubs when he was there and this disturbed him. He didn't like to party with his mother and her gang around.

One gentle Christmas the two of them reached a compromise: they divided up the various eating establishments and watering holes in New York and they promised each other they would never intrude on the other's territory. Gertrude Tone would regard "21" as off-limits and Franchot would not enter the Stork Club and so on, right on down the line. They had New York well marked, like a ranch in the Old West where the cattle cannot roam. This unorthodox mother-and-son agreement worked well for them.

Franchot and I remained close friends from that first meeting with his bride until I spoke at his funeral.

First Journey
to Hollywood

THERE WAS a small unpaved landing field near my home in Mount Ivy, New York. It was from there that my first Hollywood trip began. There were five of us, including the pilot. We struggled into the air (our small twin-engine plane was overweighted) and churned heavily in the direction of Hollywood. For the first four hours we were in a blind fog; and this presaged our entire journey to the land of gleaming sun and celluloid stars. I had never been to Hollywood before, nor had my wife, Margaret Perry.

Bolstered by my new fame and, more important, fortune, I had launched myself into adventures I'd only dreamed of in my youth. One of my new enthusiasms was flying, and as a student pilot I needed mileage for my license, so I took the controls most of the way. Leaving the Yankee landscape behind, I saw, for the first time, the tawny colors of the Midwest. The mottled wastes of Kansas, the functional Boulder Dam, the sculptured Grand Canyon. Then, as a finale, we sailed over the Sierras to the endless, grassless, geometrical stage-set that is Los Angeles, Hollywood,

Beverly Hills, and in those days, Greta Garbo, Mickey Mouse, and Charlie Chaplin.

A thrilling sight it was, rimmed by the foaming, cudgeling Pacific Ocean, which expressly cools the brows of California's cinematic gods.

California's landing fields seemed enormous. We were awed by their size. Later on we learned that California's malted milks were bigger, California's hopes were higher, fruits riper, breasts fuller, limbs tanner, art cheaper, and sales mightier than any port in the world.

In a few golden hours we disembarked, visited the inner city of RKO, shook the hand of my producer, Pandro S. Berman, drank a scotch and soda with my director, Alfred Santell, and settled Margaret and myself in the Château Elysee Hotel. Finally, as an initial gesture to the western climate, I came down with bronchitis.

Wheezing, I lay in bed, tended by Lloyd's insurance doctors. I was threatening the start of production. Pills, nurses, masseurs, colonics, and general determination cut down the span of my illness. Exactly on time, on the twenty-third of July, 1936, I reported for my first day's work.

I walked onto the set feeling confident. I was dressed in my original *Winterset* costume. My face had been swabbed a golden brown (panchromatic number 27; very handsome). In my mouth I had two onion-skin porcelain caps for my lower teeth. These had been fabricated by a Hollywood alchemist who pasted them on with a powder called Corega. He said they added greatly to my appearance. These caps required fifteen minutes to set in place, but they still kept falling out in the love scenes. They made Margo wear caps, too — I could never figure out why. Her teeth looked perfect to me. Dental appendages were a *res necessaria* in those days.

As to the studio we used for *Winterset*, a half century later I remember the first moment I walked on that stage and saw the enormous structure for our film. The Brooklyn Bridge had been duplicated! A hundred, maybe two hundred workmen beavered and banged around the great spans and parapets. I was bewildered by the torpedolike cameras, the blaze of high-flung lighting fixtures, storm effects, winding streets, substructures. I thought,

"With these implements, we'll bring iambic pentameter to the whole, wide, ignorant world! No stopping us!"

I remember vividly the opening shot. It was a sequence from the second act of the play: Mio's first entrance into the festering Esdras household. Margo and Moscovich (the father), Edward Ellis (the judge), and I walked through our designated paces. Because we were all stage actors, the director suggested we subdue our performances. He said, "Stop projecting — there is no audience out front. Speak only to the person addressed. The camera will overhear you." He advised us to reduce our facial expressions. "Do less. Think more!" This was good advice. Most stage actors had to learn it when they transferred their craft to film. It's a known and fully understood precept today, but back then it was not.

I had played *Winterset* hundreds of times in the theater, before big audiences. Now I had to find a way to speak with less projection yet not lose vitality.

We rehearsed for hours while the scene was lighted. Then our stand-ins were called. Next, we were re-called and lighted again. Finally, the whistles blew, orders were shouted, gongs banged, and the great sound doors gloomily lowered.

It went well, that first day. No one was impatient. They gave us time to settle and to learn.

The next morning someone brought me a suit of rubber underwear. I was told to put it on under my regular outfit. No one explained the reason, but I soon learned. It was rain. Many of my scenes had to be played in the rain. On the stage the audience imagined rain. But that doesn't do in films. I was placed under perforated pipes, which spilled water over my head and body. To heighten the effect, stagehands pumped Nujol oil onto my face. They used bug-spray Flit guns.

"Turn 'em over!" someone shouted. "Action!" yelled the director . . . and the first scene began.

But I couldn't talk. I was incapable of uttering a line. I somehow communicated to someone that I'd swallowed my porcelain caps! They had taken leave, so to speak. The announcement brought quick results.

A hurricane of voices shouted:

"Hold it."

"Save the lights."

"Kill the rain."

"Cut the arcs."

"Open up."

"Settle down."

Lights switched off. Cameras stopped. Stagehands hustled about and that enormous guillotine they called "the sound door" lifted its head and growled.

There are always two unhappy men connected with a film. They are called "assistant directors." Nice fellows, mostly. But their jobs are difficult. Their duty is to stop things like porcelain caps from hampering production. They led my wet, trembling frame to a dressing table and watched while the makeup man glued the caps back into my mouth. The A.D.s explained the situation:

"This production runs into ten, twenty, thirty thousand dollars a day. So figure what that fucking tooth cost us!"

I couldn't figure — and it wasn't my problem.

Finally my caps were restored and I returned to the battlefield, shivering and desolate. I had not yet spoken a word.

My recollection grows dim at this juncture. The rain must have recommenced, the Nujol oil been resprayed, the action restored, and there is, canned up at RKO, a celluloid copy of that film, showing me in the drenching rain, my face full of Nujol, saying lines like:

"Pardon me . . . I am trying to earn my tuition fee by peddling magazines . . ." and so on.

Whatever the rain-soaked words were, I said them as best I could.

Thereafter, for twelve weeks, on that water-logged set, we worked in the rain and the fog, in the hot and the freezing. I recall a kaleidoscopic series of rubber underwear, and instruments called "matchboxes" and "bon-bons" and "mikes." I conscientiously tried not to hold up production with personal problems. I found a good friend and a sound coach in our director, Al Santell. So the work proceeded until miraculously it looked as if we would finish on schedule. Then, as now, working within budget was the aim above all aims, the cynosure of all cynosures in Hollywood.

The reactions meanwhile were amazing. The atmosphere of RKO changed from cold observation to hot enthusiasm. Producers, writers, actresses, cutters dropped by our set. They said they liked the early rushes they had seen, and the secretaries and delivery boys, producers and presidents began to smile at us.

Once, for fun, I got up on a white horse I spied awaiting her cue on an adjacent set. We trotted up and down the studio alleys awhile. Higher-ups rushed out of their offices and lifted me down. They explained that my idea was enormously amusing, but there must be no accidents until the picture was finished! Then I could break as many legs as I wanted. The horse and I were led back to our stalls. I don't know about her, but I was more closely watched over until the picture was finished.

The good news about our rushes spread. Word got around that Al Santell was a genius. Pev Marley — the cameraman — was a Rembrandt; Pandro Berman and Anthony Veiller were the bravest producer-writer team on the West Coast. Friends phoned to tell me that good news about our picture was spreading.

I began to rap on wood — any pieces of wood I could find.

Those early reactions helped our work. The crew and cast adjusted to the brooding bridge and flooding rain and we all began to smile a little and work with consecrated fervor. The simulated East River (which actually flowed for a hundred feet across the set) began to look like the Nile under a full moon. Nujol oil was everywhere. It sparkled like dew on everything and everybody.

Time and budgets were forgotten. Expenditures were overlooked. During the last week, the producer said to me, "It's one of the five great pictures ever made!"

I kept on rapping wood.

Because I was in almost every scene, I had no time off until three days before the final shot. My agent said I should take those three days off because I needed a breather. There were only two or three more close-ups left to do. So my wife — who had been working simultaneously in a Mae West picture — and I flew to Catalina Island for a quick holiday.

Catalina is a sort of American Gibraltar. It was then owned

and operated by a chewing gum king. It is bespangled with flying fish, buffalo, and free samples of gum. The most genuine of its attractions back then were the deep-sea-fishing boats. They were picturesque and manned by Portuguese fishermen. We hired one for three afternoons to trail marlin. We didn't catch any, but we heard fascinating fish stories from those who had. What I did succeed in catching was a severe and painful sunburn. My face blistered and my lips swelled up like sausages.

When I got back to the studio, my appearance created the expected furor. A scurry of executives inspected me and halted production. I was ordered to bed and ministered to by the same familiar insurance doctors. The bosses were worried but reasonably good-natured about it. They said they had high hopes for the movie so, although a lesser production would have eliminated the unphotographed scenes, *Winterset* must be reeled intact.

The scenes were filmed and the cast gathered for a farewell party. Words of relief and gratitude were exchanged. I made a toast:

"I leave tomorrow for New York to play in what you movie folks call a 'Medicine Show.' I will miss you. And, by God, you will never know how much I thank you!"

Next morning Margaret and I and a newly acquired Great Dane puppy called Tor boarded the New York–bound *Chief De Luxe*. We felt happy and — for the moment — vaguely triumphant.

L'Envoi
Here is the telegram I received a month later:

SNEAK PREVIEW OF FINAL CUT BUFFALOED AUDIENCES STOP DINKY THEATRE HIGH LANGUAGE NO STAR CAST CREATED LACK OF INTEREST STOP HICK AUDIENCE LAUGHED AT WRONG PLACES STOP SEVERAL PEOPLE LEFT THE THEATRE STOP CUTS NECESSARY ALSO PRESTIGE OF PICTURE MUST BE INSTILLED IN THEIR UNSUSPECTING MINDS STOP PRODUCERS TORN BETWEEN CUTTING POETIC FLAVOR FOR LOWER AND WIDER APPEAL STOP DON'T WORRY THOUGH YOU ARE ONLY AN ACTOR AND IT IS THE PRINCES OF HOLLYWOOD WHO GRIND PAY CHECKS AND THEY MUST MAKE FINAL DECISION STOP (Signed) AL SANTELL

So there I was, three thousand miles away, not knowing what had happened. But I kept rapping wood and speaking in iambic pentameter:

> Oh Prince, bring us our desperate work entire;
> There are people who will buy such things . . .

The picture didn't make much money. It got good notices, won a few prizes, had a short burst of glory, and still plays once in a while. Today I look back on my first Hollywood venture with a smile and a touch of nostalgia.

On that first visit to California, many years ago, I was asked my impressions of Hollywood. For three-quarters of an hour I talked to a *Variety* reporter who wrote down everything I said. The next day I bought five copies of his paper, suitable for framing, and then read: "Burgess Meredith is in town and had the usual things to say about Hollywood." I framed that sentence.

I learned early that it was difficult to add one spark to the aurora borealis of Hollywood. Writers and columnists overdescribe the place and pick it clean. Yet, visiting Hollywood in the late 1940s and early 1950s was like riding on a roller coaster for the first time. We were lifted up, plunged down, swooped up again. Faces and places flashed past us with centrifugal fury. When we fumbled our way back East, we wondered why any sane person would go to Los Angeles a second time.

Eventually, of course, we came back. We discovered that when we had a job, Hollywood was pleasant enough; but when we were jobless, the town turned cold and cruel. Happiness was measured by the success of our latest movie and the fate of our last option.

Very gradually, the concept of Hollywood as the center of wild parties and swimming pools filled with actresses in evening clothes has faded. The job of making pictures became as industrialized as making motor cars. At first we worked from seven in the morning until late at night and went to bed when we could. Sundays we slept all day. Long hours of work kept the actors and actresses exhausted. Gradually, through strikes, the Screen Actors

Guild cut down the working hours and made both Saturday and Sunday holidays.

I recall the first trip my wife and I made to a nightclub called the Trocadero, a haunt for the famous. The headwaiter didn't know us, so we were quarantined at the bar. From there we saw our first flurry of stars — Johnny Weissmuller, William Powell, Jean Harlow, Clark Gable, and George Cukor, each, despite naughty reports to the contrary, going into the proper washroom. We also spotted Osgood Perkins make a telephone call, but I had seen him do that in New York. The only swimming pool I got to see was Misha Auer's — it had no water in it at the time.

At first I felt depressed, but life got better as time went along. We met and made friends with some of the natives. One evening, James Stewart, Humphrey Bogart, Joan Blondell, Dick Powell, and a number of us chartered a fortune-teller, a handwriting expert, who had become famous and charged high prices. We heard that her psychic revelations were startling. She arrived at Bogart's house where we were gathered, and told the guests hidden truths in a hushed voice. Everyone was amazed.

Finally she came to me, and asked for a specimen of my handwriting. I scribbled: "Hello, Mable! Haven't seen you since Tenth Street."

The oracle cried: "My God, Buzz! What are you doing out here?"

And that is a hint of what Hollywood was like in those far-off days. A gathering place for the talented and the fraudulent. The place where the rollicking American dream culminated, Hollywood collected the powerful and attracted the powerless. It blended beauty and the bizarre; magical illusion and cold cash reality.

Gradually, the scene changed. The captains and the kings departed decades ago, and the stars commute from Montana or the Ozarks. Today I defy anyone to figure out who runs what. The last great emperor was probably Jules Stein and after him his designate, Lew Wasserman, at Universal. Now the big bosses change weekly, and the Japanese are becoming the biggest stockholders . . . they are buying everything. However, in March of 1992, the papers hint that Sony is starting to lose money just like the rest of us.

Back in New York, a New Kind of Theater

I STARTED my career working with Katharine Cornell, Guthrie McClintic, Maxwell Anderson; and before that with Eva Le Gallienne at her Repertory Company. These people, along with the Lunts and Helen Hayes, were "The Establishment," so to speak. Their names lit up the Broadway firmament. A smart kid joined 'em if he could.

Then, as time rolled on, I began to hear more and more about a new movement called the Group Theater. Especially from Franchot Tone, who advised me to investigate what he called "The Method." He said I would find it useful. "It'll help you to stay sane."

At one point I approached Harold Clurman, one of the founders of the Group, and asked him about joining. He turned me down cold. He said I had too many interests already. "You wouldn't stay the course, Meredith," was his verdict.

I should mention that my friends in the "Establishment" were, at first, not sympathetic to the idea of a "Method Theater." For them, "Method" seemed a derogatory word, a euphemism for bad acting. "Acting is not a *'method,'* for God's sake. It's an *art!*"

However, time taught me that actors, like athletes, need to keep working. They lose their edge if they don't stay in training. I remember Hume Cronyn and I studied with a Stanislavsky expert, Benno Schneider, and found it helpful, particularly the improvisations.

Then, inevitably and dramatically, I caught a glimpse of Lee Strasberg in action. The Group Theater had dispersed and become the Actors Studio, with quarters on West 44th Street. One day I was invited there to watch three well-known actors do a short twenty-minute scene. No scenery, a few props, general lighting. After they finished, there was no applause. The actors sat down on the prop chairs and faced the audience.

Lee Strasberg was in the front with thirty or forty actor-members. He asked the performers if they wanted to tell us, in general, what their intentions had been in the scene and what problems they had faced.

The actors described what they believed the author's meaning was and how they worked to bring it about. Their answers were brief and tentative. There was a short, ritual pause, evidently allowing Lec to get his thoughts together.

What followed was extraordinary. In a concise twenty-five-minute speech, Lee evaluated what the actors had and had not accomplished from the audience's point of view. His words were meaningful, helpful, precise. His speech had form and content, as we find when we read his recorded lectures, which are now used in acting schools everywhere. If tape recorders had not come along there would have been no testimony to his perceptive skills.

Visually he used few gestures, none wasted. Occasionally he made a kind of clicking sound in the back of his throat. I learned later this "tic" seemed to be an indication of inner emotion or excitement. Otherwise his speech was even, his syntax faultless. No matter how long the sentence, it came out complete and in context. Thinking on his feet, without missing a beat, Lee sized up the effort and evaluated the results. He intertwined humor, praise, reproval, and, once in a while, a touch of rabbinical wisdom.

With my mother, Ida Beth Burgess Meredith.

In 1918, wearing a soldier costume, probably because my brother was in the army.

Playing Peter Pan in a play at Cathedral Choir School.

(*Front, center*) The board of editors for the Hoosac
school paper, *The Owl.*

Famous aviatrix Amelia Earhart made a guest appearance on the *Red Davis* radio show (1934).
(*Ben Pinchot*)

In *Battleship Gertie* (1935).

With Katharine Cornell and
Brenda Forbes in *Flowers of the
Forest* (1935). (*Vandamm Studios*)

With Margo in the movie *Winterset* (1936).

Opposite: With Lillian Gish in *Star Wagon* (1937). (*Vandamm Studios*)

With Lon Chaney, Jr., in *Of Mice and Men* (1939).

With Orson Welles in *Five Kings* (1938).

Often in Lee Strasberg's classes we watched scenes that were unforgettable — scenes done on a bare stage with no props other than perhaps a couple of chairs and a table. The lighting consisted of a few electric bulbs or small "spots." I remember Geraldine Page, on a bare stage, performing all the major scenes as Hamlet's mother, Gertrude. When Geraldine finished, we felt as if we'd been inside the castle in Denmark and we imagined that Geraldine had worn fourteenth-century costumes.

Lee asked her what her "intention" had been, and Geraldine said, "Well, I figured out that the queen is the most important character in the play. Everything revolves around her, every action is caused by her or because of her — so that's how I tried to play Gertrude. I found that in the play everyone loves me and I love them — and that's why we all die!"

"Well, Geraldine," Lee said, "however you did it on that empty stage, you made us visualize the surroundings, the costumes — the whole court . . . quite amazing." Then, after a moment's silence, he said once more, "Quite amazing."

It was a transcendental experience, and everyone who attended Lee's sessions had many experiences like that.

Eventually I joined the Studio, was made a member of the board, became a friend of Lee and his family, and under his tutelage I ran the West Coast branch for a season.

In 1964, Lee asked me to direct James Baldwin's *Blues for Mr. Charlie* for a Broadway run. He and Cheryl Crawford had raised enough money to do two or three shows on Broadway. But after the cast of *Blues* was chosen and we were ready to go into formal rehearsal, Lee and Cheryl called an emergency meeting and said they suddenly didn't have enough money to build the scenery we had decided on. Some backer had reneged.

So, they asked, what should we do? After a long pause, I reminded Lee of how many beautiful scenes we'd seen acted during rehearsals without scenery. I told him that I wouldn't miss the scenery and then I asked, "Have we enough money to hire Abe Feder to light the play? If we have, Abe could light up the actors and the audience would do the rest."

Lee said something like, "That's what I hoped you would say."

And he did get Feder — a lighting genius — and we fared very well. We were complimented by the critics for the "starkness of the staging" and our author, Jimmy Baldwin, was delighted.

One day Lee and I were scheduled to discuss something or other and I drove to pick him up. He climbed in the car and sat next to me. He looked straight ahead, not listening to my small talk. I asked, "Shall we go to the Studio?" He glanced at me and I saw, behind his glasses, that he was in distress. Something had happened.

"It's a fine day," I said. "Let's drive someplace." He nodded, and I drove aimlessly toward the Pacific Coast Highway. We rolled along the water's edge for an hour or more, beyond Trancas, saying not a word. I have forgotten what my thoughts were, but Lee's were evidently despondent.

Then, just before dusk, he took a deep breath and said, "All right." I turned the car around and headed home. By the time I dropped him off, he was relaxed and thoughtful.

I never learned what had upset him that day. It had something to do with the Studio.

As he left I said, "Lee, I like your long silences. They teach me more than your long soliloquies!"

He laughed. "So what did you learn?"

"I learned from you that the best way to solve problems is to shut up and think."

He smiled and said, "Yes, that helps; that certainly helps. Next time you think and I'll drive."

In 1969 Lee Strasberg suddenly resigned from the Actors Studio and started his own school, the Lee Strasberg Theatre Institute. It was an out-and-out commercial venture and an instant success.

Lee said he was happier because he no longer had to deal with the various advisers and boards of governors of the Actors Studio. There was only one assistant, his wife, Anna Strasberg.

The old Actors Studio still exists on both coasts, and though

I seldom get to their main office in New York, I have remained on the board of supervisors. However, a while ago I showed up at a council meeting and proposed a plan to raise money to keep the Studio going. I called my plan "The Visual Theater" and it will probably come to life in some fashion. I think that the West Coast branch might give it a try.

This was the original idea:

When we read a novel or a play the first time, we imagine in our heads what the scenery, the "props," the sticks of furniture look like. But when that same novel or that same play is theatrically performed, the things we imagine are replaced by three-dimensional objects conceived and built by someone else. It is always a different vision from our own (and the author's). Sometimes the "designed" conception is better than the imagined one and sometimes it is not.

Movies don't have that problem. In the film *The African Queen*, John Huston went to the rivers of Africa. In *Lawrence of Arabia*, the director went to the very sands T. E. Lawrence described.

On the stage, of course, exact duplication of the written word is impossible. In the stage version of *My Fair Lady* the horse races were imagined — and that worked beautifully. You never saw a horse. In the film, you saw the horses running. In both versions the scene worked fine — and that is the point: *both* work.

Harking back to our production of *Blues for Mr. Charlie*, I'd like to suggest the possibility of creating another kind of theater. The idea developed after a meeting at Paul Newman's when he asked for suggestions.

I pointed out that producing a play on Broadway is like riding a crocodile bareback: it's no fun and it seldom goes in the direction you want it to. And above all, of course — it's dangerous! You can get swallowed in one reptilian gulp.

"The Visual Theater" would not try to compete with twenty-million-dollar English musicals or Lincoln Center or the late Joe Papp's Public Theatre. It would take its cue from what was always great about the Actors Studio — Lee Strasberg's advanced sessions.

Those sessions were performed by different members of the Actors Studio — without scenery or costumes. Let me fantasize one way such a concept might work for a paying public.

We could rent four walls of an off-Broadway theater. Or to start, we could try it a few times in our own small auditorium. The *paying* audience comes in. Sits down. There is no curtain. The stage is bare. Absolutely empty. *They expect to see — and they are going to see — an evening of "The Actors Studio at Work."*

At curtain time the house lights go out and the stage lights go on — good lighting is essential. The first performer to come in is the "property man" — an actor or actress dressed either in black (as they do in the Chinese theater) or dressed like a stagehand.

He tells the audience the name of the first scene; and, as he talks, he arranges the various props and furniture. When the lights start to change, the other actors begin to take their places for the first scene. They are not in costume — though that could be optional. When a complicated prop is not available or desirable — like a horse, for instance! — the same property man brings out an imaginary animal and the actor takes the reins; or gets into the car, or whatever. (This could be the director's choice.) If it was the balcony scene from *Romeo and Juliet,* this would require a stepladder, which the property man brings in. Or he brings a guitar if there is music. Or a piano.

Then, when all matters are in hand — the property man looks out at the audience for a moment and offers the famous pantomime for "opening" the imaginary curtain. Then he goes offstage and the play begins.

It need not be a complete play. It could be any length. The *whole evening or any part.* A scene by a contemporary author or by Molière. The Jewish theater or the Irish — or the Japanese. Authors dead or alive — Hemingway, Beckett, Simon, burlesque. It could also be a well-rehearsed part of a work-in-progress written by the Writers Studio group. There could be one or twelve characters in the action. It could be comedy, pantomime, choreography. It could (for box-office reasons) be Marlon Brando doing Falstaff in the tavern scene from *Henry IV.* It could be Newman doing *Candida* with Joanne and a student as Marchbanks. Any of us old ones would take a swipe at Lear. Or Prospero. Or three different actors/actresses doing different interpretations of the same scene from Tennessee Williams. Or O'Neill. There could be one play or parts of five plays on the same subject or different subjects.

But *no scenery!* The Visual Theater means as few costumes as possible. The audience does the visualizing. And the audience pays to see it!

The idea is that the public pays to see what happens when good actors and good directors are rehearsed and ready, but before they have the scenery, the costumes, or all the props. It is called the "final run-through." It is the moment when the play first comes to life before an audience, on a bare stage. The way it used to happen many times in Lee's classes, and does today in acting classes on both coasts. Though it is never seen by the public, it is an exciting time in the theater — a creative time.

There are probably very few members of the Actors Studio who would not like the chance to do scenes or full-length plays if they could be done without the life-and-death problems of costumes, scenery, without the savageries of out-of-town engagements and first-night holocausts with bloodthirsty critics in attendance — of long runs, and gut-curdling closings.

Best of all, the whole concept could evolve slowly, modestly, sanely, and (praise God) *economically*. I have the feeling it would work. I remember how many times it worked in the past, before costumes, scenery, and tensions set in.

If it works, fine. If it doesn't, it might lead to something better which would lighten the fearsome costs of Broadway production.

If there were star names, the ticket prices could be lowered by half . . . which in itself would be a major achievement.

Equity and the Federal Theater Project
1938

BY 1938 I had developed a pretty full résumé: eight Broadway plays, two movies, a host of radio shows — and I was elected acting president of the Actors' Equity Association by a margin of one vote. This small, calm trade union had been trouble-free for many years. You couldn't say it was moribund; *sleepy* is a more precise word.

The late thirties was a time of political ferment; breadlines, strikes, and unemployment were the headline news. And Franklin D. Roosevelt was trying to sort it out.

Equity elected me president because there were serious disagreements in our guild between the conservatives and the progressives; and they hoped I would act as a sort of pacifier, a Warren G. Harding, so to speak. They considered me politically neuter.

They were not only absolutely justified in this feeling, my life had become a three-ring circus. I was playing eight times a week in Maxwell Anderson's *Star Wagon*. Besides that, I had become chairman of the National Advisory Committee of the Federal Theater, chairman of the Arts Union Conference (a united front of art unions to lobby for a national endowment of the seven arts), and was promoting a "Merrie England" village at the World's Fair. I was young but already exhausted.

It is hard to understand why I accepted new responsibilities. It was partly ego, I suppose. I moved into the paneled, impressive offices of the supreme council of one of our most respected white-collar unions; the third president, in twenty-eight years, of the Actors' Equity Association.

Becoming president of Equity, chairman of NACFT, chairman of AUC, starring on Broadway, two marriages: saying I accepted these responsibilities because of ego isn't enough. What was going on? Manic behavior? A healthy young man out to change the world? Eventually I would find out that what I needed and finally got was psychiatric help. Much later I learned I was suffering from a disorder called cyclothymia, described as "a mild bipolar disorder characterized by instability of mood and a tendency to swing between euphoria and depression." It would be some years before I became aware of this problem.

I actually wasn't too bad for a while. I developed a Rooseveltian technique of calling in advisers and delegating work to anyone with an eager eye and progressive thought. I spent late hours after the theater in conference and whole days in conflict, attempting to bring about what I thought were "reforms." I ran to Washington every month or so and lobbied senators and department heads into writing bills for a national theater, and increasing appropriations for the WPA. I conferred constantly with Orson Welles and John Houseman and other progressive friends. I pounded the gavel and glared at the cold, menacing eyes of the reactionary; I shuddered at the religious fervor of the Communist; I smiled at the puzzled, questioning faces of the liberal. I felt the pulse of fascism, communism, Catholicism, nihilism, liberalism, all these and more, beating and bellowing, rising and falling, inside our union. I wondered if, in a minute way, as through a microscope, the ideological struggles of the whole political world were reflected in our small operations.

Equity was, and I guess still is, a brother — or sister — union of the Screen Actors Guild, the American Federation of Actors, now including television (AFTRA), the Burlesque Actors Guild, and others in the entertainment field. Until the Great Depression, these organizations were a dignified, paternalistic group of guilds. We kept a haughty aloofness from the hardboiled stagehands, the musicians' local, and such like. When, however, the Depression came, Equity's paid membership fell from 12,000 in 1928 to 4,000 by 1937. Unrest set in, beginning with the radicals and the unemployed. The result was a revolt stretching from New York to Hollywood. It lashed the older established officers into a counterattack. As a result, if my metaphors are not too mixed, Thespis, for years sterile, developed labor pains.

We were treated to the spectacle of progressive-minded actors, who that same night would play in musical comedies, pounding their fists against their palms, screaming for parliamentary procedures, calling for obscure points of order — all with such vitality and suddenness that the older, respectable, white-haired officials — undisturbed for thirty years — trembled and fumbled among the law books. Finally in bitterness and humiliation they shouted "Ruffians! Ruffians!" — and called for diminishing votes of confidence.

My strategy was simple. It was to appeal to the intelligence of everyone concerned, asking the members to vote on every question raised, regardless of its origin, in the light of its actual benefit to our organization. I hoped this tactic would bring progress and order into the proceedings. It was effective for one meeting only, while the boys and girls caught their breath and sharpened their teeth.

At the end of that first week, and from then on for seven or eight months, when I gratefully retired, the fires roared. Instead of getting together to help the WPA establish a national theater, etc., etc. — the membership was divided by agitators who whispered that the battle against communism was being lost . . . Equity's home office was being undermined by the USSR!

Gasoline was thrown on those embers when a brother union (with which we were waging a jurisdictional fight over chorus girls) suggested to the New York papers that our council was financed by Moscow. We were radicals, all of us, including the chorus girls. The conflict raged beyond belief and, in this instance, unintentionally I may have fanned the flames.

As the small radical groups were rising, and the united fronts were growing, Equity decided that Billy Rose (who produced "girlie" shows) was underpaying his chorus girls. They deserved a raise, those lovely babes. Impatient with our committee's work, I sicced some of our militant members onto Broadway's Little Napoleon. This group reported that our regular lawyers were useless against Billy. They suggested a new man who, they said, had galvanized every tough union on earth.

I agreed to give this "new man" a try; and I went along with him to Rose's office to do a bit of bearding. Rose and I had become friends and he was shocked to see me show up. He told me to get the hell back to my greasepaint. He threatened that if I picketed his "palace of wonders," he would picket Equity — with elephants! He ordered us out of his office, and that ended negotiations. We fired the "new man," by the way. He was too hot to handle.

In a continuing effort to bring pressure on the federal government for WPA funds, I made a united front with the Workers Alliance, the musicians' local, the Artists Alliance, and other active groups that wanted money for their projects, but we found that the idea of a freewheeling theater, financed with taxes, was frowned on by the U.S. government. The bureaucrats started to move in and take over. Our funds began to dwindle.

I'll digress here to tell an anecdote or two about those feisty days.

I worried when I saw the ranks swelling behind a large Italian fellow from the WPA, who stood up in meetings and told the members to demand the resignation of all "Reds." He seemed to be a portent — a local Mussolini. He was a rousing orator and got people to make fists and yell. I never learned what plays he'd acted in to perform so well.

About that time the *Pins and Needles* company (a play produced by the International Ladies Garment Workers Union) was asked to join Equity. The president, David Dubinsky, thought members should not have to pay double dues to a brother union. But when

we told him that all the actors would start sewing tiny garments
if he didn't agree, he said okay. But he also said he hoped his
whole organization "wouldn't start thinking they were actors,
for God's sake!"

Our council got mad and told Dubinsky that the Ladies Garment Workers must also put up a bond just like the Rockefellers.
If he wanted to produce a play, he had to play by Equity rules.
Mr. Dubinsky felt hurt. I persuaded a Jewish editor I knew to
write Dubinsky a long, sentimental letter, which I signed, as if
I'd composed it. The letter explained how great a favor it would
be to all actors if Mr. Dubinsky would post the bond. This melted
Dubinsky's heart. He sent the bond and asked to meet me
personally.

We sat for an hour over a couple of glasses of beer. I told him
the troubles I was having as president of a union.

"You shouldn't do this United Front with the Communists,
son. It don't work. Never has! I abuse them, disassociate myself
from the C.P. Sometimes I fight the same enemy as they do, but
with my own army, and on my own front. There can be a militant
democracy," he said to me, "one that goes forward after democratic goals.

"If the Communists have any good ideas, *use 'em yourself!* In
my union they wanted soccer games once, the Commies. I gave
them not one but *four soccer fields! And two swimming pools!* Not
one! Two! The Fascist boys gotta work hard to lump us and the
Reds together," he said. "Why? Because — we got a boxing glove
on both hands!"

I thought about this a lot — this experience. As I sadly put
aside my chair in Equity, I was sure of only one thing . . . I was
not a union organizer! I don't know whether it can be done, this
"militant democracy." But it can't be done by people like me,
who want to keep a good right hand on the knob of a stage door.
Those were my conclusions, my summations, falteringly drawn
from that brief experience in a miniature society.

In our small union things happened pretty much the way they
did in the grown-up world — wheels within wheels, little fleas

on bigger fleas; perplexities and conflicts and small, well-meaning generals.

I returned, like Alice, to my dressing room; but you can bet I learned what rabbit to follow down what hole next time around.

It was the one and only political office I ever held. Or ever will. The only committee I've worked on since then is the Red Cross. No harm in that; or none so far.

Punished with Pleasure

IN 1938–39 I came near to a nervous breakdown, especially when my marriage to Maggie Perry broke up. She couldn't take my wild swings of behavior anymore and left. In retrospect, I didn't blame her. We divorced in July 1938, though that was not to be the end of the relationship.

Earlier that year I finished the run of *The Star Wagon*. I also resigned my presidency of Actors' Equity, quit a dozen other things I was faltering at, and I sailed for France, ushered aboard the S.S. *Ile de France* by a jazz band led by Orson Welles.

It was a crazy journey and it ended with my falling into the arms of a very romantic, very rich lady of German descent, who had a chauffeur and a car, and a mild desire for my company. So, instead of going to Ireland as planned, I went first to Germany, at the height of Hitler's regime, with this newfound friend.

She finally confessed to me, as our traveling vacation was coming to a close in the south of France, that she was being kept by a very rich lesbian . . . who showed up, and we became a ménage à trois for a brief period. She immortalized the occasion in one sentence: "If I acted like a woman last night, I apologize!"

Nothing seemed easy or normal in those days. Every move was frenetic, and I lugged my problems with me. Looking back, I can see that in our search for it, we were punished with pleasure. I had come to Europe to rest and to straighten out my head and I had backed into a hornet's nest with my lady-love, plus her lesbian girlfriend.

Erratic behavior was not unusual in that turbulent period, but it has been told by Scott Fitzgerald and Hemingway, and I would be ashamed to mention my small experience, beyond saying it seemed to be pervasive. It returns to me through a haze; in fact, it was a self-indulging, purposeless reign of pleasure. The world was having a "last bash," a last carousal before the inevitable war started. I met a great many people there, including Elsa Maxwell and Marlene Dietrich. Life on the Riviera was strenuous. I was more exhausted at the end of that vacation than I had been in the beginning, if that were possible.

My psyche took a very bad beating in the late 1930s. My vitality was high, because I was young. But I couldn't handle the extraneous activities, the drinking, the frustrations, and the neuroses that I was accumulating. With all that ferment, I was hard pressed to keep my status as a star. There was a dimming of talent and health. It's a miracle I didn't physically collapse.

In the middle of this hysteria, I tried to do several movies, some good, most bad, all in turmoil. Somehow I found the energy and the time to film *Idiot's Delight* (1938), *Of Mice and Men* (1939), and several more. In January I also appeared on stage as Prince Hal in *Five Kings* with Orson Welles, as I've mentioned, and in November 1939 I began hosting the weekly radio series *The Pursuit of Happiness*.

Finally, as though I hadn't enough trouble, I decided to try to win back Margaret Perry. She had moved out West. (She seemed to have a habit of moving to far-off places.) She was living in Utah and I followed her there and tried to woo her back again; but just as I had almost done that I'll turn the pages quickly to say I met Paulette Goddard.

Looking back on it, I realize I was a child of the crazy late

1930s and the emergent 1940s — a restless young actor of the period who tried to save the world, gather pleasure, and still work at my profession — all at the same time. Somehow, the work kept coming — not just movie and radio, but theater work, too. I managed to act in *Liliom* on the New York stage with Ingrid Bergman, who came over from Sweden for the play. It was her first American appearance.

The Depression was rampant and World War II loomed on the horizon. Samuel Goldwyn summed it up inimitably when he said, "Don't we have enough troubles without a war?"

On radio, I had become a leading narrator, guide, voice of authority. I jumped from *The Pursuit of Happiness* to *The Spirit of '41*, which became *The Army Hour*. For *The Army Hour* I went from training camp to training camp, showing how America was preparing for the war that was threatening. At any moment I expected to be drafted. I rushed to Hollywood and did a movie, *Tom, Dick, and Harry*, with Ginger Rogers, followed immediately by *That Uncertain Feeling*, with Merle Oberon and Melvyn Douglas, directed by Lubitsch. It was one of my best performances, for some reason. I seemed to get it all together.

As I walked off the set the last day of *That Uncertain Feeling* and drove to the house I shared with Jimmy Stewart — technically I was his guest — we discovered that both of us had been drafted into the army that same day. He was to go immediately and I was to go a few weeks later.

Being a bachelor once again, I had moved in on Jimmy as soon as I arrived in town to do a picture, and I contributed a key member to the household: Malcolm the valet. I brought him out from New York, after which he took excellent care of Jimmy, and eventually moved on to Hume Cronyn. The photographer Johnny Swope was another more or less perpetual guest, rounding out the group.

Jimmy and I were opposite personalities, but for a while we made a harmonious household.

One of the most amazing things about Jimmy was the ease with which he got things done — a prodigious amount of things.

And he never seemed to hurry. He had a magnificent slow-motion rhythm — so slow that his friends felt a sense of relief whenever he got across a street without being killed.

He seemed to be saying, "Gee, I wonder when I'll ever get this done." But it always was. I was a greyhound on a treadmill compared to Jimmy. In the end, he always got more done than I did.

Jimmy Stewart has a positive genius for doing much with minimum effort. I never found him mopping his brow. Seething citizens wind up with high blood pressure, but the Stewarts live long and useful lives.

I don't mean that all Jimmy did was work. He contributed his share of nonsense, and he attended his quota of parties — but he managed it better than most of us.

Jimmy's screen roles reflect his real-life personality: a boyish, shy, rather inarticulate individual. But he capitalizes on these weaknesses, if that's what they are. Instead of trying to be someone else, he plays himself under various circumstances. That has been true of many great movie stars, such as Cary Grant, John Wayne, Gary Cooper, and Spencer Tracy.

Jimmy has a gift for storytelling, though he pretends he doesn't. He launches into one of his yarns in that uneven, faltering tempo of his, until he stumbles. But is it a stumble? Somehow he always stumbles at the right spot. And it brings down the house. The truth is Jimmy is a self-satirist — he pokes fun at himself. Or does when it is appropriate.

Another of Jimmy's qualities which amazed me was his thoroughness, his discipline. You'd think a man with his apparent languor wouldn't be as tenacious as a bulldog for detail.

Nowhere was this more apparent than in his flying. Before Jimmy took off on a flight, he studied every mile on the maps littering the living room floor. By the time he climbed into his eccentric little plane with its yellow-striped tail, he was as well posted on emergency landing fields as J. Edgar Hoover was in those days on Fifth Columnists.

"Anticipation — that's the key to flying," he told me with typical simplicity. "The only other thing you need is luck."

It will come as no surprise that he was not impulsive. He enjoyed taking his time. At the theater, when the rest of us would charge out at intermission, making quick judgments, he would nod to everything we said. Then later, an hour after the performance, while we were off on a different subject and having a nightcap, Jimmy would say: "I'll tell you about that play . . ." He'd do it in one sentence. Maggie Sullavan said, "He likes to chew his cud a little before he talks."

Regarding his acting, on rare occasions he might ask me, "How do you think this scene ought to go, Buzz?" But I was no fool. "I'll tell you when I see it on screen," I told him. "Your instincts are better than mine."

Over the years his acting became more subtle and more varied. The first time I saw him act was in a play called *Goodbye Again*. I saw a tall, lanky guy, bemused and bewildered-looking, make his entrance wearing a chauffeur's uniform and bring down the house with one line: "Mrs. Vanderlip is going to be sore as hell."

Looking back, social life in the mid-1930s for Broadway actors who hadn't yet arrived was minimal, to say the least. Occasionally we rented a basement opposite the Herald Tribune Building, every guest kicking in two dollars, which paid for all the beer we could handle, and we bought it in barrels. We were a species of young stage animals, and some of the names I remember were Hank Fonda, Margaret Sullavan, Rose Hobart, Barbara O'Neil, Ruth Gordon, and Myron McCormick.

One night I wandered in to find a weird concert in progress. Jimmy Stewart was behind an accordion, with Dick Foran providing harmony. As an ex–boy tenor, I was invited to join them — it didn't require much prodding — and that was the beginning of the Stewart-Meredith partnership.

Anyway, it wasn't long before Hollywood spotted Jimmy's one-of-a-kind charisma and he was making pictures. He set up housekeeping in Brentwood with Henry Fonda and John Swope. When I came out, Jimmy made an unexpected offer of hospitality, and I moved in. We established a bicoastal pattern. When Jimmy or Hank or Swope came East, they were automatically a member of the Meredith household; and when I winged West, it would be vice versa. There were plays on Broadway and movies in California, and we had the habit of flying east or west every chance we got.

One view of Jimmy I remember in particular. That's the sight of him at the breakfast table — or lunch or dinner, for that matter — his six and a half feet or so of languid good nature wrapped around the table. He seemed all legs.

The meal over, Jimmy would get out his accordion and play it awhile. He played the piano, too. He loved jazz — good jazz. He was a discerning critic and would leave if the orchestra was mediocre.

Years later he and Hank Fonda played in a film I produced, *A Miracle Can Happen* (also known as *On Our Merry Way*), which linked several stories. Their episode was about two broken-down musicians. John O'Hara wrote the script and one of the finest directors of all time, George Stevens, was in charge. It was a brilliant team — but it could not save the picture.

At one point Jimmy tried to fill out his spare frame with some muscles. One of those radiantly healthy trainers came by three times a week, while I hid behind a magazine. But no amount of heavy eating or heavy weights could change Stewart's thin-as-a-pipecleaner physique.

Jimmy cherished privacy. When the publicity department was lucky enough to get in touch with him, they asked: "Anything happen to you today that might make a good story?" His invariable reply was, "Nope. Nothing at all." He was a press agent's nightmare.

This privacy was part of his nature. He never discussed his good deeds or his private life. Now and then I heard of them secondhand. We never discussed it. It was a closed subject.

Jimmy had an honest dislike for formalities and he rarely gave parties, but I remember that once, before the war, under pressure from me, he and I gave one.

To begin with, we both arrived late from work at the studio. As we drove up, the porch and lawn were swarming with guests. But Jimmy took charge, apologizing and steering the guests toward the bar.

"What'll you have?" he asked the first customer, as though we were a saloon. The guest scanned the few bottles of assorted spirits. "A Bacardi," said he.

Jimmy glanced at the bottles. No Bacardi! Stalling for time, he asked another guest: "And what would you like?" "I'll have a Bacardi, too," she said sweetly.

Excusing himself, Jim beat a retreat to the bedroom, where I was scrambling out of my work clothes.

"I'm leaving," he said. "Think I'll go catch a movie."

"Oh, no you don't," I said, grabbing his lapel. "Let's face our guests together."

"*Our* guests?" There was a definite tone of "I told you so" by now.

"Jim — for God's sake — tell them one of your slow stories."

It worked. In the time it took Jimmy to tell a slow joke, Malcolm, the valet, ran to the nearest liquor store for rum and was pouring Bacardis.

I don't say Jimmy was a financial wizard, but in his diffident way he handled his money better than any of us. One day, for instance, he said, "I've got so much insurance and annuities that I've just decided to turn most of it into cash."

"Might be a good idea," I said, "but don't trust my judgment."

That night when I came home I found Jimmy in conference with a new counselor.

"Did you liquidate some of your holdings?" I asked.

"Nope," said he. "I bought some more."

Eventually Jimmy hired a business manager. But he let three weeks go by before the poor man had a chance to talk to him.

"What's the use of paying for his advice," I asked, "if you're not going to use his brains?"

The next night Jimmy brought in the financial expert. I arrived in time to hear the man say: "Mr. Stewart, I guarantee there's ninety-five percent profit in operating a popcorn concession! All you need is a place twenty feet square and . . ." It was the business manager's last appointment. Malcolm ushered him out in a hurry.

Malcolm was impeccably trained by my valet Wood, a personage in his own right — a storybook gentleman's gentleman. He was incapable of finding fault with the person he chose to work for.

A case in point was the night a woman fainted halfway through the third act of *Winterset*. The audience was panicked and so was I. I rushed back offstage and shouted, "What the hell do we do?!" Wood drew himself up and in his best Wodehousian accent said, "Congratulations, sir! That hasn't happened since Valentino!"

When I returned to Hollywood to start work in *Second Chorus*, with Fred Astaire and Paulette Goddard, of course I called Jimmy first.

"Come out right now and we'll have dinner," he said. "Olivia is here and I'd like you to meet her. We're going to the theater after dinner, if you'd like to join us."

Well, I arrived late to find they had already left. But Malcolm was there to welcome me and he drove me to the theater. En route I told Malcolm I hoped Jimmy and Miss de Havilland would not be angry with me.

"Shall I send her flowers?" Malcolm suggested. "I'll see that they are delivered at the intermission."

"Fine! Thanks!" said I.

They were delivered, all right. I watched Miss de Havilland open the box. There were many roses, with a card that read: "Dearest Olivia, again I am late — and again, forgive me. Much love, Buzz."

The touch too much!

Olivia and Jimmy were "an item" for a while. Jimmy later found and married his lovely Gloria, but I remember those bachelor days with amusement and affection, when Malcolm played Cyrano to my Christian.

That pleasant period came to an end one day early in 1942 when Jimmy and I arrived home from work to discover we'd been drafted. We sat there in the house thinking about it as we listened to one of the first recorded radio programs, a performance of Archibald MacLeish's *Fall of the City*, with a cast of hundreds. I played the Announcer. Stewart and I listened to that extraordinary broadcast without giving it our full attention, realizing we'd soon be wearing uniforms.

The next day Jimmy went in to report. I drove him there, and two weeks later Henry Fonda and I gave him a party on his last day before going to camp. We borrowed various props from MGM and had fake snakes hanging from the trees and stuffed alligators in the driveway. Jimmy had brought his commanding officer, who was a bit startled to see a sign up in front of the house where Jimmy and I were living, which said "Anti-Military Headquarters." There were effigies hanging from the trees and a bunch of bearded men cooking on the lawn; all part of our idea of being funny . . . a crazy celebration before we joined the armed forces — a farewell to Hollywood for the duration.

We all went willingly. We were glad to go to war! I had been cochairman with Helen Hayes of "The Fight for Freedom" — a movement that urged the United States to join the Allies against Hitler.

So, in some strange way, being drafted was a relief — a surcease. A curious sense of well-being came over me when I put on the uniform. I went into basic training and there the feeling of security grew as all decisions were made for me. The army air force was where I eventually landed. It made me happy. I slimmed down and felt pleased that this enforced discipline had overtaken my life. At last I was in command of my fate — a soldier and an actor.

The euphoria lasted from February 1942 until October 23, 1944, when I received an honorable discharge from President Roosevelt to play Ernie Pyle.

But there were many events in my life as a soldier before that happened.

They Couldn't See Us, but They Sure As Hell Could Hear What We Were Saying

PEOPLE SELDOM MENTION Norman Corwin's name today, but in the late 1930s he was the top writer-producer in what was radio's Golden Age. In 1939 he directed a series for CBS called *The Pursuit of Happiness,* and I was its master of ceremonies.

Corwin is not as well remembered as some of the other directors of that era because he was never seen by the public. He liked to be the man behind the deed. Yet of all the producers and directors I worked with in that period, I most admired Norman. He was in his mid-twenties, and he operated quietly and efficiently. That was essential when every broadcast was "live" and the tensions were high. He was always in control.

In those days, as I've previously mentioned, there were no audiotapes — so mistakes were forbidden! We rehearsed until the last minute and asked God to get us through. When we got in trouble, as we occasionally did, we had to stop the broadcast and the announcer would say something like, "We are having technical difficulties. Please stay tuned and we will be back in a few minutes."

Critics praised Corwin's programs, calling them special, innovative, and vivid. He was told by CBS to be experimental. His instructions were "Make it new!" . . . "Break ground!"

Corwin's choices fascinated the public and pleased the network. He used the finest music, poetry, and drama for his shows. Above all, he was an accomplished storyteller, and he liked "spoken drama" to be spoken and not seen.

I told him I could see his ancestors sitting around a fire at night, spinning tales, singing. No movement — just voices stirring the imagination.

As a measure of Corwin's work, in 1939 Robert Saudek, assistant director of NBC, a direct competitor of the Columbia Broadcasting System, wrote to congratulate Corwin on one of his broadcasts.

I don't think Corwin ever slept. He claimed, "I was a prisoner of those shows — editing, producing, directing, casting, and calming actors. I didn't have time to pray, except out of the corner of my mind. I prayed quick things like, 'Give me a break, God!' "

The year we did *Pursuit,* Norman had the job of writing, producing, directing, and staying alive. He was friendly (when he had the time) and he kept a half grin on his face. But he was never rattled. The rest of us might rattle, but he didn't have time for that — not in live radio.

The Pursuit of Happiness was broadcast in a large auditorium at CBS, with three or four hundred people in the audience, and an orchestra on the stage. I can't remember the name of the hall, but it worked like a legitimate theater, except that in the theater we rehearsed for weeks.

It still makes me sweat to think about that show. We were lucky to get two days of rehearsal before we had to perform live for millions of people. They couldn't see us, but they sure as hell could hear us. And the audience listened carefully in those pristine days, more than half a century ago.

Radio is an old story now, but when it first arrived it was exciting to hear words and music come out of the air. It was the edge of the miraculous.

The threat of television loomed in the future but we thought it would never happen — or if it did it would take centuries to develop. But TV arrived quicker than that — and immediately short-circuited the glory of radio. Overnight, radio was reduced to background sounds you hear when driving a car or washing dishes or making love.

But in Corwin's day radio was magic. Great artists joined us on *The Pursuit of Happiness* — musicians like Woody Guthrie and Leadbelly, comics like Danny Kaye, who came to us straight from the Borscht Circuit in the Catskills and went from us to stage and movies, where he became a colossal star. Charles Laughton gave his Bible readings for the first time to millions of people and made a hit doing it, and Paul Robeson shook up the country with his performance of "Ballad for Americans."

Many of our radio plays were written by important authors, and Norman Corwin himself wrote some of the best. He also had an elegant eye for editing the scripts of others.

On a more unpleasant note, for a brief moment in the witch-hunting 1950s Norman appeared on the blacklist as a Communist sympathizer! The same thing happened to a lot of us. We didn't know why, and yet it happened. The procedure was mindless and almost enveloped the country.

But talent was hard to beat down in those days. Mr. Paley, the head of CBS, who was as conservative as you could get, defied the right-wing radicals, at least at first. And even those radicals found it hard to object to plays like *The Bill of Rights*, which celebrated the one hundred fiftieth anniversary of those first amendments. The program starred Jimmy Stewart and an all-star cast and it was carried on four networks.

Another fine script by Norman was *On a Note of Triumph*, commemorating VE Day, May 8, 1945. He also wrote *Lonesome Train*, which is still used today as an ode to American presidents.

On the commemoration of the passage of the Universal Bill of Human Rights, Corwin wrote and directed another program that stirred the country. He called it *We Hold These Truths*, and in that production I played a leading role.

It was a happy, experimental time and we felt lucky to be a part of it. Today, the public doesn't regard the media with the same awe it once did — the magic is gone. We no longer sit around campfires telling each other stories.

While I enjoy working in television, I have a nostalgia for those glorious days when radio was an audacious and motivated medium.

Orson Welles
1940

ALTHOUGH Orson Welles and I were contemporaries, I never was a part of his great theater until *Five Kings* was produced in 1940, just before the war.

Orson had come along the same time I did, and we got to know each other. It was incredible how famous Orson became in the middle and late 1930s — especially after his Martian broadcast. There never was and probably never again will be a theatrical event with such international impact. Hitler mentioned Orson in a speech. He told the Germans they shouldn't worry about Americans as enemies: *"They are a race who hide under tables at the sound of an actor's voice."*

Welles approached me to do *Five Kings* with him. As I have mentioned, this was immediately after I had promised to play the lead in Anderson's *Knickerbocker Holiday,* but my role had become a dim accessory. Out of loyalty, I said I would do the play in the fall after I'd gone to Europe for a rest. I had gone through a divorce and wanted to heal myself.

Two days before I sailed, Orson got hold of me. He was one

of the most persuasive and entertaining males I ever knew. First he drove me to a country place he had in Sneden's Landing and provided me with a lovely French girl who made me forget my marital troubles . . . and then finally, late in the evening, he read me his new project.

Five Kings was a voracious piece, gobbling up hunks of Shakespeare's *Richard II*, parts I and II of *Henry IV*, and *Henry V*, and it was all spliced together with passages from Hollingshead.

Orson's proposal was that I would play both Prince Hal and Henry V and he would direct and play Falstaff. He also said I should have top billing — it was a heady proposal. But at first I couldn't persuade myself to break my contract with my pals Weill and Anderson.

Orson assaulted my hesitancy in the grand manner. He hired a five-man band from Harlem, which serenaded me, troubadour style, over most of Rockland County and finally Manhattan. This crazy fiesta lasted a day and two nights and was joined by various columnists, actors, picaroons, lovers, enemies, well-wishers, including Toots Shor, Courtney Burr, Jed Harris, and Walter Winchell.

A hundred witnesses to that scene must still be living. But I was finally piped aboard the *Ile de France,* the party was washed ashore, and the ship sailed. At long last I lay alone in my disordered stateroom . . . in my hand a signed copy of a contract with Orson to do *Five Kings.*

Next day, at sea, I felt guilty. I composed a hundred-word cable to Kurt and Max, trying to explain things. I never got a reply. They had already read about what had happened in the papers.

I find that the memory of that episode is sadder than I'd realized. Yet, if I had to do it again, I'd probably repeat myself. Such is my nature — cycles of rebellion and regret.

Five Kings never got to New York. But it sure as hell was an earthshaking experience out of town. The concept was brilliant. Welles had dreamed up a big, revolving, segmented stage. The set was quite wonderful. The battle of Agincourt was staged like a long dolly shot, the set turning full circle and thirty or forty extras running in full heat; cannons booming, smoke billowing, trumpets blaring, and myself shouting, "Once more unto the breach, dear friends . . . Once more!"

But I'm getting ahead.

In Boston, the morning of the opening of *Five Kings*, we had our first complete dress rehearsal.

The play turned out to be ninety minutes too long; not twenty minutes, not a half hour — ninety long, well-rehearsed minutes overtime.

It ran four and a half hours! No one had timed the spectacle under full sail. But more troublesome than the length was the machinery that drove the revolving stage. It broke down — suddenly, completely, and often.

Orson, dressed as Falstaff, stepped to the footlights and commandeered twenty or thirty Harvard boys, guests at the rehearsal, to rush to the cellar and push the stage around by hand. Those young Ivy Leaguers responded with courage and enthusiasm — it was the decade of socialist idealism. Thus the dress rehearsal was able to proceed in some fashion, though the loudest voices in the house came from the cellar, where stage managers were shouting "Push! . . . Pull! . . . Forward! . . . Halt! . . . Go . . ."

On opening night, the curtain was delayed an hour. We were still working, cutting, rehearsing. All the critics were out front, fretting in limbo, while Orson tried to shorten the play by eliminating entire scenes. Things got farcical.

Downstairs the Harvard boys, like galley slaves, chafed at their oars. Quite a few of them, I'm sorry to report, became inebriated. Before my entrance I remember that Orson-Falstaff grabbed me and hugged me; "Courage!" said he.

"How'd we get ourselves into this frigging nightmare?" My voice was weary, my body fatigued.

"Don't worry," said Falstaff. "There is a thing called magic — theater magic — it's here — wait and see! Now take this pill. It's potent. It's called benzedrine."

Our cue came, we walked onstage, and the first tavern scene started. So help me God — it went beautifully! Every speech, movement, nuance burned swift and bright and spread like prairie fire over the audience. Laughter, appreciation, empathy flowed. Orson's miracle was happening.

Finally, the other actors left the stage and I, Prince Hal, was alone for my first soliloquy.

"I know you all and will awhile uphold the unyoked humor of your idleness; yet herein will I imitate the sun. . . ."

These few beginning words I spoke splendidly — I was at my best in poetic drama — but soon the miracle began to flicker. First, my spotlight went out. It collapsed. Still speaking, I fell on my knees and found another light — it happened to be emerald green. There was a rumble from the cellar. . . . The stage began to spin! Somebody had fixed the motor. It took off in high gear.

I was snapped offstage like the end boy in crack-the-whip. A stagehand caught me as I flew by. I held him tight and said, "You're going to hear the rest of this, goddammit!" . . . and I finished the speech. It was the best I ever did it, but there was only an audience of one.

Ted Emery and I had a sword fight scene that was violent. I was playing Hal and he was playing Hotspur. This scene had been choreographed by Raspelli, a saber champion who conceived many Broadway duels. Because we were agile and young, Raspelli gave us the business of leaping from parapet to parapet on the huge revolving stage — we battled with sabers, shields, and words in iambic pentameter.

I rushed on with a substitute shield — a stagehand had mislaid mine. The replacement felt light, and at the climax of the fight Ted split my shield and fractured my hand. In a hot reaction I struck out at Ted and hit him on his bare skull. He sank to the ground, muttering. Thus we finished the evening; he with his mind stunned and I with my hand splintered. I have a memory of standing there, wavering in the fading light, Emery talking nonsense lingo — the words of Shakespeare coming out back to front — until he bravely died and the curtain fell.

Very little went right in that production. For years I relived it in my nightmares.

Orson had too many responsibilities. He was playing Falstaff, directing us all, supervising the sets, the costumes, the script. He found, too late, that he needed a full-time genius to solve the logistics. John Houseman tried to help, but he was never given the leeway for some reason.

You can blame Orson only in the sense that he should have demanded the kind of help he needed. The confusion threw us all — befogged everyone who was in it. We will always remember it as a towering drama that almost came to pass, but that finally turned into a nightmare. It was a brilliant concept of a great man, but the mechanical problems were never solved. None of us came up to the vision, because of fatigue, logistics, and time.

I can still see Orson playing Falstaff. In those days he was thin, and in order to achieve "fatness" for the role he used a then new substance called foam rubber, which no one had heard anything about. He "bloated" himself with that, and he looked vast. He grew a great greasy beard, and he wore high heels to make himself tall — his ideas were lofty in every way. Later, of course, he filmed another version of Falstaff — but his stage rendition was awesome, while it lasted.

Perhaps I should have tried to play for another month or so, but at the time I felt physically and mentally unable to go on. I had a broken hand and a broken heart and was tired of those great leaps and bounds and duels. I was not endowed for the job of leaping from crevasse to crevasse on a revolving stage. In the end I had no breath or heart or mind to speak the mighty words of Shakespeare.

Orson and I remained distant friends in spite of *Five Kings*, but I never learned how disappointed he was that I had left the production until near the end of his life. One day I mentioned something to him about *Five Kings*. He looked at me and said, "Do you know why we closed that show? The only reason?" I said, "No. Why?" He said, "Because you quit, you ran out!"

So after all those years he had concluded that I was basically at fault. He said that when I left he was so loaded with troubles already, my leaving was the last straw.

So *Five Kings* was an inspired concept which, unlike *War of the Worlds*, never came to pass.

*   *   *

It was only a year before *Five Kings* that Orson did his *War of the Worlds* broadcast. I was on my way home to my place in the country. I had stopped for something to eat, and the radio said the Western World was shaking with excitement about a Martian invasion that was under way. I listened to the broadcast and learned it was Orson! I couldn't comprehend the worldwide impact until I got home. The radio waves were burning with excitement.

I think Welles was surprised and delighted at the panic that broadcast caused — it became the most famous broadcast in history.

He told me later he knew it was a "goddamn good theatrical piece of work," and if you staged it as a live broadcast, it might have a strong theatrical effect; but not to the extent it did. John Houseman was the producer of the event. He knew Orson's feelings about the production and Houseman said Orson thought a few people might take it seriously, might be scared for a few minutes — that would be good theater. But Orson never foresaw it would be volcanic, that it would erupt and spread fear over the world.

I have one story about the making of *The Magnificent Ambersons*. I went to Orson's home in Los Angeles when he was shooting the film, and he was in a wheelchair. He had broken a lot of bones, including his leg. He told me he had been trying to set the stage and direct all at the same time. He said, "I was up on the high balcony about to come down those long, steep stairs. I was talking to the actors about their lines and their entrances, and to the cameraman about camera movements. 'Have you got it?' I asked. They said, 'Yes, fine.' I said, 'Lights, camera, action!' — and I fell head-over-heels down the concrete steps. When I got to the bottom, I yelled, '*CUT!*' and they rolled me to the infirmary."

In the early days, when Orson first arrived, Hollywood was a tyranny. Actors and directors were treated like hired help. They were permitted very little artistic or creative freedom. The studio bosses, the men in charge — the five or six or eight men who ran the industry — dictated policy, and if you deviated from their instructions, you were in deep trouble.

In that atmosphere, it was hard for Orson to function. Later on, he had some independent money, but by then he was no longer at the top of his health and he tended to go beyond budget and beyond reason. In still later years, when his body was bloated and his health worse, I think Orson became impractical. But when he was at his height, and fired with genius, they did not treat him well. He made the bosses uneasy and he angered Hearst. He became an enemy of the Establishment.

Orson was enormously likable. He laughed uproariously and constantly and made you laugh with him. And he was an appreciative listener. Like any genius, he must have had his share of demons but he handled them well.

I never heard a word of despair from Orson — he seldom discussed the past. His childhood is rumored to have been troubled, but he said little about it to me — though I remember he asked about mine.

John Huston lived in my house in Malibu just before he died. During that time we often talked about Orson. John was fascinated by the man and his talent. He said, "If Orson ever needs me I will go." And that was pretty good, coming from John, who went to nobody.

Later in life, I got closer to John and further from Orson. They both relished food and relished liquor, and they both were touched with genius. And they got the job done!

Like John, Orson finally faltered because of his health. His mind was lively and never dimmed — but he could not keep himself from bloating physically. He was a man of delicate tastes and I am sure he regretted what he looked like in later years, carrying so much flatulent weight.

That flaw, that lack of discipline, diminished his genius too soon. But the films he made are unsurpassed — they get better over the years.

His supreme *Citizen Kane* was rereleased in 1991, fifty years after it was made. It was a hit with a new public, and critics have long since called it the greatest film ever made. Few motion pictures have returned to such accolades. It seems to improve with the years.

It is too bad Orson wasn't around to enjoy it. He would have been seventy-six years old.

"The Free Company"

IN 1941, Europe was boiling into World War II and the Nazis were advancing on all fronts. Back in the States, Franklin D. Roosevelt was trying to wake us up. One of the jobs he gave Attorney General Francis Biddle was to urge the American radio networks to "make democratic propaganda on behalf of liberty and free speech." Mrs. Biddle was a playwright and a poet, and I had met the Biddles in Philadelphia a few years before he became attorney general. I was impressed when he persuaded the Columbia Broadcasting System to put on a radio series called *The Free Company*, and asked me to host the program.

James Boyd was appointed writer-producer of *The Free Company*, and his job was no more and no less than defending the Bill of Rights!

The first thing Boyd looked for were the best writers in America. It was impossible to have a program of that scope without great writing, and that was what he got. He enlisted Archibald MacLeish, William Saroyan, Robert Sherwood, Maxwell Anderson, Stephen Vincent Benét, Paul Green, and others — the top authors of the time. He signed up equally fine actors such as Canada Lee, Paul Muni, and Elia Kazan. None of them refused if they thought they were right for the part they were offered.

The Free Company was a good title — it described the problem and the purpose, and it was an honor, at least at first, to be on the show. It was listened to by millions of people.

As master of ceremonies, my job was to introduce the play and the players, and I acted in some of the programs. I helped the program in any way I could, mostly by persuading friends to offer their services. I asked George M. Cohan, Ernest Hemingway, and others to write and a dozen stars to act. None of us made money from it; we worked for scale. We worked hard and we made our point.

In retrospect, the ones who deserved praise were the CBS staff and William Paley. They were patriots at first — but, alas, they soon grew timid.

Francis Biddle phoned me regularly during the weeks we were on the air. He said he felt like a midwife, responsible for the birth of the series. And, in a way, I guess he was.

Orson Welles's contribution was a play called "His Honor, the Mayor." At that time Welles not only had his burgeoning career and the upcoming war to contend with — William Randolph Hearst was out for his scalp. Hearst's attack was violent; he was determined to stop or sabotage the opening of Welles's film *Citizen Kane*.

Just before the live broadcast of Welles's program, I was taken aside and warned not to ad lib on the air anything about Hearst and instructed to give Orson the same warning. I was startled. The CBS bosses were worried that one or both of us would interrupt the program and shout our personal opinions about Mr. Hearst! It was a foolish fear and must have been planted by somebody — but there it was. Those were peculiar times.

Looking back, I remember I was annoyed by the warning, and in some corner of my funnybone, I was tempted to ad lib something like, "Down with Citizen Hearst." But I didn't do it, thank God.

Welles's broadcast was on April 6, 1941. He used his own

company of actors, which included Ray Collins, Agnes Moorehead, Paul Stewart, Erskine Sanford, and Everett Sloane. The play started with a speech to the effect that this broadcast wasn't intended to be uplifting or inspirational. It was about a mayor who had difficult problems, and if we listened carefully, we'd learn how problems are solved in the right way.

The mayor's problems were solved okay, but Orson's were not! After the broadcast, Hearst attacked *The Free Company* in earnest and we were splashed all over the chain of Hearst papers. His editors trumpeted that the majority of the actors and directors on *The Free Company* were Marxists! It was a crime against society to allow *The Free Company* to pollute the airways! Our program was "odious, like a faulty sewer."

The rest of the newspapers were divided about the whole matter, but everybody was disturbed and angry. And behind it all was Hearst's drive to stop *Citizen Kane* from being released!

None of this was helpful to the high purpose of the program. CBS got jittery when we were called Communist by the Hearst papers. While at first none of our other plays were attacked, eventually the whole project came under fire.

Nevertheless, to their credit, CBS let us go on. Somebody got to the bosses and pointed out that the attack on us had to do with Hearst's fury about *Citizen Kane* — nothing else. Looking back, it makes me shiver.

Hearst also found out that a group of us on the program had signed a petition for Harry Bridges, the left-wing labor leader, who was about to be put in jail. Although we didn't particularly like the man, we thought he had the same right of free speech that President Roosevelt asked us to praise in our broadcasts.

The *New York Times* editorialized that Hearst had paid no attention to our program until he heard that Orson Welles would appear on it, and then he attacked everybody at once.

I discussed this by phone with Attorney General Biddle and he told us to stay cool and carry on, which we did. But Hearst had drawn blood. The CBS executives became increasingly nervous and I'm sure they were relieved when we finished the series.

The uproar and the smear nearly finished Orson's career. He was trying to get other movies started and was still struggling to get *Citizen Kane* released. Although Hearst went to amazing lengths to stop that picture, he failed.

Today, *Kane* is considered by many serious critics to be the best film ever made! But Citizen Hearst didn't care, he just wanted blood, Welles's blood. And he almost succeeded.

I was both in front and behind the scenes during that stormy process, on stage as master of ceremonies, and through the back door of the White House. Those events were a sample of how the radicalism of Hitler was spreading, how the Nazi propaganda and fear of the Reds worked their way into the back channels. The enemy was inside the gates, so to speak.

Life was precarious back then. Fear was everywhere, as anyone who lived through those days will remember.

Our series' high purpose got lost in a conflict between the ego of Hearst and the creativity of Welles; between a man with power and a boy with genius. Had *Citizen Kane* been a mediocre picture, the whole controversy would have been forgotten by now, but it turned out to be a glorious achievement and it outlasted all the other participants. Hearst is gone, Hitler is gone, the war is long over. Paley and Welles and most of the people involved are dead. But the film seems to improve with time.

I don't know exactly what the moral to this story is, but I'm glad I was on Orson's side. He and the attorney general and Paley were the good guys and they won.

A year or so later I discovered that even ''friends in high places'' are powerless when the juggernaut of the ''paper war'' takes over.

After I was drafted for the army, the attorney general took the trouble to write to the secretary of war, asking that I be stationed at Moffett Field in California, where the base commander had requested me for special duties he outlined in a letter. The commander of the Induction Center and everyone else agreed on my military fate. Pretty high-powered advocates for one humble private!

March 6, 1942
My dear Mr. Secretary:

I wish to call your attention to a matter involving Burgess Meredith. I am interested in him because he has helped the Department on a number of occasions and has helped the Government in a great many ways during the past few years. As you know, he is a motion picture actor.

A few days ago, he was inducted into service. The following is a copy of a letter dated February 23, 1942, sent by General Ralph P. Cousins, Major General, U.S.A., West Coast Air Corps Training Center, Moffett Field, California, to the Selective Service Board, Brentwood, California:

"Mr. Burgess Meredith has been engaged in public relations activities connected with air corp functions.

"It is particularly desired to utilize the services and experience of Mr. Meredith for particular functions under my command.

"It is requested if Mr. Meredith is inducted into the service that he be assigned to Moffett Field. It will then be possible to utilize his services pending his obtaining a commission in the Air Corps."

I learned from Mr. Meredith that this letter was presented to the Selective Service Board and that he was requested to carry it to the Induction Center at Fort MacArthur, California. He showed it to Colonel France, Commanding Officer at Fort MacArthur, who told him that the request, of course, would be followed.

However, it seems a slip in the Classification Office at Fort MacArthur routed Meredith to the Signal Corps at Camp Crowder, Missouri. Meredith wrote me about the situation and asked me if I could assist in getting him transferred to General Cousins at Moffett Field.

Apparently, General Cousins and Meredith worked out a tentative program in which Meredith can be particularly helpful, and that is all Meredith is interested in. He wants to serve where he can be most useful.

Perhaps General Cousins has already requested the War Department for this transfer. However, I thought I would advise you of my interest in the matter because I want to see Meredith in a position where he can use his excellent talents to the best advantage in helping the Government. Since General Cousins is anxious to have him, I thought it would not be an imposition on my part to bring this matter to your attention.

Sincerely yours,

(signed)   Francis Biddle

Attorney General

But in spite of the attorney general and in spite of several army generals, I ended up at Camp Crowder, Missouri. A thousand miles off base. The faceless bureaucrats win every time. It took two weeks to get me back in circulation.

John Steinbeck

I'M NOT SURE when I first met John, but the occasion was casual and must have been during the making of the film *Of Mice and Men*. His wife, Carol, was with him and the three of us became friends. I saw him later on in New York, more often than California; but by then he and Carol had separated.

He came to visit me with Gwyn, his new girlfriend, when I lived at Mount Ivy, New York, and they stayed two or three months. He came back to that house several times and even later he wrote two books there. One was *The Moon Is Down* and the other was *Bombs Away*. He also wrote a play there, *The Last Joan*, about Joan of Arc, for Paulette Goddard, then my wife, to be performed in Dublin after the war.

In 1942, I was an army air corps lieutenant and I persuaded John to write *Bombs Away* for the air corps, encouraging young men to enlist.

John read *The Moon Is Down* to me as he wrote it, chapter by chapter. I remember those readings. I can see him there by the fireplace, and can hear his quiet voice. I recall that I suggested a title, a quotation from Carl Sandburg — "The Stars Make No Noise." John lifted "The Moon Is Down" from Mercutio's speech in *Hamlet* — a much better choice.

That period of John's life was a happy one, because he was in love. He had left Carol and was on the run with Gwyn, soon to be his second wife. While that marriage did not work out either, they had two sons.

When the war began, John and I were sent to England as it was being bombed. He was writing for the *New York Herald Tribune* and I was a captain, assigned to Intelligence in the Air Force Transport Command. When I told him my assignment he responded: "You, in Intelligence?! We're going to lose the war."

We spent our free hours talking and walking around London. We would meet at his hotel on Picadilly and at a little off-hours restaurant named Le Petit Club Français, which was a rallying spot for the French underground forces. I discovered it and told John and other friends about it. It was a fine hangout, squalid and secret, with the Frenchmen filling us in about the black underside of the war. Even today, I can picture it, with a strange cockeyed lady bartender dishing out drinks.

The times that Steinbeck and I got together in England had no historical significance to us except dodging bombs. But there were amusing episodes.

The first was when I was making a picture called *Welcome to Britain*, an orientation film that Eisenhower had ordered. Its purpose was to show GIs how to behave in the British Isles. The Yanks were just coming over by the millions and were ignorant of living conditions and British ways. In the process of making this picture, I had to drive around to pick out film locations, and Steinbeck took two or three trips with me to look around the country himself, getting material for his column. I doubt he had been to England before, and I had only been in London briefly.

It was our good luck to be given a car and driver by General Lee of Eisenhower's staff. We went to Wales, Cornwall, and other areas outside London, seeing Britain at war. I remember that journey well — John and I talked about it in later years. He wrote a couple of columns about our driver, Eddie. Eddie amused us, because he could imitate birdcalls. He was proud of his gift and relentless in the art of producing bird noises. All the while we traveled around looking for locations and dodging bombs, we were accompanied by an obligato of birdsongs, with many descriptions and footnotes.

Another story I recall was about a friend of ours named Maurice Williams. He was the husband of John's literary agent in New York, Annie Laurie Williams. Annie was gray-haired and fussy, a close friend of John's and evidently capable, for she handled all of John's books and essays for movie sales. Maurice was a timid, quiet man. In New York he must have had some kind of a job, but he was under the shadow of his wife, a major literary agent. At any rate, compared to Annie Laurie, Maurice was considered a dim personage.

When the war started, he decided to make a mark for himself, so he joined up as a tailgunner in the air corps. Although he seemed old for such a hazardous job, the air corps accepted him and, after training, shipped him to England to take part in the 8th Air Force bombardments of Germany.

One sad day, word came that Maurice was lost in action over France. The report was: "He went down with his plane in a ball of fire."

John was shaken by the news and wanted to write a column about his friend, giving him a glowing epitaph. First, he had to verify Maurice's death, so he used his influence as an important correspondent to demand a military countdown. Intelligence told John that his pal was indeed missing in action. Officially dead.

So quiet, timid Maurice was given a hero's farewell — a glowing two-column obit in the *New York Herald Tribune* and associated papers. Everybody back home, especially Annie Laurie, was moved: not only by the man's brave deeds but by the beautiful words that John Steinbeck bestowed on him.

The only trouble was that Maurice was *not* dead. He had been rescued by the French underground and shipped back across the Channel good as new. "Like a resurrection!" Annie Laurie Williams said.

It struck me that somehow Maurice's life might become difficult now that he was alive and kicking. Some of the catharsis went out of the event, some of the heroism. Of course, we all saw Maurice again when we returned to New York. However, I don't think the subject of his resurrection was brought up often, beyond asking him questions about his health and so forth. He said the escape was quick and smooth and accomplished with finesse by the underground.

"Quite interesting," he said. "The technique was very skillful." He had the proper modesty of an almost-dead hero.

After the war John went back to New York and he and Gwyn bought a brownstone house in Manhattan, deserting his beloved California that he had written about for so many years. There they brought up two boys, Tom and John Jr. Gwyn died a few years ago after a long estrangement from John. He and his last wife, his widow Elaine, were happy, but because I moved west we seldom met.

During my marriage to Paulette Goddard, however, I saw John Steinbeck often, and under happy conditions. Paulette and I were living in my country house in Rockland County, twenty minutes north of the George Washington Bridge. The Steinbecks came to visit us there and we went to his home in Manhattan. During the postwar period, I witnessed the disintegration of his marriage to Gwyn and the growing up of his children. Later, he rented a country house near me, a fine hand-built home belonging to the artist Henry Varnum Poor.

During that period John Steinbeck decided to write the play *The Last Joan* as a vehicle for Paulette. It began one evening at our home. John said he was fascinated by the legend of Joan of Arc and his notion was to write about a modern-day Joan who hears the voices of God over the radio, and for all I remember, the television. A voice that no one but she could comprehend. I cannot, looking back, imagine why the idea seemed so good to us at that time, but we were enthusiastic and Steinbeck wanted to start writing at once. That very night, in fact. He began to wonder how we could get some information about Joan of Arc on which to base the play.

Maxwell Anderson lived close to me in New City. I had

introduced Steinbeck to Max and we knew that Max himself was writing a play about Joan of Arc! It was a play eventually performed by Ingrid Bergman. At any rate, I remember that we had a hilarious, not too sober conspiracy that night — John, Paulette, and myself. The conspiracy was to steal some basic information about Joan of Arc from Maxwell Anderson without raising his suspicions that we were writing a rival play. After a few drinks, we decided to extricate a volume or two from the *Encyclopædia Britannica* we knew Max owned.

We phoned and asked him if all of us could come over to borrow his encyclopedias. We explained we needed some historical data about ancient France. He said sure, so we went over there and had a few drinks with him and returned home carrying the volumes without raising a speck of suspicion. It makes me smile to think about that episode; but whatever John read in those volumes was enough to make him sure he could write the play, as indeed he did.

Before John finished it, we announced to the press that Paulette and I were going to perform *The Last Joan* in Dublin, and that the head of the Abbey Theatre, Ria Mooney, was signed to direct it. There was much excitement in the press here and abroad.

The Irish public, having heard about our forthcoming drama and, being a suspicious and inexplicable people, decided that any play written by Steinbeck must have Communist propaganda in it. We tend to forget, in this present age, that those were perilous times and the fear of communism, particularly among Irish Catholics and later among the McCarthyites, was awesome.

But a month before leaving for Dublin, we received a telegram from John, saying, "The play is not good enough. I tried my best, but it didn't come out. I'm sorry, but I don't want it done."

Paulette and I were in trouble. While the incipient rage of the Irish public might be appeased, we had a commitment with the head of the Abbey Theatre to do it and they had announced it. There was nothing to do but wire Ria Mooney that the play had been withdrawn by Steinbeck.

Ria took it in her stride. She suggested that a production of *Winterset* be done instead. This engendered new problems.

Whereas the Steinbeck play was suspected of being communistic, the Anderson play was rumored to be atheistic as well as communistic! A terrible combination. When we arrived at Shannon Airport, we were astonished to be met by a hostile crowd. Some of the mob ran up to our car and began hitting the windows and yelling, "Go back, go back, you dirty Communists!"

I was smothered into silence by all this, but Paulette, who was always quick with a riposte, called out: "Roll down the window and I'll hit 'em with my diamond necklace!" That became our favorite story for many a day. We were finally rescued by the mayor and the airport police and escorted to our hotel. When the play opened it did well, despite occasional boos from the audience.

Let me now throw in a lugubrious note. John Steinbeck had given me a copy of *The Last Joan*. I kept that copy for many years and I carried it from New York to California when I moved there. About four years ago, looking through files, I found the play again and kept it in front of me thinking, "I must make a copy of this!" In the time since it had been written, John Steinbeck had been given the Nobel Prize and he had died. Therefore, this unproduced play, this lost project, had become an object of great value. So the play rested on my desk while I figured what to do. One day when I was packing to go to New York, I decided to take *The Last Joan* with me and ask advice. I put it in my briefcase and went to New York. And that is the last I ever saw of that misbegotten play. It was lost in transit.

Such terrible things happen only once or twice in a lifetime. They leave a scar on your memory. I had not made a copy of *The Last Joan*, and I had lost the original. I looked through my files for a copy. Other people looked through their files. We offered rewards. Never a trace of *The Last Joan*. It was indeed "The Last Joan" as far as I am concerned. I believe the estate of John Steinbeck has no copy. Small consolation: it was probably not a good play. It "never came off," in John's words. His heart wasn't in it, he said.

Another less than successful venture I had with John Steinbeck concerned *Cannery Row*. I was fascinated with *Cannery Row* and

spent many days with John and Doc Ricketts, the real-life hero
of the book. We three passed the time telling stories and enjoying
life. At that period of my life I considered *Cannery Row* the best
book ever written — it fitted my view of life.

Ricketts and Steinbeck often gave high-voltage parties of various kinds, and John described those parties vividly in *Cannery
Row*. I witnessed a few of them. A phonograph was always playing. Mostly the music would be Palestrina or Monteverdi — ancient Italian devotional music — as a solemn background to the
everlasting drinking and noise-making of the guests. The decor
was unusual too. There were dozens of laboratory bowls and
glass cases filled with different species of aquatic monsters, live
and angry. There were anemones and weird crayfish peering and
blowing at us from inside the bowls. Once I stuck my finger inside
one of those cases and was bitten by a small monster of some
kind. I recall Steinbeck laughed so hard at me he fell off the chair.

In the book *Cannery Row*, John made up a large part of Doc,
the character who resembled Ricketts. But some of what he wrote
was true; Ricketts was an interesting man but not mythic as John
made him out; no human could be. John described Doc as being
a man of great sexual prowess. And indeed he may have been.
Doc had a couple of girls to whom he seemed pretty faithful during
the time I knew him. John became intimate with one of them
after Doc's death.

Once Doc introduced me to a girl and I went with her to some
private beach and we had a lovely affair, or so it seemed to me
then. Doc asked me about it later and said wistfully, "I envy you."
That did not sound like the womanizer, the satyr, the attacker
John painted Doc to be. There was a great spirit in Doc, but he
wasn't a devil either — not in respect to women or in respect to
morals. He was, in my opinion, an example of the relationship
between model and artist. A moderately attractive woman can
inspire an artist to paint her as a surpassing beauty. And so it is
in literature. Doc, as a model, was given certain dimensions that
he didn't altogether possess in life. Steinbeck's literary version of
Doc added devilment and wit and extraordinary capacities to the
original character. Those who remember Doc firsthand remember

him with love; those who have read about Doc remember him in mythic ways. John Steinbeck clothed Doc in many colors.

And so it is with the little house that Doc turned into a laboratory on Cannery Row. The events that happened in that house were happy or sad, dull or amusing, just like any other laboratory or studio of its size and character. But not every event had the panache John describes in *Cannery Row*. It is a lesson in the magic of art . . . and the magic continues. Even to this day, whenever I go by Doc's lab, my memory is colored by John's stories — not by the simple happy times we spent there.

I asked John whether I could attempt a dramatization of *Cannery Row*. John said okay, and I went ahead. His agent, Annie Laurie Williams, drew up a contract. I remember we made pretty good headway — I would write a scene and read it to John, and he would laugh or snort or make a suggestion. We got most of it finished, but it became less a play and more a screen scenario as it went along.

One day, Humphrey Bogart, a mutual friend, dropped by and we asked him to read it. He was excited by the idea and took the script home. We had told him that the best role for him was Mac, chief of all the bums who lived next to Doc's lab. I said I wanted to play Doc.

Bogie returned the next morning laughing. He read aloud the opening description of Doc, my role — it characterized Doc as "half goat and half man." It went on to say, "Doc was irresistible to women and had a brilliant mind."

Bogart closed the script and handed it to John. "Well, this sounds like a good thing for Meredith, but what the hell do I do against a character like that?" He went on: "I got an idea . . . you finish this up and I'll buy a ticket to see it." And that was that.

A few years later, John himself dramatized *Pipe Dream* for Rodgers and Hammerstein. It was based on *Sweet Thursday*, the sequel to *Cannery Row*. It was quite different and less wicked than our early effort, polite even, and as it turned out, forgettable. And more recently, in 1978, *Cannery Row* was finally diluted into an even more forgettable screenplay.

Around 1957, a new character named Kevin McClory entered

Steinbeck's and my life. Kevin was out of work at the time and was living in my house in Rockland County. He ran up a nine-hundred-dollar phone bill, I remember, attempting to get an expedition started to find hidden treasures in the Bahamas. Kevin is an adventurer, always was. He had heard that pirate ships had been sunk in the waters off Nassau, and was determined to find them. He was persuasive enough to enlist me in his group of adventurers, and through me, John Steinbeck.

Kevin and I bought diving equipment from Abercrombie & Fitch, and took diving lessons from a man who taught scuba in the swimming pool of the St. George Hotel in Brooklyn.

John and his wife, Elaine, Kevin, Peter Gimbel — a famous deep-sea diver and heir to the Gimbel department stores — along with his wife and myself and my wife, Kaja, made the trip. When we arrived on the island of Nassau, there was a general strike going on, which involved the entire resident population — it was an ominous start. Nobody on the island would take our luggage, or drive us anywhere. Only a few locals would speak to us at all. Finally, we got our equipment into a hired boat and took off to seek our fortune in the adjacent seas.

But the trip was doomed and the karma was bad. Steinbeck became annoyed with the whole project. He turned dour and sullen. It was a raspish side of him I'd never seen.

But the rest of us went forward seeking this sunken treasure and we had a couple of scrapes with death. Peter Gimbel, our professional guide, once dove off the side of our boat just as dusk was coming and stayed below so long that we lost track of his bubbles. Darkness came and we despaired. We kept howling into the deepening twilight and the rising seas, hoping to raise Peter from the deep . . . then finally his wife heard him. Far off. We spotted him, at last, and he crawled back into the boat, a chastened man.

I also had a close call. I got the idea that if I were towed behind the boat, I could, with my goggles and scuba equipment, peruse the ocean's bottom for treasure. This turned out to be a dangerous concept. It was like trolling a fish as bait. I was hauled in, just in time, away from a school of pursuing man-eaters.

It was one of the world's least successful treasure hunts; it became tedious and it had a side effect: it began an alienation between Steinbeck and me that was never quite repaired. Our friendship was diminished, our good times never resumed — a sad and senseless turn.

Kevin, on the other hand, found several treasures. First, on that voyage he found his future wife, Bobo Sigrist, a beautiful lady, and very wealthy. He also found Ian Fleming, the author. From him, Kevin bought the first James Bond story, *Thunderball*, which was made into one of the most successful of all Bond pictures. So are the ways of the world: because Bobo Sigrist and Ian Fleming happened to be on Nassau at the time of our treasure hunt, Kevin McClory's fortune turned bright. The rest of us became disgruntled, snarling at one another like prisoners of war.

John Steinbeck was basically a simple man. He liked good food and he liked pleasant surroundings; but underneath he was a farmer and enjoyed country attitudes. There was a dichotomy in his nature, though. For example, he dined often at the "21" Club and the Colony Club in New York; and yet he never let a meal pass there without making some deprecating remark about New York life. Maybe deep down he felt that he should never have left California or left his beloved "Pastures of Heaven."

Some critics have said he never wrote well after he came East. John would talk about that problem openly, saying that he often thought of going back, and part of him wanted to, but he could not force himself to do it. Yet he never stopped writing about it; and his books became more and more successful.

From memory he could write about Monterey or Cannery Row or Salinas or Soledad with such freshness of mind and sharpness of detail you'd think he'd never left the West Coast — but he ended up with homes on Long Island and on the elegant side of Manhattan. Whether the quality of his writing diminished or was sustained, time will tell. But it's interesting that in the days when Steinbeck was alive and at the top of his career, most critics considered him a lesser talent than Hemingway or Faulkner. As time went on, this estimation began to change. He received the

Nobel Prize. And today, bookstores sell more Steinbeck novels than those of Faulkner and Hemingway. Even some of his shorter works like *Pastures of Heaven* and *Cannery Row* and *Tortilla Flat* are more highly regarded now than they were when they arrived on the scene. Steinbeck was always famous — he was always a star and always a best-seller — but high acclaim and deep respect come to him more and more as time rolls on. American authors do not ripen as well as the English and Irish authors; but time seems to favor John Steinbeck.

Odds and ends of memories of Steinbeck float into view: I recall his childlike pleasure with tricks and gadgets. Once he conceived the notion of bringing helium tanks into his house, not for therapeutic purposes, but for the purpose of changing the quality of people's voices.

If you inhale helium and try to talk, something fantastic happens to your voice. It becomes eerie and strangled, an octave above its natural range. The first time Steinbeck tried it on himself, he took a gulp of helium, and spoke the words, "It is a far, far better thing that I do than I have ever done." He sounded like a suffocating cat or a querulous corncrake. It was one of his favorite amusements, and often in those carefree days when we went to Steinbeck's house all of us would amuse ourselves by inhaling the stuff and saying foolish things in an altered voice.

This so intrigued me that years later, when I was directing a play called *The Frogs of Spring* (a play by Nathaniel Benchley, about Steinbeck, by the way), I had one of the characters come on stage with a lungful of helium and say something or other in the hopes that it would brighten the act. The audience laughed at the gimmick but the critics were not amused. They said we were trying to cover up a bad plot with secondary tricks — but right or wrong, we had fun doing it.

The other thing I recall about John was his early fascination with his sons. He had wanted very much to have children — he said he felt incomplete without them. He wrote a play about it, *Burning Bright*. It had to do with a circus performer discovering he could not have children. Then one day his wife became pregnant by someone else. At first the performer was murderous and vengeful, but in the end he was persuaded that all men are related and all children are everyone's sons and daughters. That was the plot . . . but John personally would never have been guided by such a gentle philosophy. His own children meant a lot to him.

I made up a poem about John's son Tom, when the lad was five or six years old. It went: "Tom, Tom, the writer's son, stole a plot and away he run." For the life of me I don't know why this struck John so funny, but it did, and I can only guess we were easily amused in those carefree times.

John was a seeker after women and he enjoyed them. I had the sneaking feeling that John liked to appear more unbridled than he really was. This, of course, is a tendency of many artists and, I guess, nonartists. But artists particularly, because they are in the public eye and often feel they should hide their sensitivity and their shyness. John's defense was to thrust out his chin very hard after he had a few drinks — I think he believed his chin receded a little. It looked to me like a perfectly good chin, but he wanted it to be more than that. Finally, in the last fifteen or twenty years of his life, he grew a full, thick beard. After that he apparently didn't feel the need to act pugnacious.

John usually was a humorous man. He gazed on most events with an antic eye. He wrote seriously when he wanted to, and his serious writings are probably his best — but in his life, John had a humorous slant on people and events. He enjoyed most of the things that happened to him and many of the people he knew. It comes back to me strongly, that enjoyment. When he laughed, his face got red, like Santa Claus's. It did not get rosy, it got painted red! There is a portrait of him that Lewis Milestone owned, which caught John's high coloring exactly.

There was another, darker side, that sometimes showed through; underneath, there seemed to be an ocean of sorrow. Yet I never saw John out-of-hand while drinking. I did not ever see him totter or stumble or show hostility, as they tell me Faulkner and Fitzgerald sometimes did. I never witnessed him disagreeable or dangerous. He was a large man, over six feet, and well built, but he never took exercise. I don't recall him running or playing

outdoor games. Yet I feel he often fancied himself a rugged individual resembling many of the characters he wrote about. One
time in a pub, I saw him arm-wrestle quite a few people and get
beaten regularly, which seemed to surprise him. A lot of us act
that way. We think we are in better shape than we are. And, of
course, until late in life John's eating habits didn't always en-
courage good health.

On the other hand, his writing habits were disciplined and
very scheduled. In the years I knew him he wrote early in the
morning — from five to noon. Originally, he wrote in a wonderful
longhand on legal paper with fine blue lines — his earlier manuscripts are handsome as a monk's scroll. His handwriting was
small and tight, and he seldom had to rewrite. It is interesting to
note that Maxwell Anderson's handwriting and John's writing
were somewhat similar. They both wrote in small careful script
and they both used a finely lined legal paper; a coincidence that
interested me, because otherwise they were totally unlike.

Years after John and Gwyn separated and she was living in
Palm Springs, she showed me the original manuscript of the novel
Of Mice and Men. It was faultless, with few corrections, and hand-
written. Gwyn was about to sell the manuscript to a college or
a university or to a collector for $50,000. She was, she told me,
broke. Her health was bad and despite suffering from emphysema
she smoked constantly.

John wrote passionately and with absolute concentration. He
seemed to be totally involved in the process of creation and in
the formation of words. In the 1950s, when John moved to New
York, he confessed to me that he was starting to use a dictating
machine. He said it felt pretty good. He told me that *Travels with
Charley* was partly dictated. His manuscripts are now extremely
valuable — particularly his earlier ones that had to do with California and were written in his clear, precise hand. I have a half
a hundred unpublished letters from him written in that very
fashion.

East of Eden was finished about 1951 in New York at the Bedford Hotel of all places; but I don't recall if it was written in
longhand. He told Nathaniel Benchley and myself he wanted to

write it for his children, to make them aware of their heritage. He struggled to make it instructional and simple. In the end, with his editor's urging, Steinbeck the novelist took over. *Eden* was his last long look back at California. He wrote it while his powers were still mighty and while his feelings about the West Coast were vivid.

Three fine motion pictures were made of the works of John Steinbeck: *The Grapes of Wrath, Of Mice and Men,* and *East of Eden.* I was with Elia Kazan and John at the Bedford Hotel, when they phoned Darryl Zanuck and made the deal for *Eden.* I felt left out of the proceedings, a poor cousin.

After the death of Doc Ricketts, John took over the laboratory and assumed the financial obligations of Doc, who had not been a great hand at making or saving money.

I remember John phoning me about Ricketts's death. He spelled out the details of the tragedy with great exactness: how a train from Monterey had run into Doc's car and killed him instantly. Knowing Doc as I did, and knowing how close he was to John, it was moving to hear John tell it so slowly and so clearly. I wish the exact words he used were in my memory; in times of tragedy, the mind can't always hold the full picture.

The two of them collaborated on *The Sea of Cortez.* The original book was an expensive edition with many color pictures taken by Doc of the sea creatures they collected on the famous voyage to the Sea of Cortez. A beautiful book it was. I still have a copy of it and I look at it often. John's words are the fourth dimension.

One day I was sitting in the "21" Club with Harold Ross, editor of *The New Yorker* magazine. *The Sea of Cortez* had just come out. I talked about it with some enthusiasm to Ross. He said to me, in his shoulder-raising, head-scratching manner: "That book is nonsense. It was just an excuse for Steinbeck to get away from his wife with some jackass friends of his. You can't expect much of a book under those circumstances." This is not a precise quote, but it is the exact gist. It was not an accurate observation, since Carol, Steinbeck's wife, was the cook on that trip. I was taken aback, because I respected Ross's opinions; but recently I reread

The Sea of Cortez and to me it is one of John's most enduring works.

Steinbeck, whatever his reasons for writing the book, had enjoyed the trip. Later, he told me — and this was after Ricketts died — that Ricketts had not written any of the diary, and so John felt justified in reissuing it without Ricketts's pictures and scientific data. In the original edition, there are many technical descriptions given in the enormous index at the end of the book. Apparently that index, plus the pictures, of course, were the extent of Doc's contribution. John also told me that his publisher begged him not to use Ricketts's name as co-author, but that John had insisted that his friend be so designated. John immortalized that trip; he was the one who made it work. He did it for Ed Ricketts's sake, and all of us have benefited.

One time I was sitting up in Doc's laboratory with John and Doc. We were drinking California wine. Martin Ray, a winemaker and a colorful character, had just made some Chardonnay and we were tasting it. John was in a wistful mood and started to talk about the golden past of California. He regretted that much of the beauty had disappeared. He said that the Spaniards came here to find the fountain of youth and they found gold in the ground and they found gold in fields and golden weather as well. The California hills were gold and the earth was gold, and so California attracted adventurers from everywhere — she seduced them with golden promises.

But then, in less than a century, the scene changed. The mines were closed, the gold rush was over, and the hills and the valleys were overlaid with cement and asphalt; the golden groves of oranges were covered with housing developments and factories; the Pastures of Heaven were subdivided . . . and so California, the seductress, took away the platinum weather and bright sun and covered the gold coast with a veil of smog. The shiny beaches and the adjacent palisades looked gray and foggy . . . California wasn't the same golden gal she once had been.

I said to John maybe California was not as pristine, not as virginal as before, but didn't he think there were other seductions still around . . . like the golden movies, the golden aura of Hollywood? John said he didn't think movie studios were seductive to begin with, but whatever they were before, now they were dismal and commercial.

"But there is one bright promise," John said. "There are the vineyards . . . the gold and rose and red grapes of California. Vineyards are good." He looked at the goblet of Chardonnay he was holding in his hand and said, "I like vineyards very much . . . and they will stay here for a long, long time." He proved to be right. Vineyards are beautiful to look at and, for the moment, they are holding off the ruthless cementers.

A last thought about Steinbeck. He had been "schooled," but his was not a professionally trained, intellectual mind, like Huxley's or Anderson's or Shaw's. Sometimes John would surprise you with his knowledge about books or facts, but his talent was raw and native. He said he had not been a steady reader when he was young, but later he read everything he could.

So far in this century, Steinbeck's writings hold up with the best of American authors, which should make him happy — particularly if it includes Mark Twain, his favorite.

Weren't You Married
to Paulette Goddard Once?

WE MET during the making of a picture called *Second Chorus*, produced by a man with the unlikely name of Boris Morris. The film was independently made and in the cast were Paulette, Fred Astaire, Artie Shaw, Charles Butterworth, and myself. It was an offbeat musical with a good deal of high jinks going on backstage. The subject was "jazz," and it got good reviews — a cult picture. It still shows once in a while. But, to me, the importance of it was that I met Paulette . . . and Fred Astaire. In later years, I often saw Astaire at the racetracks and we reminisced about that picture and about Paulette. Fred was attracted to her as we all were — Artie Shaw, the entire cast. Paulette was legally separated from Charles Chaplin at the time, but not yet divorced.

I was fascinated by the impact she had on people. Her presence was strong; she was more attractive in life than on film. She sometimes became tense facing the camera — not all of the spontaneity and fire of the lady came across. But in life she was bright, funny, sensual — you felt the vibrations when she walked into a room. She had an intuitiveness, a kind of ESP, that told her where people's thoughts were. She understood the id of the male animal. She was flattering in conversation and attractive physically. I was lucky enough to get her attention and we had a quick, clandestine affair, which bowled me over.

She worked hard on the set but in the off-hours found time to play. I had a few evenings with her, which she made romantic and mysterious. There were secret telephone numbers and bursts of passion. The next day she ignored me, became unavailable . . . the kind of behavior that churns up the psyche. Then, after a spell, she would call me and we would rendezvous, sometimes at the home of Jimmy Stewart.

An amazing phenomenon happened, after we finished *Second Chorus*. Among our friends was a man by the name of Anatole Litvak, a very skillful European director. His nickname was "Tola," and he had been a pal of mine, but we parted company when I met Paulette. He had accumulated money and knew how to spend it. He had a large, attractive beach house, lived elegantly and, of course, fell in love with Paulette. He had the resources and the common sense to ply her with presents — jewelry, oil paintings, and so forth — and she was happy to accept them.

Overnight a blazing scandal arose about Litvak and Goddard. Early bulletins claimed that one night the two of them had made love, in public, at Ciro's, an expensive nightclub on the Sunset Strip.

I remember I learned of the "shocking revelry," as they then called it, when I walked into the studio commissary. Ralph Morgan, a very antic fellow, called me aside and said, "Did you hear what happened at Ciro's?" I didn't know what he was talking about. He went to a pay phone, put in a coin, dialed a certain number, and put the receiver to my ear. The phone emitted a weird mechanical tone that sounded like a moan of passionate ecstasy. Ralph began to chuckle and choke in that famous way of his. I asked him what he was talking about and he told what had allegedly happened between Paulette and Anatole.

It was whispered that Anatole went down on his knees and made love to Paulette in the French fashion, in full view of the world. The horoscope must have been right for a scandal of this sort because it certainly caught on. Like prairie fire the scuttlebutt spread from one end of the country to the other — details and embellishments were added every day.

The story became so famous that the School of Journalism at Columbia University investigated this phenomenon and learned that nobody was ever found who had actually witnessed the event! For legal reasons the newspapers did not detail the story or publish names. What it finally came down to was that it was a momentous event which no one witnessed! Or so the Columbia survey concluded.

Of course eventually I talked with both parties about it. Litvak laughed and denied it. Paulette said it was "a fable" — and she laughed, too. I never pursued it beyond that. I felt if they wanted to tell me, they would. If nothing happened — what was there to tell? Today, after all these years, I still find people who heard of the event and swore that it happened — but were not present. Nobody was ever found to verify the story of that exotic display. References were made to it in vaudeville and television. Whatever it was, it certainly split Anatole and Paulette. They didn't dare, or didn't care, to be seen together again.

Paulette moved in a kind of roulette d'amour during that period. She flew from man to man. She was beautiful and flirtatious. I was surprised and hurt when she suddenly left me and moved on to other conquests.

In quick cycles, she would avoid me for a while, and then hug me like a long-lost lover. I took the next step and gave her a good-sized diamond. I remember she looked at it, surprised, and said, "Well, this starts a new set of rules, doesn't it?"

In the middle of my early dates with Paulette, the war started, the draft came, and I joined the army. Paulette sent me off to camp with her black lace nightgown as a souvenir.

Paulette collected jewels the way ordinary folks collect matchboxes. She was careless and had no insurance — she said it was difficult to get a policy. Actors and actresses had trouble that way and still do. Paulette stored some of her precious jewels in a small black leather case, the size you carry on an airplane. More about that jewel case in a moment.

Early in World War II, I was stationed in Texas with the USAAF Training Command and was assigned by my commanding officer to go to Hollywood to persuade one of the famous songwriters to compose an anthem, not for the army air force — "The Wild Blue Yonder" was theirs — but for the "Glider Command."

The gliders were a new branch of the army air force, a subsidiary development. The concept was that these gliders were to be filled with troops and pulled behind a big plane and then released to swoop into enemy territory. It was a dangerous assignment. Somebody found out that I had connections in Hollywood and I was sent to persuade "somebody like Cole Porter" to write the words and music for this emergent command. I was delighted to get out of Fort Worth to make the trip.

Of course, when I got to Los Angeles the first thing I did was contact Paulette. She suggested we drive out to the beach, where she had a house. It was a pleasure I looked forward to beyond any desire I knew in those days. I was an excited soldier when I met her in the late afternoon. We had a lot to talk about and she said it was time she "got into my psyche" — a new phrase in Hollywood in those days.

The drive to the beach was blissful and carefree . . . except for her jewels — they worried me. She carried them in her black leather bag and it was my assignment to guard this bag — a precarious job. There must have been $300,000 worth of precious stones in that bag — and those were just her carrying-around jewels, her working jewels, so to speak. The great ones were stashed in safe vaults around town.

In a quiet, expectant mood we drove down Sunset Boulevard until we got to Pacific Coast Highway, turned north with the sea to our left, and stopped at a small bistro secretly owned by the mysterious and powerful Joe Schenk and his brother Nick, both top studio executives. We went in for a final drink before arriving at Paulette's house.

I remember this much: I took the jewel case inside and placed it beside us at the bar. We were happy; we had a whispered conversation, love-talk, and a bottle of Dom Perignon.

The next thing I knew we had left the restaurant and were settling down in her house farther up the beach. I got out of my uniform. Paulette kissed me, took off her earrings, and asked casually where I had put her bag of jewels. I stopped breathing . . . I couldn't remember bringing the case from the restaurant! In a dead panic, I pulled on my clothes and drove back to the Schenk bar at eighty miles an hour. The restaurant was closed — black and silent.

I pounded on the door, shouted, and tried to climb the stone fence. Finally the door was opened by the bartender, who was packing to leave. I told him I had left a large handbag at the bar. He said, "No, no, no, there's no bag here, there's no bag here! As a matter of fact we noticed you took that bag with you when you left. You went out with it, I remember." Then he added mysteriously: "The one with the purple on it." He said, "You'll find it, you'll find it when you get home, the purple one."

Though I didn't realize it immediately, this was a fatal slip of the tongue; because the outside of the bag was black — only the inside lining was purple. But, as I say, it didn't strike me that he had made that mistake. I felt that the bag must be somewhere at the beach house. "Maybe in the driveway when we got out — that's where I left it!" I said to myself.

I roared back to Paulette and told her what had happened. We looked — but the bag was nowhere around. I told her exactly what the barman had said, and Paulette pointed out that he could only have known it was purple if he had opened it. I was frightened by my stupidity — I was losing my brains, no question about it.

The two of us got into the car and went back to the restaurant. This time there was no answer to my knocking. I tried to climb the outside of the building. I often pass this building now and I don't know how I crawled up that sheer stone wall on the side facing the ocean. I climbed because I saw a light in the upper story. I reached it by some superhuman effort, while Paulette waited below. I looked in the lighted window and saw a man in bed, a very old man, with a nurse beside him. I yelled, the nurse shrieked and pulled the window shade down in my face, and I climbed down the wall again — falling the last ten feet. That's all I ever knew about that old man in bed with a nurse. To this day I couldn't tell you what that scene was all about.

Next we found a phone booth and called the police. The police said that if there was nobody in the restaurant section, there was nothing they could do; they told us we could file a claim that night or wait for morning. We decided on the morning. I was a wreck when I fell into bed that night. All the glamour, all the anticipation of love was gone. I was demoralized and apprehensive. What would tomorrow do to us? Dark omens were gathering.

The next morning we made our report to the police and they contacted the people in the bar and the restaurant; but there was complete denial. No one knew anything about anything. They said I was mistaken: there was no bag — black or purple.

I was a depressed soldier. There seemed no way to recover Paulette's cache of jewels, which I had single-handedly lost. It was painful to acknowledge my ineptitude, my stupidity. Here was the woman I loved, and the first thing I do is lose a quarter of a million dollars' worth of her jewelry.

In order to justify my staying in Los Angeles to look for the diamonds, I called Cole Porter about the "song for the gliders." I had known Cole and he invited me to his home. I described to him what I needed for the air force. He wrote down the pertinent information and said he would give it a whirl. He said he was eager to do something for his country and he promised to call me in a day or two. I wanted to tell Cole about the jewels — but I didn't. Life was complicated enough.

The following day Paulette decided to see Joseph Schenk, and said I should go with her. The two of us went to his office, and were admitted to his inner sanctum. Joe Schenk looked very much like a stone Buddha. He asked us to sit down and politely listened to our story. Then, without a word, he picked up the phone and told someone that two friends of his had been in his little restaurant and he would appreciate it if their jewels could be returned. He said one of his friends was a soldier who had no money and the girl was a close friend of his. He hung up, turned to us, and said, "That's all I can do; but anything might happen," then bade us farewell.

Later in the afternoon we got a call from the police who told us that two of the diamonds, a white and a gray one, had turned up in a pawnshop! The person who had pawned them had disappeared. Paulette repurchased the two diamonds, but the rest of the jewels were still missing.

In the meantime I was busy telephoning my headquarters trying to buy a little more time and getting more and more warnings. The general was losing patience. "What the hell are you doing? There's a war going on, soldier!"

Paulette was filming at Paramount Pictures and she phoned me a few hours before I had to leave town. She said she had received a telephone call from somebody out in Tarzana, who claimed they had found her jewel case, and would I go and get it. She told me if they had really found it I should give them a thousand-dollar reward. I didn't have a thousand dollars, so she said, "I'll give it to you." I went to the studio, got a thousand dollars in cash from her, and then drove to Tarzana. There I came to a little old broken-down house where a woman and two children were waiting for me. They had learned it was Paulette's jewel case because among the jewels there was a medicine bottle with Paulette's name on it and the telephone number of the studio.

This good woman had called the studio and got through to Paulette. She said her children had discovered the bag under amazing circumstances. Her two boys, nine and eleven, had chased a rabbit over the fields and into a culvert and in the culvert they had found this bag. The children forgot the rabbit-chase and took the bag to their mother, who opened it and found it was loaded with precious jewels! Fortunately, the woman was honest and contacted Paulette. I thanked everybody, including the two boys, and left them the thousand-dollar reward.

Incidentally, I had taken the police with me so the whole transaction could be witnessed. Thus, all the jewels were returned to Paulette, but it was anybody's guess as to what had happened. My theory is that the culprits who stole the jewel case in the restaurant got frightened when Schenk put pressure on them and decided to hide the bag temporarily . . . but they chose the wrong place to hide it.

By then it was past time for me to leave; but I got a phone call from Cole Porter, and I made a hurried trip to the great man's home. He said, "Burgess, I've got something and I don't know if it's right or not, but here's the way it goes." He sat down at the piano and sang me the song, the tune of which I forget; but I recall the first words were, "Glide, glider, glide, through the soaring air," or something close to that. I had a hunch it wasn't the composer's greatest composition — but I was grateful for his efforts, more than he would ever know. Cole Porter was an elegant man, talented and impeccable. Above all, he had provided me the excuse to finish "The Case of the Missing Jewels." If the jewels had not been found, what would I have done?

(That same bag of jewels was to trip me up again, in Switzerland, two years later. Paulette and I were checking out of a hotel. I reached down to pick up the famous black bag, and as I reached for it the memories were so painful that I fell in a faint on top of the bag and was taken to a hospital.)

When I brought the song back to the Training Command and to the Glider Division, the major, my superior, said, "You can't seriously tell me you've been out there all this time to collect a crock of shit like this! Don't try to kid me that Cole Porter wrote this blobber — he couldn't have. 'Glide, glider, glide,' for Christ's sake! You don't want me to take that to the guys, do you? They'd eat me alive!"

The following winter Paulette came to New York, where I was a soldier on leave from the army, playing Marchbanks in *Candida* opposite Katharine Cornell. Paulette liked my performance as the young poet. She also liked the attractive farmhouse I owned in Rockland County, just outside New York City. The house, which Maxwell Anderson had found for me, was an eighteenth-century colonial dwelling listed as the "original residence of Mad Anthony

Wayne during the Revolution." It was surrounded by sixty acres of woods and I had spent all my money restoring it.

Paulette and her companion and coach, Constance Collier, moved in. They said they "never wanted to leave." They almost never did.

After New York, *Candida* played a limited run in Washington, D.C., and Paulette came to Washington for the opening night. Harry Hopkins was in hot pursuit of Paulette at the time, and he and Paulette sat together in the audience.

Following the performance, Harry invited Paulette and me to come back with him to the White House. During the Roosevelt years he lived in the White House, in the "Lincoln Room." We very eagerly accepted. Paulette had visited the mansion before with Harry, who told me she had flirted "outrageously" with the president, who in turn enjoyed the whole procedure. FDR needed a little divertissement now and then.

So Harry, Paulette, and I went to the White House and talked and sipped wine until the morning hours. I remember that the evening became a subtle, good-natured triangle. I knew that I had the "inside track" with Paulette for the moment. She was interested in my "ambience," as she called it, but she felt free to flirt with anyone she chose and Harry Hopkins was no exception. Paulette had an uncanny ability to engage people emotionally. This was a dynamic and attractive period in her life. She was beautiful, famous, and witty. I was fascinated by her — and on that night, so was Harry Hopkins.

However, as much as I'd like to report otherwise, nothing outrageous happened. We were a little too boisterous, perhaps, a bit hilarious for the White House in time of war — too talky maybe . . . but about 2 A.M. Harry properly saw us out the famous front doors.

A few guards were in the shadows, deliberately paying us no attention. I will always remember the sensation of being there in the moonlight, staring out over the White House lawn . . . in the center of the world . . . the three of us — a private in the U.S. Army, a famous, flirtatious movie star, and the righthand man of the president of the United States . . . a fond memory.

When the limousine came, Hopkins excused Paulette and himself and the two of them stepped for a moment or two into the shadows, while I climbed, happily enough, into the car to wait out their farewell whispers.

God knows, more interesting events than this one have happened in the White House, but to me the evening was splendid . . . Marchbanks, the army, the war, Paulette, Harry Hopkins, and a late, late night ending on the moon-drenched White House lawn, in November of the year 1942.

Within a few months I would be sent to England, a captain in the U.S. Army Air Force. Within a year after that, I would be back in the States, getting married to Paulette.

And three frenetic years later we would be divorced.

As far as Harry Hopkins is concerned, I don't believe Paulette heard from him for a while. One day I told the story to Garson Kanin, who guessed that somebody in the White House had a little talk with Harry. After all, the world was in flames and Hopkins held a delicate position, second only to the president. Possibly Mrs. Roosevelt or even the old man himself pulled Hopkins aside and said, "Look, Harry, a war is going on. We'd better stop this movie-star business, drinking in the Lincoln Room, and midnight meetings on these sacrosanct premises in the center of the Universe!"

I look back in wonder at the wild attractiveness of that girl. She had an extrasensory perception of what people were thinking and what they wanted — how to engage them. When she walked into a room you could feel a sinuousness, a danger. On top of this she produced a nonstop flow of speech, witty, cutting, touching. She attracted Chaplin, H. G. Wells, Anthony Eden, the Duke of Marlborough. Alexander Calder was fascinated by her. All diversities of men and many varieties of women were drawn to her. For a period, she was the top sex symbol in Hollywood, not as an actress, but as a girl around town. Something was filtered out on the screen, but as an individual she was incomparable.

I remember one time John McClain and Jock Whitney were talking about "P.G.," as they called her. Jock said, "Who's eventually going to get that woman?" McClain said, "Lord Mountbatten."

He was wrong, but the two of them did "pass in the night," as they say.

The way Paulette and I came to be married was singular. Paulette had been living, from time to time, in my "Mad Anthony Wayne home" back East while I was away. She liked to go there with the aging actress Constance Collier, her old pal. When I returned from Europe, Paulette was in an altered state of mind. She hinted she was experiencing a strange desire to settle down! She found that she missed me and said she probably wouldn't say no to a proposal. It was that simple.

Many people were surprised at our marriage — they hardly realized we had been "going together." Mervyn Leroy said it was the greatest surprise since Pearl Harbor. Louella Parsons, the columnist, called. She said, "How dare you do that without telling me?"

Paulette and I were married in a quiet, regal Hollywood way, at the home of David Selznick. Irene Selznick was matron of honor, and Lewis Milestone the best man.

We saw Harry Hopkins one last time after the war and after Paulette and I were married. Harry, Robert Sherwood — who wrote the majority of Roosevelt's speeches — Paulette, and I had dinner in New York City at a Chinese restaurant Harry liked. I remember the dinner was given for him by the owner of this small place serving exotic food, somewhere on the East Side. The main thrust of the evening was to urge Harry to write a book about his personal life, the Roosevelt regime, and his political career. We all felt it was essential to get Hopkins started on the intimate history of those fevered years — but he never did.

When I was making *The Story of G.I. Joe* (1944), Paulette became pregnant. She said it was important for her to have a child and I felt as she did. But she developed severe pains, which worried the doctor but which she tolerated. She whispered to me she would see it through. I was called on the set the next day and told that Paulette had been taken to surgery. When I got to the hospital, they said the fetus was not in the normal womb area.

It was a torturous condition and necessitated an immediate abortion to save her life.

Both of us were in despair, which I suppose brought us closer than we had ever been before. Our child would have been a boy. For a long period the doctors were worried — Paulette's depression became constant and deep. It was weeks before the pall finally lifted.

I wonder what sort of man he would have become, the offspring of Paulette and myself; what change would our child have brought into our lives? It is a wondering that bears no fruit, of course. It is food for a daydream, nothing more.

Our divorce had no drama, no quarrels. Our separations just became sadder and longer, until one day our lawyer, Bill Fitelson, informed me that she was seeking a divorce in Mexico. He said she had to find a "new life." Ten years later she married Erich Maria Remarque, the author, in Switzerland; and went there to live, apparently in peace and luxury until he died in 1970.

Ernie Pyle

IN WORLD WAR II Ernie Pyle was a man of immense influence in the United States — he was the most respected and widely read correspondent of the common soldier. It's hard to think of Ernie Pyle as being such a hero; he is almost forgotten these days. The war he covered is over and past, but he was a mighty figure who wrote, as John Steinbeck said, a "worm's eye view" of the war and that was the view most people responded to, in those exploding years.

There was an effort afoot to make a film of his life, and William Wellman was chosen to be the director. The producer was Lester Cowan. They asked Pyle who he wanted to play his part . . . and Ernie thought he would like to have me do it, if I wanted to. The producer knew I was in the army, but because it was Ernie Pyle there would be no trouble about getting me extricated — what Ernie wanted, Ernie got.

I was in the United States, about to return to the European Theater of Operations, when I got a call from the White House.

It was my friend Harry Hopkins, who told me that Pyle had requested me for the part and that General Marshall was anxious to do anything Ernie Pyle wanted — so if I cared to play the role they would give me an honorable discharge.

Hopkins was very blunt and said, "Do you want to, or don't you want to?" I said if I had to answer right away, I certainly did. He said, "Very well, you stand by, and the orders will come through . . . good luck, nice to talk to you again." And, while Hopkins and I were speaking I presume our minds went back to the last time we'd seen each other, with Paulette at the White House in the Lincoln Room, two years before.

My discharge came through within a few hours, so I "reported to duty" and was sent to meet Ernie Pyle at his home in Phoenix, Arizona.

In Phoenix, Ernie and I spent a week or so talking things over and assuring each other we would do the best we could. He said, "You act me and I'll try to keep my reputation clean." He was a very spicy-tongued fellow and was always threatening to break his Christ image, which he felt was undeserved. I remember once he said, "If I hear another fucking G.I. say 'fucking' once more, I'll cut my fucking throat."

We talked a lot and drank a bit — Pyle was good at both. I was surprised to learn how antiwar he was — the great chronicler of the G.I. was a pacifist.

Ernie came to see me again just before leaving for the Pacific and we reminisced for hours. Then he wished me luck with the movie and took off. It was the last time I saw him.

He was killed a few months later on Okinawa . . . and he never saw a foot of the picture. I was half listening to my car radio on the way to look at the final cut at Goldwyn Studios, and when I pulled into the gate, I heard the radio announcer say: ". . . this most beloved friend of the foot-soldier and the most famous war correspondent this country has ever —" Before he said the name, I turned off the radio. I knew it was Ernie. I couldn't look at the film that day. I didn't look at it for months, his death so affected me. He was gone for good . . . and I became his shadow.

The Story of G.I. Joe gave Robert Mitchum his first good part and made him a towering star overnight. I got good notices — but he was the new find, the discovery of the year. He was personable and helpful to me in the crisis I had during that picture when Paulette and I lost the baby we wanted so very much. Mitchum talked to me and tried to help as best he could and I appreciated his kindness.

Over my desk even now is a picture of Ernie and myself wishing ourselves luck back in 1944. I wondered and worried then if he would have liked the way I played him and, from time to time, I still do.

Renoir, Huxley, Paulette, and Me

I N HOLLYWOOD years ago I had the privilege of writing a film script with Jean Renoir, for *The Diary of a Chambermaid*, which he directed. I coproduced and acted in it and my wife, Paulette Goddard, played the lead. The idea for the film was taken from a series of short stories by a French playwright, Mirabeau.

Many wise people think that Jean Renoir was the greatest film director of all time. I agree with them. And aside from his genius he was a witty, compassionate friend. There are few moments of my life I enjoyed as much as I did when I worked with him.

The films of Renoir do not lose importance as the decades roll by — they remain vivid and moving, close to perfection.

The Diary of a Chambermaid does not rank with his great ones, but it is quite wonderful; a very special work of art.

The memory of working with Jean Renoir stays with pleasure in my mind. When we wrote the script he would fill me in, partly in French, and I would try to equate his ideas into English — find the equivalent phrase. For example, the French phrase *"J'en ai suppé!"* I translated as, "I've had it!". . . that was one of my less-inspired contributions.

In his films, Jean never wrote the actual dialogue. We sat at his feet and heard what he had to say, and put that into screenplay form. I succeeded pretty well, but I was always constricted by budget problems. In America the "backers" said, "It's all right for French films, but in America you've got to say it different!" It was a tricky task, but time has treated our picture well.

Renoir improvised on the set. Suddenly he would be off shooting a new scene he felt was needed. I had the job of saying, "We have to get back on schedule, Jean!"

"No," said Renoir, "what we have to do is to make a fine picture!"

It was at a screening of *The Diary of a Chambermaid* that I first met Aldous Huxley, who liked the film very much. We discovered we had a close mutual friend, Christopher Isherwood. So when Huxley moved to Los Angeles, we saw each other for a couple of years.

I was in awe of Huxley and I told Paulette he seemed to be wiser than any person I ever met — and very amusing.

During that period Aldous was in an experimental frame of mind and his comments and his analytical conclusions were amazing.

I told him I wanted to make a film of *Brave New World,* but Aldous said at the moment he was interested in hypnosis and was writing a thesis on the subject.

"Wouldn't it be more interesting to do a film on hypnosis?" he asked. "I wonder how it would affect the audience?"

I thought it was an intriguing idea and I set to work trying to find an angle for *Brave New World* that would work as a film, and at the same time learn something about hypnosis!

We got hold of a specialist, Dr. Leslie Le Cron, who brought "subjects" to our apartment. Neither Huxley nor I had ever witnessed the phenomenon of hypnosis and we were fascinated. We watched those subjects regress into their childhood, suffer attacks of asthma, bouts of fear, frenzy, joy, and pain — reliving the past.

I've never forgotten nor ever witnessed again that unsettling experience.

Incidentally, I tried once or twice to be hypnotized, but for some reason I could never "go under." Stubborn, I guess.

One demonstration Huxley suggested was especially bizarre. Paulette came to that session, but never came to another. The doctor had brought along a patient, a businessman who the doctor explained was a "good subject." Huxley suggested that if the subject was that good, the hypnotist should thrust the man, not *backward* in time, but *forward* into the future!

The hypnotist said the notion was new to him, but he would give it a try. He said to the subject, "You are not going into the past. . . . You are going down the river of time. . . . You will float into the future. . . . You will travel forward. . . . Yes, you are sailing slowly, slowly, beyond today, beyond tomorrow. . . . You will arrive at a day five years from now. . . . You understand absolutely that my suggestions will let you fly ahead on the winds of time . . . forward, onward."

I don't pretend to remember the exact words he spoke, but the session stays vivid in my mind, because it was an unsettling experience — subjects under hypnosis seem peaceful, unworldly, disassociated. Then, after ten minutes of silence, he said he had made the voyage!

Le Cron asked him where he was. The subject told us he was in a certain house, giving the number and address. He also told us the day and date, which *was* five years into the future! The hypnotist said, "What's happening in the papers? Anything special? What's the political situation?" When the subject began to answer, I had the sensation that we were witnessing a miracle.

The subject described the news of the day very concisely. He said that Congress was in a turmoil, and the public was angry at such-and-such a senator for a tax law that had been passed. I don't recall the details, but it was a natural, realistic discussion such as a person sitting at breakfast with his newspaper might have with the family.

The hypnotist asked: "Is there anything you would like to read to us?" and the subject said, "Yes, I would like to read you my favorite cartoon, my favorite funny paper." He assumed the position of reading a newspaper and described a funny cartoon, something like a Little Orphan Annie strip. It was a casual reading, very relaxed, as though he were seeing the words and looking at the pictures for the first time. He had the attitude of a man who enjoyed comic strips. So far, so good.

The hypnotist was at a loss for a moment — the success of the experiment seemed to surprise him. He asked the subject: "What else is happening in the world?"

The subject shrugged and said, "Well, of course nobody is talking about much else except the assassination of Vice-President Wallace."

For years afterwards I read the headlines, wondering and worrying if our probe into the future would turn out to be true.

Huxley wondered if the man's statement came from a subconscious desire to get rid of the vice-president. Wallace was a controversial figure at that time. So our subject could have been politically motivated — disliking the vice-president. Or maybe he was trying to astonish us. Probably the latter.

We did not know where we were heading, but while it lasted it was a little fearsome and a lot of fun. I also began to think about regression in relation to acting. It is distantly related to what actors and actresses are asked to do when they play a role. It is a question of text. One has to be written and the other lived. On a stage, the actor's words are not his or her own, but a playwright's. In hypnotic regression, the patient writes his own text, or more specifically, lives it. It is his own show.

Huxley asked Le Cron how many times a patient could "relive" old terrors and still continue to be terrified. And I asked him, in fun, how many times an actor could play Romeo and still shed tears. Clinically, the theory is that a patient can be "cured" or relieved by a good therapist after regression.

Romeo, on the other hand, doesn't want to be cured! His job is to find a way to keep weeping, suffering or laughing, night after night. On cue!

I suppose there is an answer out there somewhere, but I don't know it. Unless — no, no, I am not serious — either regressive patients join the Actors Guild, or actors learn hypnosis. It might be interesting.

One evening Huxley brought along an old friend, Edwin Hubbell, one of science's great theoreticians, the man who proposed the "exploding universe" concept. Hubbell seemed less fascinated than Huxley and I by hypnotism. He politely pretended to be mildly interested, but I got the impression that, compared to the origin and nature of the universe, hypnotism was not so important. A question of priority.

Huxley and I worked for a time on a dramatization of *Brave New World* but, unfortunately, one day we discovered that his publisher had sold away the rights in some forgotten deal and they couldn't be reclaimed. "I am not a good businessman," said Huxley, "and this annoys me very much."

However, something enduring did result from our *Brave New World* episode. I had earlier remarked to Huxley that *Brave New World* was pessimistic about the way the human race was headed; and I wondered if he had a different concept of how things should go in this day and age.

This was a casual question, but it intrigued him.

Yes, he answered, he had theories of how things should go — otherwise, he had no right to criticize!

The next week he wrote an essay on the ideal way to live today and the ideal way to wield power; and this essay was used as an introduction to special editions of *Brave New World*.

There arose a faint rumor that possibly Aldous Huxley was attracted to Paulette. If so, it had a quirky logic to it — Paulette was a universal flirt, and if the great man was interested in such divertissements, his regard for my wife was natural, perhaps even to be expected!

So possibly, after Paulette and I separated, there could have been a "rapprochement." After all, as I say, she was a flirtatious lady.

I don't seriously believe that it went that far, and I mention it only because a couple of reporters asked me about it in a manner that insinuated I might have inside information on the subject. I told them that I didn't know, but if it were true, I hope all went well!

I observed that Paulette was never as interested in hypnosis as we were; in fact, she told me she was a little apprehensive about this "regression business." She said she had more secrets in her head than all of us put together and she didn't want them made public!

I suppose she believed her past flirtations were private matters. She knew the way to handle famous men — and if you wanted her love, you had to forget her past and all that went with it — from Charles Chaplin to, finally, Erich Maria Remarque.

Erich was her "last love," and between the two of them they accumulated a large fortune. After he died, she continued to live in their home in Switzerland. She had other homes too — in Paris and London, and she always kept a suite at the Ritz Towers in New York.

One time, long after we separated, she telephoned me to say that once again someone had offered her a large sum of money for her life story, but she didn't want to waste time giving anyone that kind of help. "Don't you agree?" she asked. She said she didn't want to spend the rest of her life helping strangers write her biography. "If anyone writes anything bad about me, I'll do it myself! If they write good things, it's not interesting."

But years later, when I last saw Paulette, in Switzerland, she was carrying a tape recorder and recording my conversation, explaining it was for an autobiography — only this time she said she was writing it in collaboration with Andy Warhol!

There was publicity about the book, and Warhol told me later he was "enraptured" by her. He said that the two of them were indeed going to write a book about her adventures, marriages, loves, distresses, and so forth; I suppose with illustrations by him! But nothing came of it — and they are both gone now.

Most of the tales about Paulette have dramatic content — her life was livelier than the film scripts she acted. I wondered if she was going to beat us all to the punch. It wouldn't be the first time.

In 1991, I was approached by a woman who was doing a biography of Goddard and Erich Remarque. I lied and said that I remembered absolutely nothing about the lady . . . hadn't thought of her in decades. "Goddard who?" I asked.

When Paulette died, the *New York Times* and other newspapers called me asking for reminiscences. I said I had none that came to mind.

But I thought to myself . . . if I were a reporter I would have gone to the famous sale of her jewelry at Sotheby's in 1991. Every one of those diamonds and pearls and precious metals would have legends to tell — those jewels were gifts to her, every one of them . . . from men who loved her. She told me she refused to buy gems or flowers for herself. It was a matter of principle — a principle she observed to the end.

If there is doubt about the impressiveness of Paulette's jewel collection, Sotheby's auction catalogue is stunning proof positive — not to mention her twenty-million-dollar bequest to New York University.

God bless her.

Charles Laughton

M Y ASSOCIATION with Charles Laughton lasted over twenty
years, until his death in 1962. His fatal cancer was first
diagnosed by a doctor in my house in Mount Ivy, New
York, a place he often visited and was always welcome.

I first met Charles when I was master of ceremonies for *The
Pursuit of Happiness,* a CBS radio series in which Laughton read
passages from great works of literature. The first writings he chose
were from *Look Homeward, Angel* by Thomas Wolfe and passages
from the King James version of the Bible — it seemed heavy going
for radio, but it worked.

Charles Laughton was a meticulous performer and in the early
rehearsals he was dissatisfied with his Bible reading and said he
needed to sit down — he felt stiff and formal standing there like
a preacher.

So the director, Norman Corwin, got him a great overstuffed
chair and lowered the microphone close to him and that was how
Charles achieved the "intimate feeling" he wanted. I remember
at dress rehearsal the network president, Bill Paley, came in and

laughed — "Is everybody going to want leather chairs?" he asked.

To everyone's surprise, the Bible was the biggest hit — more than Wolfe, more than Dickens. The studio phones rang and the mail was record-breaking. Later Charles toured the country with an armload of books — including the Bible — and made a fortune. He started a new trend in one-man readings — but no one did it as well as he.

After that our paths crossed often — he enjoyed hiding away in my country house and we worked together in films and theater.

Laughton fell in love with a series of young boys but he was constantly afraid of being "found out." He felt he couldn't stand the exposure — it would ruin his life and his career. His most constant fear was that his wife, Elsa, would expose him — he could not be dissuaded from this dark terror. We assured him she would never do that, but he was filled with guilt and fear.

In 1946 I directed Laughton in a short film, *A Miracle Can Happen*. It could have been very good. I had this idea about stories tied together — about how a child affected your life.

We finished a magnificent sequence — which was the main reason I did the whole thing — with Laughton. Charles played a minister whose life is changed by a little child coming to his house and saying, "You've got to come see my father — he is very sick." So the minister followed him and they came to the house. Then, suddenly, the child disappeared.

The bedridden father said, "I didn't ask for anyone, but I'm glad you're here." And Charles read the Bible to him and the man felt better. And as the minister was leaving he saw a picture of the boy who had brought him to the house. "Oh, that's your son. . . . Where is he?" the minister asked. The father answered, "Was, *was* — he died many years ago." It was a magical moment.

But Ben Bogeaus said "the backers" wanted more comedy in the film. They wanted that section thrown out — and out it went. I showed the film to David O. Selznick and he offered a half-million dollars for that section — he wanted to throw everything *else* out and start all over with that one scene. But Bogeaus refused the offer and the film was destroyed.

This siege of bad luck bound Charles and me together and led to our doing *The Man on the Eiffel Tower*. The picture was shot in Paris in 1947, a period when I was breaking up with Paulette. Our mutual friend, Franchot Tone, had purchased the rights to a Georges Simenon book, *The Man Who Watched the Trains Go By*, and he persuaded Laughton and me to be in the picture, which he retitled *The Man on the Eiffel Tower*. I directed the film and played the role of a knife grinder. Franchot played a rabid murderer, and Charles played the leading role, Maigret the detective.

It was one of the most colorful experiences of my life, and although we were always short of money — the film was financed by Franchot's personal fortune — we came out with a good picture. It was filmed on a newly invented color negative and there was always a two-week delay on the rushes, but Laughton and I pre-planned every scene of the story. I would spend half the night drawing pictures of the shots we needed the next day. Most of it was filmed on various levels of the Eiffel Tower, and vertigo became a serious problem. Laughton couldn't go near the outside rails — it made him dizzy — and after a few days, all of us felt the same. Only Franchot was immune — he could walk along the outside handrail with no fear at all. I couldn't watch him, let alone direct him. Down below, the automobiles looked smaller than beetles.

Although Franchot was not afraid of heights, he was a bad businessman. He signed a contract that allowed Simenon to destroy the film any time he felt like it — it was the most incredible agreement ever conceived. Tone's rationale was that if the picture was bad it didn't matter — and if it was good the author would cherish it. What Franchot did not anticipate was that Simenon was an antic fellow, famous for his unpredictability, and later he ordered every copy of our film seized and destroyed. There are a few pirated 16mm prints around, and occasionally it is seen on public television. It was one of the best roles Laughton ever played — and I was proud of my direction. But it seemed that an unfriendly spirit was pursuing us, a ghost that didn't want us to collaborate.

Years later I showed an old, worn 16mm print that Franchot's son had to Jean Renoir, who said, "These are pictures of Paris you can never photograph again." It was made right after the war and it was the first single color process — Ansco — and quite beautiful. But then we couldn't get it printed by a single process and the prints were made by Technicolor.

The end of filming *Man on the Eiffel Tower* found me in a ragged state. Between the personal unhappiness of my marriage, the inadequate film budget, Simenon's strange business practices, and the constant problems of danger and vertigo we were experiencing, the job had been heavy going, and Laughton said later there were times when he wondered how I kept my sanity; but we got it done, in spite of the slings and arrows.

In 1956 Charles directed a production of George Bernard Shaw's *Major Barbara* in New York. The cast included Cornelia Otis Skinner, Eli Wallach, Glynis Johns — and Charles and myself. I am happy to report it was a sellout. The tides had turned.

Our friendship deepened and Charles spent a good deal of time with me and my family — and we learned about his mind, which was creative, and his sorrows, which were profound.

During this same period Laughton codirected me, with Paul Baker, in an unusual version of *Hamlet*, at Baker's theater in Dallas. It was an avant-garde concept, in which Hamlet was surrounded by three other Hamlets, playing different aspects of the melancholy Dane! The production caused a national debate among the critics — *Life* magazine gave it three pages. After a few months I felt the experiment was over and called a halt.

Following *Hamlet*, Laughton and I made preparations for a two-man tour in which we would perform classic scenes written for two people, such as Lear and the Fool and Plato and Socrates and so forth. That came to a halt because Charles was taken ill — he had cancer of the bone.

That was the beginning of the end of the life of Charles Laughton — he never recovered and his pain never ceased.

I was with him much of the time, whenever Elsa needed me. At first he stayed at the St. Moritz Hotel in New York and then, finally, he was brought back to California. This decision was made by a triumvirate of Otto Preminger, Taft Schreiber of MCA, and myself. I had the job of telling Charles he had cancer. I didn't say it was lethal — I could not do that. I told him the doctors wanted to try an operation even though the chances of success were small — but Charles refused. He only wanted to get out of New York and fly home to California where he belonged.

It was a dark experience to watch that great man waste away. Toward the end he wore a mustache, which he had grown for his part in *Advise and Consent*.

My work brought me to California and I visited him almost daily in his old surroundings. He wanted to see a young lad he liked, and I brought the boy around. As a curious postscript, this same lad married Charles's nurse after Charles's death, and years later I received a book of poetry from the girl. It seems she and the boy had broken up and she was writing poetry and having it published! The intricacies of the world are astounding.

Finally Charles was moved to Cedars Sinai Hospital and there he stayed until the end. Because of the painkillers they were giving him, Laughton could not recognize anybody. He was under sedation constantly, but I visited him because I felt it was a ritual I wanted to continue — attending, standing guard, for a close friend and a surpassing artist.

Elsa stood on guard too. I have to admit I was never close to Elsa — she was a bit sharp-tongued for me — but I grew to admire her tiger instincts and her courage.

I knew that Laughton had left the Catholic Church many years before — the two of them were agnostic and through the years Charles told stories of how he was able to give up Catholicism in World War I — he was proud of it. But, as he got weaker, his long-lost brother appeared from England and wanted Charles to see a priest. In a moment of anxiety, Laughton asked me, "What should I do?" I said, "Well, if you feel like seeing a priest, for God's sake see one! It won't hurt you," and Charles said, "Oh, I don't think I would know how to pray anymore."

At any rate the decision was made for him, because one day Elsa told me she "caught a priest" entering Charles's room and she told him, "No! Get out! Get out! Don't try to sneak in here by the back door." The priest left, but as he was going she added a parting shot. I didn't think Elsa should have ousted the man, but I have forever admired her grim and humorous phrase: "That man, my husband . . . he dined out for years on how he quit the Church."

However, as things turned out, Charles saw the priest several times — Elsa let down the bars. The good man blessed Charles and talked with him . . . and we were all relieved.

Soon after that, Charles lost consciousness. I walked into his darkened room at the hospital and I reached over and touched him. His arm was no bigger than a baby's; it had wasted away. To my astonishment, he whispered, "Is that you, Buzz? Buzz, is that you?" My hair stood up — because of his drugged state, I had not heard him speak for many days. I said, "Yes, Charles, it's me." And then he said, "Listen close." I said, "Yes, Charles — what?" He said, "Do you think this director knows what he's doing?"

I didn't know what director he was talking about, but I said, "No, I don't think he does, Charles." Then Laughton said, "We'll have to take over, won't we?" I said, "Yes, I think you will." Those were the last words we ever spoke together.

It's too bad Laughton couldn't have taken over — he would have made things right.

Ladies of Great Beauty

LADIES OF GREAT BEAUTY learn ways of starting and ending friendships gracefully . . . particularly ladies with European backgrounds. Let me reminisce a bit:

Hedy Lamarr and I met in France. Hedy was floating free at that moment in her life, and I was feeling lost and romantic. We left the friends we were with and the two of us made our way across Europe, stopping where and when we pleased.

A popular song that summer was "The River Seine," a haunting melody with smiling French words. "It rolls and rolls and it winds and winds, the River Seine," was the mundane translation.

I remember, we ended up in Vichy — not a breathtaking town, but that's where we finally stopped. We found an inn that had bright-colored wallpaper in our bedroom. The prospect was pleasant and there was a great towering elm tree outside our window. Our time together was not long, but memorable to us both.

I saw Hedy a few years ago. We met at a vineyard, in the Finger Lakes country in New York. I had not seen her since Vichy, and often wondered how she was doing. She arrived in a Rolls-Royce,

escorted by not one but two handsome men. She and I got together in a corner of the vineyard and reminisced while the winetasting ceremonies went on. We were happy to remind ourselves
of how well things went years ago in Vichy; as we sat there, she
composed a toast to our friendship: *"Vichy soit qui mal y pense,"*
a pretty good ad lib in an American vineyard.

We drank a toast and I thanked her for a gift I received from
her after we parted, years before. She had sent me a recording
of "La Seine," the song we had listened to that summer in France;
and that same package also contained a small piece of wallpaper
she had torn from our elm-shaded room in that small hotel in
Vichy.

Marlene Dietrich was magical. Aside from her beauty, she was
wise and witty, and helpful. People always expected many things
of Marlene, but never got quite what they expected. She loved
to cook for people she cherished and she was a blue ribbon chef.

Also, Marlene, in contrast to many beautiful women — and
in particular Paulette, who during moments of passion cared
mostly for her own pleasure — was extraordinarily giving. In the
act of love, Marlene was unconcerned for herself, and focused
on what she could bring her lover. Quite the opposite from her
reputation.

Anyone writing about past affairs runs the risk of crossing the
boundaries of good taste. God knows I was not a dashing swain,
but in a kind of mongrel way I chased the foxes. My intention is
to give a backward glance at girls I adored like Betty Bacall, before
she met Bogey, and also — No! Enough is never enough, but it
is all there is to say at the moment. Most of them are still alive
and well.

I sit here in my active rocking chair and smile. . . . So it goes,
so it goes. Today my dalliances are reduced to a precious few.
Time slows a fellow down, and other elements fill my mind and
heart.

It seems remarkable to me that in all the plays I was in, I don't
remember having an affair with my leading lady. I don't know

what kind of world-shaking pronouncement that is, but to me it has clinical interest. Thinking back to *She Loves Me Not*, I see the lovely, half-naked body of Polly Walters as she did a modified strip-tease before of my young eyes and I remember thinking: "She looks good, but the witch is giving me the wrong cue! Who wants to have an affair with an actress who moves her ass on my punch line!"

Then there was Margo in *Winterset*. She was exotic and desirable, and we played passionate love scenes together night after night. But when the curtain fell, the passion was over — we closed the office, so to speak. For some reason this syndrome did not apply to the movies — only to "legitimate" theater.

My next play, *High Tor*, was a case in point. Peggy Ashcroft was the leading lady in that critically acclaimed hit. She had come from England, fresh and beautiful, and saved the show, no question about it. I started to fall in love, but felt trapped by the idea, and so did Peggy. I was making the rounds with everybody I could embrace outside the show, but here was this beautiful woman, this extraordinary actress, embracing me on stage and I could not find a basis for passion. Peggy said she felt the same way. By mutual consent we kept it cool.

Next I went on to *Star Wagon* with Lillian Gish. I had a crush on Lillian, but it was an intellectual fascination — we laughed too much to get serious.

I remind myself of *Playboy* and *The Remarkable Mr. Pennypacker* and of all the countless stock plays I went through, but I had only passing fancies for the beautiful ladies who played opposite me. I wonder where they are now, my leading ladies. Maybe, at long last, we could give it a whirl!

Peggy, of course, returned to England and became Dame Peggy. If we had married and I had gone to England and worked in the classical theater, might I have become Sir Burgess? . . . And if not, I would have felt foolish being introduced, "May I present Dame Peggy Ashcroft . . . and her Yankee husband, Mr. Meredith."

P.S. I finished this chapter on June 16, 1991. When I opened the morning *Times*, I read that Peggy had died.

*   *   *

Then there was Gussie. I am speaking about Gussie Moran, the twenty-three-year-old California tennis champ who turned the English upside down when she competed at Wimbledon in her lace panties. Those panties made history in those languorous days — now they wouldn't cause a murmur.

Gussie was born and raised in Santa Monica and won the U.S. Women's Indoor Singles Championship. That was the only major title she won, but it was enough to get her to Wimbledon and set the sporting world on fire.

I had met Gussie in Hollywood. She was a friend of Sydney Chaplin and George Englund, young pals of mine, and she was a bewitching girl. She resembled Paulette, but was athletic and always happy. She had a quiet, lovely laugh that drew you to her.

Gussie and I got together in New York City. At the time she was dating Pat De Cicco, an impressive guy who knew people in high places. He was a big stud around town and the cousin of Cubby Broccoli, who later produced the James Bond pictures.

Pat was pursuing Gussie, as were many people; but I persuaded her to move to the country with me, where she could practice tennis and percolate in style. This happened just after I had directed *Season in the Sun*, when my professional life was getting better but my personal life was more complicated. As the prophets have warned us, there is a price for everything. And the price I paid for Gussie was the fury of Pat De Cicco.

People were afraid of Pat De Cicco; he was physically a very violent man who laughed a great deal — and there was an unconfirmed legend around Los Angeles that he had murdered a lady who had offended him. Pat died many years ago, or I would not have dared to write this story.

Pat heard that Gussie and I were together upstate and he told me over the phone that he was "going to get me!" He made this phone call in a loud voice at the "21" Club in New York. The owner, Mac Kriendler, overheard him and told De Cicco that kind of talk was dangerous and he would report it to the police — then Mac phoned me and warned me to lay low.

The "21" crowd was glad to see me alive a week later.

I didn't anticipate Gussie would become an international

celebrity — no one did. It was the surprise of the year. She worked hard to prepare for Wimbledon and asked me to go to London with her. She was afraid to go alone. I couldn't manage it at first, but later she cabled that she desperately needed me, so, to be with her, I arranged a quick deal to make a bad film in London, in time for Wimbledon. It was a major mistake.

I was in no shape to take the emotional beating I got when I arrived. Overnight, Gussie Moran had been transformed into a goddess of love — she became one of the most attractive women in the world — all because of her lace-trimmed panties, glimpsed beneath the short pleated skirts of her tennis whites. The paparazzi went crazy and photographers hounded her. She was followed in the London streets by mobs of people and her pictures appeared in the international press — London, New York, Paris. She became the celebrity of the year.

I flew to London to comfort a lost, timid girl; and found she had, overnight, become twice the star Paulette ever was — a transfiguration. She was surrounded by crowds — I couldn't reach her on the telephone. It was a wound on top of a wound. I had suffered rejection from Paulette, and now — as the song says — it happened all over again.

I had to fight a sudden depression . . . it was a hard job. I finished the movie as best I could and somehow made it back to New York. I had stopped analysis to go to England, but I should have stayed home and tried to solve the problems I already had. There was no need to drive myself witless.

So there I was, my career in fair shape, but my personal life turning into shambles.

And then, luckily, a miracle happened.

Family

AS FAR BACK as the end of making *The Man on the Eiffel Tower* in 1947 I was in a ragged emotional state. Directing the film in France had been heavy duty.

Problems came and went in my life, but looking back, I see that the element which shook my confidence for the longest period of time was the failure of my marriage to Paulette Goddard. I tried to beat out the answer on the anvil of my mind at the psychiatrist's office. All broken marriages bring about a sense of failure . . . and I was no exception to the rule. It took me a couple of years to realize what I had been through, to sort it all out.

So after my disastrous trip to London, as soon as I could I returned to New York — and then I met Kaja Sundsten. Almost blindly, we got together. She was eighteen years old, Swedish, and an apprentice dancer with George Balanchine's New York City Ballet.

I was almost twice her age, and very despondent. Clinically I was on the edge of a breakdown, because I couldn't find a reason to stay alive. Meeting Kaja was a roll of the dice, a lucky turn. She was beautiful and serene.

My neighbor, Kurt Weill, called her "The Quiet One." He said that if I could think of quiet words, he could write quiet tunes about her.

Silence was meaningful to me, a necessity during that period of my life. Kaja was uncomplicated and trusting. She lived in a boardinghouse in the West 70s. Her parents were musicians, and their home was in Seattle, Washington.

In a few months it turned out that Kaja was pregnant! I was delighted to hear it, and I told her that if we could have the child I would be grateful. I was leery of legal entanglements, but I knew it was absolutely essential to have this child.

Now let me go back.

A few years before, in England, when I was filming a movie called *Mine Own Executioner*, I played the part of a psychiatrist, and during the filming I had long talks with the British analyst who was our technical adviser for the picture. I told him I thought I was on the way to some sort of breakdown or collapse and I needed advice. What should I do?

In his clipped, British way, the doctor suggested, "Why don't you have children? Sometimes that helps." At first it seemed like a speculative observation that had no basis of truth. I had known too many instances when having children brought confusion and despair. But I always remembered the doctor's statement, and when Kaja said she was pregnant, a gong struck. I told her again, if she were willing, I wanted the child very much. She laughed and said she felt the same way.

Next, I told Dr. Mittleman, my own analyst, that I was concerned about our age difference. He said, "If that is the only problem, it is no problem at all. But take time — a little time is prescribed."

Mittleman let me work out my own solutions — nudging me this way and that — but he never blueprinted my behavior.

A comedy of errors took place when Kaja's mother came from Seattle to bless our marriage. It turned out that the Mexican divorce I had arranged with Paulette was not valid in New York! At that time, in 1950, Mexican divorces were suspect.

We wandered around Westchester and adjacent counties, the three of us — Kaja, her mother, and I — but we could not get a marriage license. By then Kaja was two months pregnant. She smiled constantly and she kept saying, "The ceremony doesn't make any difference to me."

Her mother wanted it legal, but Kaja wasn't worried whether it was legal or not. "Let's have it the old-fashioned way," she said.

I felt the same. I had been through three marriages with all the legal papers, all the statements of fidelity, all the documented promises — and since all three had collapsed, I saw no magic in legal rituals.

We sent Kaja's poor mother home without the knot being tied, and we moved into my house in the country. Today that is a common way of life, but in those years it was not.

So Kaja and I waited for Jonathon, our first child, to be born. He arrived in good shape and a year later we had a daughter, Tala.

Meantime, in order to ensure everyone's peace of mind, I consulted William S. Fitelson, the same lawyer who had once sued "Red Channels" for me. He said, "There's no problem here — no problem at all. I'll make up a civil marriage for you." He wrote a document, which stated that on a certain day Kaja and I had gone into the hills together and sworn to be man and wife. Fitelson said that was absolutely legal, and he would keep that document in his safe deposit vault; after a certain number of years, nobody could contest it. I put our copies in our bank files and Kaja legitimately became Mrs. Meredith. Such are the ways of law.

The document is still there and Kaja is still here and Jonathon is now forty-one years old and his sister, Tala, is forty — exactly a year apart. There never was a church ceremony, but Kaja and I are legally married. It was fine with us and the marriage holds.

The children brought me first an almost explosive happiness, and then a sudden emergence into some level of tranquility. The triple gifts of a quiet household, the birth of two children, and months of treatment with Dr. Bela Mittleman got me going again.

Bela slipped away from this planet many years ago, but by then he had done all he could for me. The old patterns are still with me, but they have become as faint as fog.

One day I was surprised and delighted to find Kaja's picture on the cover of *Life* magazine. Kaja said she had not mentioned it because — although she had posed for the picture — she did not believe it would happen.

Here is how it had come about. When Balanchine's New York City Ballet was on hiatus, the members of the company took other jobs, for income, experience, and to maintain their skills. As the related *Life* article mentions, Kaja, then only nineteen, was appearing in her third Broadway show, where the *Life* photographer spotted her. In a subsequent issue, *Life* noted there had been many inquiries about the lovely blonde on that cover. Kaja returned only briefly for her final season with Balanchine, until she discovered she was pregnant. We've kept the photo as a souvenir of her life before we met.

Later, after we married, Kaja gave up dancing, and Balanchine asked me, "Why did you take her away from us?" I told him, "I married her because she said to me, 'I will give up ballet — if you'll give up being sad.'"

Balanchine smiled and said, "Amazing! . . . hope it works!"

Kaja continued to ease and simplify my life. We shared an interest in flying and she became a skillful pilot, with a commercial license. When I had to commute from our home in Rockland County to the Broadway stage, or even to Los Angeles, Kaja was my pilot. She has given up flying now, and so have I. After all, what's the hurry?

Today, Jonathon, a musician, Tala, an artist, Kaja and myself have separate houses: in Nevada City, Borrego Springs, and Malibu. But we circulate to one another's homes as the spirit moves us and are in constant touch. We have diversified interests and activities, but we are united in our concern for each other. I believe that is what a family is all about.

1950, a Very Busy Year

1950 WAS a jammed-up period of my life, spiced with mixed activities. It was a delayed growing period. I now think Mittleman steered me away from a collapse — I didn't realize until later how close I was to a breakdown. When you are living through forlorn periods you often lose yourself in a whirlwind of activity, not understanding the dangers. My friends in that period did not consider me mentally ill — I was on the up-and-up externally and only in the psychoanalytic sessions did I probe my discontent.

About the same time I met Kaja, I made a documentary film about Alexander Calder, the sculptor — and it turned out to be one of the most successful short art films ever made in the States. It is distributed by the Museum of Modern Art, which bemoans the fact that somewhere along the line the original negative was lost so the colors are getting dimmer, but even today they sell as many prints as they have. The film anticipated Calder's enormous success and later, in a play I directed and acted in, *Happy As Larry,* Calder designed the sets for me.

When Wolcott Gibbs saw *Happy As Larry,* he wrote that the

stage was ". . . agitated by a strange group of objects called mobiles," a statement he would later regret. A few years later, if you
tried to hire "Sandy" Calder to do a set he would have charged
a fortune.

The play lasted only three weeks, but I was proud of it — it
raised my hopes about myself. *Happy As Larry* had music by Edgar
Varèse — another major artist.

When the show closed, Calder gave me several of the mobiles,
and later when I was broke — which was more or less peren-
nially — I sold a fourteen-foot black one for $50,000. Today it
would be priceless.

Also in 1950 I was invited to become a member of the "Old
Vic," in London, an offer I turned down. For years, I felt a bit
melancholy about that decision; unquestionably my forte was the
classical theater. Both by inclination and by talent I handled verse
well. At that time there were only a few classical theaters in
America, and they were second rate. If I had gone to the Old Vic,
if I had explored that path, what then? But I refused — so these
speculations serve no purpose. Still, I am proud they wanted
me — the only Yankee they ever invited until then.

Perhaps, I was too enmeshed here. Besides entering psychoanalysis, and working with Calder, one of the more interesting
events earlier in the year was directing a play called *Season in the
Sun*, written by Wolcott Gibbs, the theater critic of *The New Yorker*.

I had spent wonderful hours with various members of the *New
Yorker* staff. James Thurber I knew for more than a decade. We
generally met at the Artists and Writers Club on 40th Street, along
with Charles Addams (who was my closest friend and godfather-
to-be of my son), St. Clair McKelway, Wolcott Gibbs, and less
intimately the great editor and founder of *The New Yorker*, Harold
Ross himself.

Gibbs and I first became acquainted while he was doing a *New
Yorker* profile of me in 1936.

St. Clair McKelway was another top writer of that era, and his
most famous profile, which ran in three editions, was about
Walter Winchell. In those days, profiles could be merciless, and

I think Mac almost unseated Walter, or came close to it. He certainly started his downfall.

Wolcott Gibbs's most famous diatribe was his article on Henry Luce, publisher of *Time* magazine. The last line read: "Backward go the sentences until boggles the mind. Where it will all end knows God."

Wolcott and McKelway were both very hardworking and occasionally hard-drinking. Charles Addams was disciplined. God knows Thurber was not disciplined, but bad health stalked him most of his life. His downfall came from complete blindness and a series of strokes.

Gibbs was sometimes in his cups, but so were all of us. We spent precious hours recovering from hangovers. I constantly worked out in gyms, getting in shape for evening performances. My body was like a rubber band. It would stretch and loosen, snap and hurt.

One day Gibbs told me he wanted to try his luck at writing a play. I was astonished. Critics never wrote plays of their own. They were afraid to. But Wolcott had no fears — he wanted to try. He brought me an outline of a play called *Season in the Sun*. I liked it at once and I took the play to a flamboyant Broadway producer by the name of Courtney Burr.

Courtney had made and lost several fortunes producing Broadway plays. He tottered between being either dead broke or dead rich. When he was successful, he lived luxuriously on Park Avenue, surrounded by Kent brushes and English valets. The rest of the time he was scrounging and scrooching to stay alive, but he always managed to look dapper, and he always had a butler, regardless of the state of his income.

"It will give you class," I told Courtney. "Okay," said Burr. "Will you direct it?" I had directed a couple of off-Broadway hits, but this would be a major production. I had a hunch I could do it, although I didn't believe Courtney could raise the cash. But Gibbs's name intrigued people, and Burr went to many bizarre places to find investors, including two famous whorehouses, where the madams were friends of his.

Courtney was a friend of the brilliant writer and humorist Robert Benchley, and the two of them used to spend late hours drinking champagne in houses of ill repute, talking to anybody who would listen. The madams were intrigued by the prestige of Burr and Benchley, and with their usual hearts of gold, helped Courtney raise the money to produce *Season in the Sun*. I never told Gibbs that his play was financed in whorehouses and in fact, this interesting detail is being confessed right now for the first time.

The making of that show was perplexing and traumatic. We went to Boston for the tryout and Gibbs began to rewrite the play from top to bottom. I learned that Gibbs had an extraordinary ability to write quickly; he wrote on order and he wrote well. But six weeks later, just before the New York opening, changes were still being made. I said to the cast, "Thank you, bless you, now go to your dressing rooms. The audience will be here in two hours." Alice Ghostley, a lovely actress, said, "Can we freeze the play *now?*" ("Freeze the play" is a time-honored phrase that means "No more changes allowed!")

The cauldron of the theater is a hot experience — you live over flames and in the heat, you meet the audience — they react to you and you respond to them. It's a volatile environment, and it generates high-voltage behavior.

I've made more than a hundred movies, and they all have been produced in a kind of icy laboratory — the sound stage. Most of the hours are taken up with logistics, and you have very little time to develop anything except hysteria. A hot discussion or a blazing affair with the leading lady is difficult on a cold sound stage . . . it's too expensive and the accountants will send you home fast.

But for *Season in the Sun,* everything, including the changes, worked. So although my first major directorial endeavor had an unholy birth, it turned out well. We surprised the unbelievers who thought we'd never get it on. The drama critics liked it — one of their kind! — and they would have lambasted it if they hadn't — but every review was a rave!

The comedy had to do with Fire Island and the mixture of

whores, homosexuals, drunks, and intellectuals who sometimes inhabited that peaceful spot that lies within cocaine distance of New York City. Wolcott had a beach house on Fire Island, and I visited him there for the preliminary work. Gibbs later wrote he got inspiration from our adventures together.

The news item about *Season in the Sun* was that the leading character was fashioned after Harold Ross, editor of *The New Yorker*. The part was played by a fine actor also named Ross — Tony Ross. Tony looked uncannily like Harold, and had Ross's eccentric energy. Gibbs etched Ross in exquisite detail and savage humor — and luckily the critics and the audiences were intrigued. Everyone I knew liked Ross, and we wanted the play to do him justice. That was the challenge we accepted and that was the challenge we met.

I eventually took Ross to see the play — he had refused to go to the opening. He had stayed in the *New Yorker* office that night muttering and worrying that civilization was going to cave in because of this foolhardy step by Wolcott Gibbs. But as I say, Tony Ross played Harold Ross and was brilliant . . . and Harold himself was pleased by the performance of himself.

Later, Tony left the cast because of illness, and his place was taken by Walter Matthau, who was different but also brilliant. Dicky Whorf played the other male lead and Nancy Kelly played his wife. Dicky was drinking at that period, which at first made a lot of us nervous, but he never let us down. It's very strange how the problems of liquor can be overcome if a person likes his work, and Whorf liked it mightily.

An unknown actress, Joan Diener, was chosen by me to play the sex-appeal lead. Joan was amazing. Her acting wasn't great but she was beautiful and had the most astonishingly large breasts in proportion to her body that Broadway had ever seen.

Anyway, I was fascinated by Miss Diener and I wanted her to make good in the role. During rehearsals almost everybody wanted her out of the play. They all felt that no matter how luscious her breasts were, she was incapable of being an actress. But my attraction for her was deep and my faith in her was profound. I liked working with her, helping her. Without question we became an item and when we opened in Boston she got rave notices! On opening night when this girl walked out on the stage, the audience decided she was funny and absolutely ravishing.

I had been fighting for Joan against overwhelming odds. Courtney Burr, Dicky Whorf, Nancy Kelly, all felt that Joan would never make it, but believe me she did. We even added a song for her because I discovered she had a fine singing voice. She was only nineteen years old at that time and her problem was that she had no experience as an actress: but she learned in record time. Of course her successful career from then on is well known, notably in *Kismet, Man of La Mancha,* and other major musical productions.

It was a time of great anxiety for me. I had started psychoanalysis. After I returned from France and *Man on the Eiffel Tower,* it was Alan Jay Lerner who recommended the analyst he was consulting, Dr. Bela Mittleman. Looking back, Bela saved my sanity and maybe my life. It was interesting that in the doctor's office I saw many of my friends — Lerner, Marlon Brando, Elia Kazan — we would pass each other with a shrug of the shoulders as we went, separately, to lie down on the couch, trying to find out what brought us here and where the hell we were going thereafter.

Whatever piece of work I do, on the stage or in the movies, is always colored by my personal life. If somebody asks me, "Which was your favorite play?" I can't always remember the play — but what comes to my mind is "What was my psyche like during that period? What was the condition of my head? How screwed up was I? How happy? How out of shape had I become, physically and mentally?" Those years were a forlorn period of my life.

There is no doubt I had talent and I was sometimes able to maneuver with half my cylinders working. For instance, the critics praised my work in *Season in the Sun.* I worked day and night and I brought all the skill and talents I had to make the show a success. But it was rough going and I don't believe I would have succeeded as well if I had been acting. In some curious way, directing was easier for me.

With Ingrid Bergman and Elia Kazan in *Liliom* (1942).

With Paulette Goddard and Fred Astaire
in *Second Chorus* (1941).

Opposite, above: Charles Butterworth, Fred
Astaire, Paulette Goddard, and I . . .

Opposite, below: With Ginger Rogers in
Tom, Dick, and Harry (1942). (*RKO Radio*)

Opposite: Paulette Goddard and I surprised everyone with our wartime wedding on May 21, 1944. (*Photo courtesy of the Academy of Motion Picture Arts and Sciences*)

Right: In costume with Ernie Pyle, the person I played in *The Story of G.I. Joe* (1944). (*Columbia Pictures/Ned Scott*)

Below: In *Man on the Eiffel Tower* (1947).

With Alexander Calder and one of his mobiles
used in *Happy as Larry* (1950). (*Eileen Darby*)

With the cast in *The Remarkable Mr. Pennypacker*
(1954). (*John Erwin*)

Opposite: Kaja and I on a picnic.

Left: Starring on Broadway in *Teahouse of the August Moon* for ten weeks and on national tour for two years (1955). (*Eileen Darby*)

Below: With John Huston, Master of Hounds with the Galway Blazers, at a fox hunt in Ireland.

Opposite: As the Penguin in *Batman*, the movie (1966). (*Ruben Greenberg*)

Left: The whole family: Kaja, Jonathon, Tala, Kinvara, and I in 1960.

Below: Stepping out of her plane, Kaja, James Thurber, and I arrive for the opening of *A Thurber Carnival* in Columbus, Ohio, in 1960.

In *The Day of the Locust*, for which I was
nominated for an Academy Award
(1973).

Opposite, above: As Mickey in *Rocky*, for
which I was also nominated for an Academy Award (1976).

Opposite, below: In the ring with Sylvester
Stallone in *Rocky*.

Opposite: Charcoal drawing (life size) by Diego Rivera, inscribed "Para la casa de Paulette, Marzo 9 de 1943" ("For Paulette's house"). It was overlooked in our divorce settlement and lay rolled up and ignored for years. Rediscovered and framed, it graces my living room as an ironic souvenir. Whether Paulette is the subject has never been established, but Rivera did paint several portraits of her (1993). (*Photograph by Frank Buddenbrock*)

Left: As Ammon in *Clash of the Titans* (1980).

Below: With Robert De Niro in *True Confessions* (1980).

In my Malibu office, at work on my autobiography (1993). (*Photograph by Frank Buddenbrock*)

I had more responsibility but less scrutiny when I directed. Putting it another way, acting placed me in full view of the public where people could see my distress; but as a director, I was less visible — and my distress was less apparent.

I also discovered that a director has to meet challenges not covered by Stanislavsky, so I learned to think on my feet. Problems can blindside you in an unguarded moment.

As an editor, Harold Ross was a genius, and no one would have thought of him as a reckless romantic with the same bumbling indiscretions as the rest of us. Or so I believed, until I caught a glimpse that showed me even Harold had his Walter Mitty side.

Harold swore me to secrecy at the time, so perhaps I should not betray his confidence even at this late date, but to quote Marlowe,

> Thou has committed
> Fornication — but that was in another country;
> And besides, the wench is dead.

Some time after *Season in the Sun*, I was again in my director's role, putting a show together, when Harold approached me with uncharacteristic diffidence and said that he had a favor to ask. "You see, there is this girl . . ." I had an awful feeling I knew where this was going, and I was right. "She's young and good-looking," Harold assured me. I noticed there was no reference to talent. And then it came: "Do you suppose you could find a part for her in your new show?"

This was not Ross the Icon of the Intelligentsia, but simply a guy trying to make points with a girl.

I played Solomon and gave him my wise opinion. "Perhaps if you were to make a substantial investment in the show, Harold, I think the backers would consider giving the young lady a supporting role." Harold gave me a startled look, but he rose to the challenge — and sunk a chunk of money in the show. Unfortunately, *sunk* is the proper term. The show died an early, unmourned death. But Harold never complained, so I have a feeling it was worth it to him.

Ulysses in Nighttown

LOOKING BACK, I have come to believe that staging *Ulysses in Nighttown* by James Joyce was probably the most interesting and the most satisfying job I ever had in the theater, even though it was done off-Broadway and for very little money. It seemed to me then and still seems to me now, that all the essential elements came together on that magical opening night on June 5, 1958 — more than three and a half decades ago.

That wonderful event came about almost casually. One day a retired publicist, Oliver Sayler, and his partner, Marjorie Barkentin, called me on the telephone and mentioned the sacred name of James Joyce. I had steeped my head in *Ulysses* and had purchased as many first editions of Joyce's books as I could afford.

It is pleasant to remember the impact the half-blind Irish author had on young people in those days. Oliver and Marjorie developed the outlandish notion that *Ulysses* — which had been privately published in Paris and illegally distributed everywhere in the world — would soon be sanctioned and legalized by the U.S.

Supreme Court. "Before that happens," said Oliver, "we intend to buy the dramatic rights from the Joyce Estate!" Although I was intrigued by the concept, I was apprehensive that many of the words in the book would never be allowed on the New York stage.

"Perhaps," said Oliver and Marjorie, "but even if some of the more salacious words are censored — there will still be enough sexuality left to set fire to the whole parched New York stage!"

And so, after a month's study and after conferring with Dennis Johnson and Padraic Collum — two Irish intellectuals and writers who happened to be in the United States — I set about to fashion a play based on the Leopold Bloom sections of *Ulysses*. We chose *Ulysses in Nighttown* for the title.

Everyone agreed with me that the production should be presented in a small off-Broadway theater or hall and staged with immaculate taste and brilliant acting.

Morris Ernst, lawyer for the Joyce Estate, wrote the introduction to the first legal American edition of *Ulysses* and helped me raise money for our daring adventure.

This event brought me the gift of two striking experiences. First the play, and the second my relationship with Zero Mostel, who played Leopold Bloom. I believe my memories of that fine actor are objective, but I find it difficult to attain the same detachment toward the first experience — the actual staging of the play.

So, to offer a glimpse of what was involved within that larger frame, I asked my old friend, Robert Brown, who played Stephen Dedalus (James Joyce himself), for some of his recollections of that exhilarating 1958 theatrical milestone.

Here's what Bob remembers.

Burgess, you suggested I recall some of the moments we spent together during the rehearsals and performances of *Ulysses in Nighttown*. Your work during that period, directing all of us in the play, is remarkably worth remembering. So let me see what I come up with.

Either your friend Franchot Tone or Stanley Gilkey or somebody from your past days with Max Anderson called me to say you were directing *Ulysses* and I should contact you for the leading role of Stephen Dedalus.

I remember going down to Sixth Avenue in the twenties or thirties for the audition. On the top floor Mrs. Barkentin had a wonderful old studio. Just you and I and Zero were there. I was nervous, so you stopped the reading and talked to me a moment. Some directors tighten you up, but you brought my breath back. *Ulysses* was a book that we had all tried to read, but only a few understood. *Finnegans Wake* had put me off and scared the hell out of me. So I knew almost nothing about Joyce.

Then you said, "Listen, this scene is a story about memory, and reflection. Don't worry about the dialect, don't worry about character. Just talk to us as though you were remembering fragments of what happened a long time ago. Was it a dream or was it a fact?"

This had a marvelous effect on me. It gave me the idea. You understood that there was a very tense actor standing in front of you, and you were able to relax me. It was a wonderful help.

Then later, we rehearsed at the Rooftop Theatre building, a place that once housed the Bagel Bakers Union. It had a lot of old chairs on stage and some ancient theater seats in front. That's where we staged *Ulysses*. From bagels to James Joyce. It was exactly the place Leopold Bloom would hang out, if he came to New York. Lower Second Avenue. A perfect setting. It even had the smell of yesterday. It was very easy for the actors to slip back into the past. At any rate, you gave me the job, and rehearsals began.

The first day that jumps into my thoughts, was the day you told us about Kabuki! Zero Mostel was having trouble with a walk, a certain walk that you thought would be needed in the Bella-Bello sequence; and you brought into rehearsal a great Kabuki player who was in New York at the U.N. doing something or other. You asked him to show Zero how to do an exaggerated feminine walk like a geisha girl might do. I remember the man suggested to you — there was a translator there — that Zero put a piece of tissue paper between his knees. And you told Zero, "When you walk, hold that piece of paper between your knees, without dropping it!" And that is how Zero found the wonderful swish walk he used. It was exactly right for the scene. It was the kind of thing you found for all of us.

Carroll O'Connor and I spent most of our time together, because he was doing several roles. But the best part he played, and the one he cherished, was Buck Mulligan. We went over that many times, waiting to stage it, but, at first, we couldn't get to you. You were busy with the larger group scenes that you had to establish and it took time. Also, you said you didn't want to do the personal scenes until we had learned the words. So we went over and over them until, at last, we were ready to rehearse on stage. In the Bagel Bakers Union!

Padraic Collum came to visit us one day. He had just buried his wife, Mary, and he brought with him a walking stick that he had cut from an ash plant, in Dublin. He said, "I got it at the very spot I had last seen James Joyce. Before Joyce went to Paris. And I brought it back for the actor who plays Dedalus! Where is he?"

I was sitting next to Carroll waiting to rehearse, and you said, "Ah, here's our man. Meet Robert Brown. He is Stephen Dedalus."

Padraic asked, "You play Stephen? Stand up — do you mind?" So I did. He said, "Oh. . . . You are too athletic, aren't you? Joyce couldn't lift up a dish without help."

I remember that because my confidence was getting shaky at that point — both in rehearsal, and in life maybe. I was insecure. Carroll, of course, had been in Dublin and had played with the Gate Theatre. Also you had gathered a bunch of Irish actors — people who spoke the dialect. Like James Kinney and Michael Clarke Laurence, and that lovely actor who played Kinch . . . Tom Clancy! And there I was, trying to play catch-up while Padraic Collum is saying, "You don't look right."

So we went through the scene again, Carroll and I, until we broke for lunch. Then we went down the street to one of those little Jewish delicatessen places — I forget the name of it — while you stayed behind to work out some technical problems with the set.

At the restaurant, just as our food was delivered to the table, in comes Collum with his two cronies, and he gives me the crooked finger, waving me out, and I followed him into the street. It was a drizzly day and he said, "Walk along with me. I'd like to hear you do that soliloquy again." So we started back toward the theater, which was a few blocks away, but he decided to stop at a storefront which had a little overhang; and I realized there were gravestones in the windows! Marble gravestones! It was a remarkable sight. Instead of groceries, there were gravestones! It was an empty store, and I guess somebody had put the gravestones there so the stonecutter could carve names in them.

We stepped out of the drizzle, and he put me flat against the glass, my back against the window, and he said: "Ah, this is a very fine spot. . . . Now do it again." Well, I began the soliloquy as best I could. It was the beginning scene, you know, after Buck Mulligan leaves and Stephen stands there alone, thinking out loud. When I finished, I looked at Collum. He was staring at me, very troubled. Finally he said, "Is that the way you're going to do it?"

I was stunned! Afterwards I told you the story and you laughed and said, "That's amazing!" Then you added: "But if I were you, I would have socked him!" And that gave me back my confidence, I tell you. I was relieved and grateful.

On opening night, the excitement was high until Sean Dillon, who did the narration on one side of the stage, came down and said, "Zero, you're the deputy, I'm told. I wasn't given my contract to sign! They kept promising it to me, but they forgot about it or something. What do I do?"

Zero answered, "What do you mean, what do you do? We're all dressed, ready to go — but you can't go on! We can't open — we will cancel!"

In panic, I ran up and told the stage manager to get you. I decided I wasn't going to butt in because Zero was doing his union business and I had to act with him that evening and I wasn't going to get into a hassle.

When you finally came down, you asked, "What's this about, Zero — are you saying we can't open?" Zero yelled in return,

"That's right, Burgess, you should know, goddammit! You were the president of our union. We cannot proceed because this guy has not got a contract." You just looked at him before saying, "Zero, come on! It's an oversight. Just an oversight. The producer's been here every day, where the hell is he now! Sean's an Irish actor, maybe that's the trouble."

"No, no!" Dillon put in, "I am now an American and I belong to Equity. They don't care about me, I guess. Or they forgot me. I don't know." Even this didn't shake you because you said, "Well, we'll work it out. Come on! Get ready. For God's sake — we're opening in one hour!"

Says Zero, "No we're not!"

You asked, "Tell me why?"

"Because this actor has not got a contract."

You thought a moment and then announced, "*I am* a paid-up member of Equity, and I've got a contract with them to direct, and act too. And I'm going to do that! Act! Listen, Zero — *you're not going to close the play before it begins!*"

I guess this gave Zero second thoughts, or else he got scared. Or both. I could never figure Zero for sure, to tell you the truth. And I'm sure many times you couldn't either. Gifted he sure was, but he often rattled and confused you.

But, of course, we opened. And you did the narration, and without a single rehearsal, you gave a performance superior to what Dillon could ever hope to do. We were sorry that you couldn't repeat it every night. But that first opening was the important one.

The next morning the reviews were spectacular. The critics hailed the play, praised you, and were good to me. But Zero was the toast of the town! Not since *My Fair Lady*, with Rex Harrison, were there raves like that in the press.

Do you remember, Burgess, that a few days before opening, you brought your final notes to rehearsal? It was like a book. It described each scene of the play. It defined the meaning and the quality of every act in specific terms. It gave descriptions of every character, very concisely and clearly. At first it seemed late to receive it — or was it? It was easy to take, because you were like a conductor, giving the various musicians the final instructions of what they were about to play.

I hope you still have those notes, because they were inspirational. I don't think you slept for several nights, so you could bring to our final rehearsals those beautifully written, very specific instructions of what each of us had to do.

And there was another time when the play almost didn't go on. I don't know if you remember, but on matinee days we didn't have enough time to go out and have dinner and come back and get ready for the evening performance; so a restaurant down the street would bring in the food. And one night, between the matinee and evening, they brought us a bunch of poisoned food. There was something in it that was not kosher, and we all got sick. Some fainted, everyone vomited. It was a terrible night, and almost closed us down. But somehow we survived. You know better than anybody that "the play must go on."

I don't know if anybody ever found out *why* it *must* go on; but it does, and as far as I know, will for a long time to come.

The Saga of Zero Mostel

"What he spake, though it lacked form a little,
was not like madness."
                                                    — *Hamlet*

In spite of his immense popularity, in spite of being an honest-to-God superstar who played with audiences like a juggler plays with tinseled balls, I have a theory that Zero felt uncomfortable with people. By people, I mean the entire species, including strangers, friends, enemies, family, the whole two-legged caboodle. And at the basis of his humor, there was always sorrow.

Mostel was a big man, and in a jovial way he roared and rumbled and intimidated anyone who wandered near his territory. As far as I could tell, his behavior was genetic, like the hiss of a cat, but louder, of course, maybe like the snort of a playful rhinoceros or the subsonic rumblings of a whale. First there would be long periods of concentrated quiet, and then the dissonance would take over. Zero was never drunk and never manic-depressive — his low cycles were soft, quiet, creative; but when he was high he took off like a rocket. But high or low, up or down, I liked him very much and missed him very much when he left.

Sometimes, for instance, going into a restaurant with Zero could be like assaulting Omaha Beach. People's first instinct was to dive behind their tables like bunkers. After a while they generally recognized him and were amused by his actions, but not at first. At other times, on the stage, he would feel, or seemed to feel, menaced by the actors and audiences that surrounded him, and as his protective energies increased, he would cow them.

Julius Novick of the *New York Times* once wrote about Zero's outrageous behavior:

> . . . Burgess Meredith is persuaded to sing a Russian song, and Zero agrees to "translate." "Babushka Volga vodka narodny, ny, ny, ny," sings Burgess, or words to that effect. "All Russians have hemorrhoids," translates Zero. Burgess sings another line of Russian. "They haven't got hemorrhoids, they've got piles," says Zero.
>
> The marvel, the mystery, of which I despair of convincing those who have never met him, is that this was not gross and stupid, as it probably looks in print, but brilliantly funny and irresistibly charming; . . . and the poetry of coarseness.

The idea of casting Zero Mostel as Leopold Bloom came to me suddenly one night when I was in despair that I would never find the right actor. I thought of Zero.

After I called him, he agreed to meet me the same night at Vincent Sardi's restaurant, where I was astonished by his quotings of Joyce. In a few moments I knew I had the right man. I remember Vincent Sardi came by and heard the news. I said, "I feel I've found Moses in your bullrushes! Mr. Moses, meet Mr. Sardi."

Some time after, when we opened and were a hit, Vincent put our pictures together on the wall above the booth where we had been sitting when we made the pact. I believe those same pictures are still there, in the same spot.

At first some producers shied away from Zero because of a blacklist. He had been named in "Red Channels," as were many of his friends. However, I am sure he was never a member of the Communist party. I think he was just a radical-minded fellow, who liked to swim in those waters. As a matter of fact, I had been briefly "listed" myself, so my only reservation about Zero was that he had always been a comic and had never played classic theater. And now we were about to give him the gigantic role of Leopold Bloom in a Joycean classic. But I was justified in telling the press they would find that Zero was not only a talented actor, but a Joyce scholar! I assured them that he "walked out of the book!"

I also told them that I had found the perfect "stately, plump Buck Mulligan." That happened to be an unknown young Irish actor by the name of Carroll O'Connor. Also among the cast were Tom Clancy, John Astin, Beatrice Arthur, and Anne Meara.

I was lucky enough to know choreographer Valerie Bettis, who agreed to help me synchronize the actors' movements. I wanted the action of the play to have the discipline of dancing, of ballet. I thought of the play as a feverish series of hallucinations, and I needed the "organized unreality" of dancing.

Zero was awed by my unshakable faith in the play, and he said in an interview: "My God, when the producer said we couldn't afford the scrims Burgess thought were necessary, he paid for them himself!"

Before I began working with the actors, I broke the script into fifty-six scenes, and to each scene, I gave a color, an intention, a suggestion of physical characterization (referring to paintings by specific artists) and a metaphor to help our actors find their own reality in their creation of Joyce's surreal world. For example, my metaphor of the first scene between Buck Mulligan and Stephen Dedalus was "two Harvard men in Harlem."

These notes of mine fascinated Zero. He called the notebook in which I kept them "The Bible."

As an actor, Zero always took off like a rocket, but whenever he veered too far, I tried to keep his performance steady and focused. But he liked to experiment from time to time, depending on his mood and the reactions of the audience. One result of this trait was that people saw different performances on different nights.

This made me afraid that the purists, the "Joyce lovers" who came night after night to see our presentation, would be outraged. I begged Zero to beware of them — they were certain to write indignant letters to the press, and they often did. To them Joyce was sacrosanct.

I succeeded in a limited way in keeping him steady, and he never tried to ad lib or change the text. But when he was bored, there was a danger he would improvise the action. In that department I never saw him do very much that *was* expected. But whatever he did, the audience, other than the Joyce scholars, liked it. And, because his choices were so brilliant, I could never stay angry about it.

Later, one journalist quoted me about his tendency to stray from direction: "Zero was sometimes a rascal in that department. After sneaking into a performance every once in a while, I'd get fascinated by his variations — but I worked hard to get him back to the original staging, because his variations sometimes threw the other actors off balance."

On the other hand I felt that the unpredictable nature of Zero's performances had one great advantage — it kept his attention focused. He had a mind that was easily bored, and when that happened, he invariably improvised. He was never mean in what he did; sometimes gargantuan — but always generous. He never tried to ruin another actor's laugh, for instance. And then, since James Joyce had never been played on the stage before, most people didn't know whether Zero's behavior was supposed to be antic or not.

Zero's opinion of directors was generally low, but we got along like lovers. Here is what he said about me as director.

I've worked with all kinds of directors. Some of the big-name directors destroy the most wonderful thing an actor has. Just because he has power and importance, the destructive director tries to bend you to what he calls his sense of production instead of letting you use your own configuration, your own way of merging your own personality with the character you're playing. A good director knows how to bring out your own talent. One of the best directors I've ever worked with is Burgess Meredith.

. . . What a wonderful director he is. He can say "Aah!" suddenly to me in rehearsal and I'll get more out of the aah! than months with those fancy directors explaining my motivations to me or the other kind, the ones who say, "Take two steps forward and then turn with a gleam of ferocity in your eyes." You know why? Because he's a wonderful actor himself — very inventive and very creative — so he can do a lot of the things he wants you to do on the stage. We're on the same wave length. It's like two painters talking. You don't need explanations. Sometimes he can make a single little gesture when he steps into a part, and it rubs off on you. He sees things a cut above realism. He has a conception of what a thing is, what it means. He knows how to make use of you as an actor, but always in good taste. It's very stimulating. And I don't feel the breath of ambition on him, which is always disturbing to an actor. I feel that his concern is for the play.

Zero's physical resources were at their peak in the original 1958 production of *Ulysses in Nighttown*. As a result, sometimes that old Houston Street building would shake like the scaffolding at Cape Kennedy, so great was his energy. When this occurred, we called it Zero Hour. It was like thunder and lightning.

One famous night his emotions got so high that he bit a fellow actor, Sean Dillon, on the arm. Dillon's yells didn't bother the audience — they thought it was part of the act — but in a calmer moment after the performance Dillon asked me, as director, if I had seen what the hell had happened on stage. I said I had, more or less.

"If he does it again," he asked, "what should I do?"

"Bite him back," I said.

"He's too big!"

"Well, then, I suppose the next best thing would be to get out of his way."

And this, I believe, was the advice Dillon followed for the rest of the run. Those two somehow ended up friends.

What it came down to was that, in one sense, Mostel's performance became more important than the play; most people who purchased tickets came primarily to see him.

From Brooks Atkinson's review in the *New York Times:* "... The degree of success [at transferring the novel to the stage] ... is extraordinary. Directors [Meredith and Bettis] and actors have found ways to convey the imagery of Bloom's spinning mind as it leaps from one graphic allusion to another."

Walter Kerr suggested Zero's stage performances were "more akin to clowning — using the word in its most complimentary sense — than to acting." But others disagreed. Charles Laughton told me he thought Mostel was becoming the finest classical actor in America — in tragic as well as comic roles.

After our success in New York, we took *Ulysses* to London and Paris, where it won the same critical acclaim as it had in the States. Our production won the Sarah Bernhardt Prize, and Zero was awarded something or other every week or so.

We missed out on the movie rights through a series of slovenly maneuvers on the part of Zero's lawyer, who I nicknamed the "Wrong Cohen." I purposely forgot what the man's real first name was.

After *Ulysses,* Mostel and I were always planning and plotting to do things together. However, though our efforts were continuous, our accomplishments were sporadic. We kept trying, but none of our efforts caught fire — except possibly a television special we acted in together. The year was 1961 and the play was Samuel Beckett's *Waiting for Godot.* Our performance was taped and released on cassettes. Whenever I think of it, I take the tape out and play it for friends. The legal rights have long run out, so it is no longer available to the public, but we were proud of it. The critics said it was the "definitive performance of Samuel Beckett's most famous play."

In 1963 I agreed to direct the pilot for Zero's new television series, *Zero Hour.* There we were in trouble from the beginning, because Mostel came to loathe the whole concept. "It will ruin me!" he said.

In the end, he said, "I won't do this. It's *nothing!*" Since he felt that strongly, there was nothing for me to do but quit. When the producer asked me if I could change his mind, I answered, "No, it's beyond me."

You see, I thought he was right.

In 1966 Zero and I formed a repertory company. It was our intention to produce several plays each season, but not with a "permanent company." We realized that prominent actors would be reluctant to devote an entire season to such a venture, so we formed a separate company for each of four plays, with each play presented for a limited engagement of ten weeks each. Both Zero and I wanted to be free to work in films and television when we chose.

In the first year, our organization planned to produce two new plays — Chayefsky's *The Latent Heterosexual* (featuring Mostel and myself) and Guy Endore's *The Man That Was Shakespeare* (directed by Mostel and with me in the cast) — and two revivals — *Ulysses in Nighttown* and *Waiting for Godot* with both of us starring. Our other projects included a musical adaptation of Sean O'Casey's *Juno and the Paycock* for the second year. Paddy Chayefsky became so enthusiastic that he joined us as a partner. He was very much on the rise then and he felt our repertory company would provide a means to extend the life of his plays.

In August, however, *Ulysses in Nighttown* became unavailable, because the James Joyce Estate sold the film rights to a British producer, Walter Reade, with the proviso that no version of the play could be presented until the film was released.

So I announced that *Ulysses in Nighttown* would be postponed and *The Latent Heterosexual* would be produced instead. Arnold Sundgaard's *Forests of the Night* would replace *The Man That Was Shakespeare*, and Kurt Weill's *Threepenny Opera* was on our schedule, as was Molière's *The Would-Be Gentleman*.

But these changeable plans never came off. Opinions vary as to why. My own memory is that while our artistic intentions were sincere, we did not have the business experience to get such a complex undertaking started. Whatever else we were, we were not good businessmen.

Ironically, our most fateful failure proved to be the direct outcome of a theatrical success. In 1968 I finally did direct Zero in an independent production of Chayefsky's *The Latent Heterosexual*. The memory of that experience still chills me, although it provided some highlights I can't forget.

For example, during one rehearsal, Paddy as author and I as director were alone in the auditorium watching a run-through when "Z" evidently decided the stage was getting too small for his emerging emotions. Zero Hour was approaching, so to speak.

In the middle of a soliloquy, Zero left the stage and began to rampage in the aisles. Then, still roaring Paddy's lines, he disappeared through a far exit. We could hear him perfectly as he prowled the basement below. The other actors, bewildered, shouted their lines to the floor. And then, like a Minotaur from the labyrinth below, exactly on cue, Zero erupted from the wings back onto the stage as the curtain fell.

Chayefsky sighed and whispered, "Buzz, are we going to keep that piece of business?"

This kind of demonic behavior by Mostel was familiar to many people, and became part of his Broadway legend. Examples like this can, and probably will, fill many books.

Originally Zero had expected me to act with him in this play but later he asked me to direct. We got Jules Munshin to replace me in the cast. We opened at Paul Baker's Dallas Theatre Center. The play went well in Dallas, although it seemed a bit daring for the residents of that fair city — and we moved on to Los Angeles with our hopes high.

After *Heterosexual*'s opening in Dallas, Clive Barnes, who was then the critic for the *New York Times*, called Mostel "America's greatest actor." I agreed. On the stage he was unforgettable. And people who saw him in *The Latent Heterosexual* believed he could have played it for years to full houses. Why didn't that play continue? Here is the mournful story.

After the Dallas tryout and our Los Angeles opening, we

received a huge number of attractive offers for *Heterosexual*, including bookings from one end of the country to the other. Unfortunately, by that time, Zero and Paddy had become entangled in a feud so complicated that it would take several volumes to describe. I never really understood all of the details even though it festers in my memory. It was an unholy struggle and, as I say, it was waged on a level I couldn't comprehend. Like watching hawks fight in and out of the clouds.

The one part of the quarrel that I did understand involved a leading lady Zero had fallen in love with and Paddy loathed. The upshot was that Zero resigned and Paddy withdrew the play. We closed abruptly, canceling advance bookings of more than $100,000 — a prodigious amount in those days.

As a rule I was skillful at solving those kinds of personal entanglements, but in this case I was helpless. I tried my best to patch it up, but nothing could cool their fury. The conflict was final and fatal.

Both Paddy and Zero are long gone now, but wherever they are I hope they became friends again. Their quarrel shot down a hit play in full flight. I don't remember any situation like it in stage history. I wonder if the Chayefsky Estate would allow the play to be revived today, since Paddy forbade its production during his lifetime.

In 1974, fifteen years after our original success with *Ulysses in Nighttown*, Alexander Cohen, the New York producer, persuaded Zero to revive it at the Winter Garden Theatre and asked me to direct it. Of all the bad decisions we ever made in the theater, that was probably the worst.

The play should never have been revived at the Winter Garden, a huge arena. *Ulysses* is an intimate, oblique play. It was meant for the few who cared to think. At the Winter Garden it was advertised as a kind of blatant sex comedy. The cavernous theater, the broad staging, the Broadway hype, combined to destroy the spirit of the play. We felt we could make it, but we were wrong. It was like trying to play chess in Yankee Stadium. But we went ahead, and the result was dismal. We destroyed the memory of a play we had brought to glory — a hit show.

The revival was overproduced, requiring vast audiences and inflated ticket prices. This change eliminated students, who were a crucial segment of our public. As though that weren't enough, I had quarrels with the producer, who at one point asked me to step out of the production! No one in the cast would allow it and Zero threatened to quit; it was chaotic. Finally, because of fatigue, we got five or six days of help from John Dexter, then I came back in and brought the show to its first night.

The opening went smoothly, but, as I say, the critics were disappointed. Here was a play that had proven itself, a play that they had raved about for years; and we destroyed the memory by bringing it back with different elements. *Ulysses* was never meant to be a lavish Broadway show — Joyce's subtleties were lost in the chilly depths of overproduction, smothering scenery, and bare breasts.

It's a lesson which, as you unlayer it, onion skin by onion skin, describes the Broadway theater as it exists today. Tickets are a hundred dollars a pair and it costs millions to produce any play. The gamble is perilous, and only a few survive. Experimentation is a bad word nowadays.

Zero's quiet hours came when there were only a few people around him, or preferably none at all. In his studio on 28th Street he quietly painted hundreds of canvases, which he sold to many collectors — including me. His studio was orderly — every brush was clean and every picture neatly stacked . . . and there was quiet.

Very often as he worked, he played the music of Bach with its transcendental disturbances, and then the Big Man seemed completely happy. His paintings, unlike his public actions, were mostly small and always delicate. They were also highly disciplined, as Klee was disciplined, or Dubuffet, both favorites of his. No fearful symbols and no clashing cymbals were on his canvases. No disruption and no disdain. For this Minotaur liked to graze and ruminate more than he liked all the bloody fighting in the bullring.

Zero preferred the company of painters, and when he could get away from show business he would spend weeks wandering around, exploring museums all over the world. At such times he seemed calm and content, a planet away from the business of biting actors and pinching chorus girls and sabotaging authors' lines and directors' stage business.

Early in life, "Z" turned his back on religion, although he had been brought up in an Orthodox Jewish family and his father was a cantor. Zero never attended synagogue that I heard about, though he could sing all the services in Hebrew, and he did so at the drop of a hat, or when he was making up in his dressing room before a performance.

What he liked very much was his hideaway on an island off the coast of Maine. In summers he stayed there with his Irish wife, Kate, whom he adored and with whom he fought much of his adult life. She was the closest and best part of him; and he of her, though as I said, their love was sometimes boisterous. They seemed to like it that way.

Because Kate was a "*shiksa*," Zero was estranged from most of his Orthodox Jewish family, but he seemed, on the surface, not to be disturbed by this. Kate and he had two fine sons whom they loved very much.

I suspect it was not easy for Zero at the very end of his life. Quite suddenly — almost overnight — he became ill. With his religion torn away and a Broadway show in rehearsal, and his spirits so high, I am sure he was not ready to go. He and I wanted to do some Shakespeare, for instance. We had plans for his Falstaff!

Yet Zero was, more than anything else, a man of immense bravery; and in his will he said he wanted no memorial service, no people with sad faces. Ready or not, what he finally got was Peace and Quiet . . . and a world of people who miss him.

Hail and Farewell.

James Thurber

JAMES THURBER was destined to be two things he really didn't care about. The first was a humorist; the second was being blind. He never reconciled himself to either of those two lifelong conditions.

Jim was born, as everybody who has read about him knows, in Ohio. He came from a happy, midwestern family and went to Ohio State College with no great distinction — an average student. Suffering from cataracts and other related eye ailments continuously and painfully, he could see partially for only one-fourth of his life. Much has been written about him and about his wife, Helen, who was witty, long-suffering, and popular. The two of them were cynosures — bright stars in the New York literary world.

While he could still see, it was a whim of Jim's to draw pictures on restaurant walls. The owners were flattered, never painted them out, and some of them still exist around the city, or did a few years ago. Indeed, when Costello's restaurant relocated some years ago, they literally took the walls with them.

Underneath his panache, Thurber was serious and wanted to deal with the important issues of life. But when he did he never stayed on course long. His intellect was sharp, and he found humor in every subject, tragic or trivial. Wherever Jim sailed he flew the flag of humor. His conclusions were original, penetrating, witty.

A student of Henry James, Bertrand Russell, Immanuel Kant, and other great philosophers, he seldom accepted their somber conclusions. His most profound statement is "The Last Flower."

Only when Thurber looked at things askew did he become brilliant. You could say he excelled when he took a cockeyed view of things.

His vision was chaotic, but his writing was precise. So were his drawings; they are probably the most famous of his accomplishments — a Thurber drawing was and is recognized and enjoyed in all parts of the world.

When he discussed current politics he was not always memorable. But when he turned his secret, private eye on the war between men and women, when he considered the human dilemma, when he drew those early skeletal cartoons, he made wondrous observations. I wish I had recorded the conversations he had with his friends at night — McKelway, Ross, Benchley, all the extraordinary *New Yorker* staff making their late-hour comments, with Thurber the catalyst. All gone now, except in the memory of a few.

Another observation about Jim's behavior. He never acted like a blind man. As a rule blind people carefully organize their life. They find out where articles are in a room. They know where the ashtray is, where they put the glass they were drinking from, where the bathroom is. They plot out the invisible world in their mind's eye, so that they can live in some sort of order, move around with some dispatch. Thurber, however, was marvelously disorganized. He could never find the ashtray, he headed toward the fire escape in a hotel looking for the bathroom. He couldn't or didn't take the time or the trouble to orient himself. Well, he did after a fashion, but the general impression he gave was of a loosely organized fellow. We easily forgot he was blind. Reckless, yes — but not sightless.

You couldn't see the condition of his eyes, because he always wore glasses; not dark glasses like a blind man's, but large foggy horn-rimmed contrivances. They were scholarly and perched jauntily on his nose. He looked directly at the people he was talking to as he sprawled casually around the room, often with a drink in his hand. He acted absentminded, professorial. He was tall and angular. His speech could be vituperative and cutting, occasionally kind, but never sweet, never saccharine. He had a fierce, toothy smile — I remember the smile well. An evening with Thurber was entertaining. Sometimes he was ironic, but seldom sad, seldom despondent.

A man by the name of Bernstein published a book about Thurber a few years ago. It raised a small controversy, because it downgraded Jim. The critics felt the author went out of his way to emphasize Thurber's cantankerous nature, or worse. I know that Helen Thurber, Jimmy's widow, was distressed by the book. She dissociated herself from it. I was asked several times to be interviewed for that book, but intuitively I refused.

Helen and Jim were inseparable and I shared many adventures with them. There are two I will mention. The first concerned a couple of nights and a day we spent with a sober Brendan Behan, the Irish author. I was acquainted with Behan and he stopped me in the Algonquin Hotel lobby and said he wanted to meet Thurber. We went up to Jim's suite and passed a night and day of torrential talk, with only brief moments of separation. As I say, there was no drinking on Behan's part, and, because he was sober, Thurber, Helen, and I were temperate too. Thurber was fascinated by Behan, and Behan by Thurber. Behan had a headful of entrancing theories about Thurber's famous characters. He would imitate them, improvise their dialogue, all in a rich and very loud Irish brogue.

It ended with the manager begging for tranquility. He said, "If you gentlemen were intoxicated, I would feel justified in shutting you up, but under these circumstances it is difficult, very difficult

indeed. Keep talking, but for God's sake be quiet." We sat him
down, gave him a drink, and went on as before.

My important collaboration with Thurber was *A Thurber Carnival,* which I directed. It was a revue based on Thurber's works,
produced by Haila Stoddard and Helen Bonfils of Denver. Haila
is a well-known actress and a charming woman. She brought the
proposition to me and I got hold of the actor Tom Ewell to play
the lead. We spent many weeks in preparation, getting the revue
together. It was a "spoken" revue. We used jazz musicians, but
no songs were sung. We were out on the road for many weeks,
opening in Columbus, Ohio, where Thurber was born.

At the grand opening the mayor proclaimed a "Thurber Day."
The press conference was packed, newspeople from every state.
Thurber was handed a parchment inscribed in his honor. The
reporters crowded around and asked Thurber to pose reading the
scroll. Thurber said, "Yes, I'll be glad to do that, if I can write the
headline . . . I'm an old newspaper man, you know . . . matter of
fact I was a reporter here, in this city. So I'll give you the proper
headline for pictures you are about to take of me reading this
scroll: 'THURBER REGAINS SIGHT IN MAYOR'S OFFICE!' "

We went from town to town and from rehearsal to rehearsal,
working and rewriting the show. It was a mind-bending process.
We worked day and night in the theater, altering, correcting each
scene. Unable to see the skits and scenes, in our discussions Jim
visualized every nuance. As I look back, it seems uncanny. In all
our weeks of work and rework, he did not falter, never despaired,
never complained. It was an extraordinary accomplishment: with
no eyesight, he saw everything.

At first, during previews, I had a pretty young secretary sit
beside me in the audience, and I'd whisper acting notes into her
ear. She'd write those notes down in shorthand, and after the
show she'd type them up and I'd read them to Thurber. Then, if
he agreed with my notes, I'd pass them on to the cast.

That system worked, until I discovered a new gadget called a
tape recorder. I bought one and began to whisper my notes into
the black box.

Thurber never liked this change.

"Your notes don't make sense anymore," he growled. "They are hollow. You've lost your manhood with that damn machine. For God's sake, go back to the blonde!"

Thurber was generous with interviewers. He'd talk to all of them for hours. I'd get mad because we needed him at rehearsals. "Interviews don't feed anybody," I'd say, "if the play is no good."

Jim resented this. One day a reporter stopped the two of us on the street and asked him how he liked me as a director. Thurber said, "We don't get along well — but I'll say this much about Meredith; he's the only director around I see eye to eye with."

From a blind man, that wasn't much of a compliment, but the reporter wrote it down and published it as though it were high praise. It gave Jim a big laugh. "I gotcha!" he said.

In the play I conceived a bit of staging I called "Word Dance," which we used at the end of the second act. The music would be playing and all the actors would be dancing slowly to the beat of the music. At every fourth or fifth beat, the music would stop and one by one the characters would step out of the chorus line and say lines to the audience:

"My wife wants to spend Halloween with her first husband."

"So this girl said to me, 'Why did we have to purchase Louisiana when we got the other states for nothing?'"

"Well, if I called the wrong number, why did you answer the phone?"

"I don't mind her buying the pistol, but it makes me nervous when she holds it on her lap at breakfast."

"No wonder every man she looks at seems to be a rabbit. After all, she has eight children."

"Her husband went up to bed one night and was never seen again."

"Do you realize it took Paul Revere two and one-half hours to rouse the widow Matthews that night?"

"She says that he proposed something on their wedding night her own brother wouldn't have suggested."

"Then I had an affair with this twelve-year-old girl. Think of it, Mrs. Bixby, I was only ten at the time."

"I knew their marriage wouldn't last when they called their honeymoon cottage 'The Qualms.' "

"My husband wanted to live in sin, even after we were married."

"Where did you get those big brown eyes and that tiny mind?"

"So I said to the bank teller, 'How could I be overdrawn when I have all these checks left?' "

"He's having all his books translated into French. They lost something in the original."

"She's always living in the past. Now she wants to be divorced in the Virgin Islands."

"How could I tell him what happened when I didn't know the French for 'I have flushed my passport.' "

"It's funny, but every time I relax with a man, he gets all tensed up."

"Love is blind — but desire just doesn't give a damn!"

"Why didn't they repeal inhibition while they were at it?"

Finally the music stopped and the stage manager walked to the footlights and said to the audience, "The women now keep their seats while the men leave the auditorium. . . . God knows they need a head start." And the curtain fell.

Often Jim would object if the humor got too broad. He had the *New Yorker* sense of restraint. If laughs were too uproarious, too belly-like, he would say, "We'd better cut that down. It seems cheap." Sometimes when I was sitting with him and the audience would roar with laughter I would whisper, "That's too funny, Jim. Let's kill it." He chuckled, but he kept us honest.

When we finally arrived in New York and opened, there was not one scene unchanged. He had rewritten or remolded every act — he was a perfectionist. All of us were near collapse, but as it turned out, it was worth it.

When the play opened we received a glorious set of notices from every New York paper and magazine. The reviewers said it was skillful, funny, impeccable, "a wonderfully civilized piece of work." The play ran for over a year, despite its high production costs. The production required revolving stages, treadmills, orchestra, hundreds of light changes. It won a special, loyal audience who came to see it again and again.

The high point of the whole venture was the night Thurber went on stage as an actor. One of the cast was taken ill and I suggested casually that Thurber go on and act in one of the scenes — he was fascinated with the idea. After two or three hours of rehearsals, he went on stage and amazed us all. He was professional, disciplined, and developed an instant rapport with the audience. He also invented ingenious tricks to cover his blindness. When he was reading a letter on stage he pretended the writing went around the edge of the letter so he kept turning the page of the letter as if he were following the writing. He had a fine deadpan delivery, and he was clear and personable. His wife said he was never happier than during that brief period — not many months before his death — when he played a lead role in a successful Broadway play he himself had written.

I cannot describe the agony he suffered at the end. He was given very little physical comfort during his life, and none at the finish. He was dealt a grim set of cards. Yet he lived valiantly and left a legacy of comic American writing only Mark Twain can match.

I remember when we were in London, I was invited to a special meeting in his honor given by the editors of *Punch*. He was made an honorary member of *Punch*, the first American writer they ever honored. He occasionally asked me to go with him to these events.

We did a few wicked things too. One time he said to me that one of the worst aspects of his blindness was that he couldn't cheat! "I can't be unfaithful!" said he. This statement brought me up short. We were crossing Fifth Avenue when he said it. Taxis screeched to a stop, horns honked, but the two of us stood there talking. I said, "Why, that's true, Thurber! That's the goddamn absolute truth! I don't know why I never realized it. It's a tragedy." The people we were with at the time, I remember, rushed back to rescue us. They thought we had gone crazy, talking there in the snarling traffic. They led us to the sidewalk.

But his statement haunted me. I said as we walked along, "You're right! Here you are, a man with a lot of lust and you can't sin! Not even one goddamn single, solitary sin! It's not fair — I mean it! It's hard enough for a man to sin even with all his senses going . . . and you can't see! It takes a lot of planning, a lot of skill to sin well. Dammit, Thurber, I've got to find a way for you to break a few commandments!"

It started as a joke, but the joke began to take on an incipient reality. I told him I would arrange with a girl in the cast to help him break any commandment he wanted broken. We were kidding, of course, but I was curious to see his reaction.

"I've got a play going on," he said. "There are important things happening! Good God, Meredith," he said, "if I'm caught, what window do I jump out of? I'm blind! What flagpole do I slide down? Where are the back stairs? Where are my pants? That kind of thing!" I told him I would stand guard and be his military adviser, but as I said it, I realized the joke was over. On top of this, of course, his wife, Helen, heard about our outlandish plot. She said she would throw the girl out before she could take her dress off!

It was a half spoof, the whole rigamarole. But it set me thinking. I said to Thurber, "I don't see how I can direct your damn play, if I can't direct you in one small amateur assignation!"

I haven't read it, but if it is true that Bernstein's book about Thurber demeans him, that's worse than too bad — it is shameful. With all he had to contend with, Thurber lived a gallant life. Because his work is extraordinary and meaningful and will give pleasure to people for lifetimes to come, we can forgive the vagaries he might have had. I know I never met a fellow I enjoyed more.

It may be true that Jim's later work did not always equal his earlier writing. His most fruitful times were probably five or six years before the end. Then his health failed, in ways he never admitted. He had a brain tumor, which finally weakened him; and aside from his blindness, there were the physical irritabilities of pain and confinement. Thurber earned the right to be angry when he felt like it.

God knows his anger never lasted. Any snarl I ever saw on him was gone a breath later — and it ended in a crooked smile. He never blamed any individual; he blamed the everlasting pain which hurt him, smothered his laughter, clouded his antic view of the world, diminished his sense of mischief.

A few years ago, I had to keep a bandage over my eyes for three days. I advise everybody to try it. It will bring you a sense of gratitude when the bandages come off. Thurber's never did.

Horses, Jackie Kennedy, Wine, and Picasso

S OMETIMES IN THE PAST I put more energy into my hobbies than I did into my work. Distractions became important to me. There is probably a dark psychological reason for this kind of behavior, but the best cure I found was to go broke. Hobbies cost money. No money, no hobby.

My most expensive hobby was jumping horses. I wish it had been stamp collecting or birdwatching, but it was horses . . . and that sport is high priced. Not for nothing is it called the Sport of Kings.

I became so involved that I built an indoor riding ring with stables for twenty horses on my farm back East. I didn't start jumping until my middle thirties, which is considered suicidal. Riding a horse slowly down a country road is one thing, but jumping tall fences and wide ditches is another — yet what I lacked in experience I made up in rashness.

In Ireland I hunted with the Galway Blazers, who were mastered by my friend John Huston. I also hunted with the Essex Hounds, the West Hill Hounds, and others, here and abroad. I jumped hunter class in Madison Square Garden. I spent a good part of my income riding those lovely four-legged creatures. George Bernard Shaw made fun of riding to hounds and in his prologue to *Heartbreak House* — which he nicknamed "Horseback House" — he wrote that fox-hunting people were boring, and I admit I went through a siege of that tedious behavior for a while. What I did get out of hunting was a series of broken bones and a headful of lovely stories. Not all fox-hunting people are boring and, as I said, John Huston liked horses too, but he rode with more panache than the rest of us, as he did everything he put his mind to. He galloped and jumped like a demon.

When I sold my stable I did keep my favorite horse, Kinvara, named for the town in Galway where she was born. She won more ribbons for me than I could count. One day I cleaned out a storage room and came across a trunkload of ribbons and cups the old girl and I had won — maybe a couple of hundred or more. They weren't all big shows and only a few of the ribbons were blue, but we won them together, Kinvara and I. When we stopped jumping, we escaped with our lives, so to speak. Each prize we won had cost a fortune; and the result was a bagful of ribbons I threw away. But in some curious way the memories are worth it.

My daughter, Tala, is a grown woman now, but when I told her I was writing about Kinvara, she reminded me that when I went on location to make a film, I would sometimes ship Kinvara with me. "I wanted to go, but you took her!"

A few of my horse-capades, as we called them, are worth the memory. For instance, I fell off Kinvara just as Jackie Kennedy was riding alongside me. The president's wife stopped to see if she could help, but, embarrassed, I climbed to my feet and waved her on. That episode happened with the Essex Hounds, a fashionable hunt in New Jersey. I often fell off my horse . . . apparently I was not a natural horseman. One professional warned me that my seat was faulty! But the Master of Hounds at Essex was a lady I admired, Jill Slater. Friendship with a woman like that made the hazards I faced worthwhile.

I have memories of going to the Grand National steeplechase races in England with Tim Durant, who became famous as the "Galloping Granddad." Tim raced in the Grand National when he was sixty-nine years old, and again when he was seventy, and finally, a third time, when he was seventy-one! In each case I raised the money for him — got my friends to back him. In his last race at the National, out of a field of forty-four horses, only twelve riders finished and Tim was the eleventh. The rest of them had crashed, fallen, or been thrown. The ovation for Tim was something any actor in the world would envy — any opera singer, any rock star. The English people loved the Galloping Granddad, a man of three score and ten, riding that frightening course with jumps three yards across and ten feet deep, horses breaking their legs and riders thrown from their mounts. It made him famous.

That gallant man went on riding horses until he died a few years ago. At the end he galloped wildly along the Malibu Beach in California, until the police stopped him.

Every horseman's dream is to race in the Grand National, and at the age of seventy-one it was miraculous. When Tim finished that race he became a hero at the end of his life. If you are going to win fame and glory, that is the time to do it . . . as the curtain falls and the audience is still cheering.

The growing of grapes, the tasting of wine, and the collecting of good vintages has been a hobby of mine for years. I have wine cellars in California and on the East Coast. I know many California winemakers and I have friends in the business. I wander into the wine country when I can. Vineyards are peaceful to visit and the owners welcome you as a rule. It is part of the tradition.

Wine is a secondary pleasure that requires discipline, but pays good dividends. Drinking a great wine brings you pleasure if you savor it and restrict it to two or three glasses a meal, but it is a pleasure that stays the course. Among the knowledgeable members of the winetasting societies, I notice that the folks who have the most fun are the older men and women. They have let the steamier pleasures slip away, but when they raise a glass of Lafite to their noses, their eyes glisten and their minds sparkle. For all I know a kind of cerebral orgasm takes place, harmless fun. Wine was my friend, always. Hard liquor was the enemy.

One of the friends I have in the wine business is Robert Balzer, the wine editor of the *Los Angeles Times*, and former wine and food editor of *Holiday* magazine. He publishes a newsletter, is known as a "professor of wine," and gives classes to students, old and young.

Because of Balzer I have been, for many years, a judge on the *Los Angeles Times* "Wine Tasting Panel." Every summer a group of us — I am the only nonprofessional — make blindfolded decisions on what wines are best and those decisions are published. It is hard work and gets small thanks. We taste wine for two and sometimes three days. We obviously cannot swallow much of it — we sometimes judge a hundred wines. We roll a vintage around in our mouth and spit it out! As I say, it is hard work, but I suppose somebody has to do it.

I don't intend to do biographies of everybody I know in the wine business, but I value my friendship with the Mondavis, the Gallos, Tom Jordan, Rodney Strong — all the great vintners. Also I salute Sam and Michael Aaron of Sherry-Lehmann Wines & Spirits of New York, who are friends and comrades. We are all bound together by grapevines, and wear tendril-bearing cissus rhombifolia in our hair.

I approach this avocation with gusto — it has few rewards, except that I get invited to fine dinners. I don't have time to accept many invitations, but when I do, people break out their best bottles.

Picasso is generally thought to be the greatest artist of the twentieth century. He stands supreme in his field, as Einstein and Joyce and Freud and George Bernard Shaw do in theirs. No one can surpass them; there isn't time. The century has only a few short years to go before the curtain falls.

And, the trouble is, those geniuses have left behind a cluster of annoying problems that they didn't have time to solve. Gaping holes have been discovered in the ozone layer. Despite the end of the Cold War, nuclear bombs remain at the ready on their pads. Reports of acid rain and cosmic disturbances appear each day in the news. Everybody will have to duck and dodge through the next few thousand days.

Now you ask: What do such solemn subjects have to do with the joys of wine? What connection do they have with the quality of great vintages? With the heady aromas of Burgundies? With the complex enchantments of Bordeaux?

Here is the connection: Wine is the opposite of Gloom, the opposer of Fear. Wine is a redeemer, a pleasure maker. Wine is the still, small center of the cyclone . . . and here is a case in point:

The closest I came to meeting the great Picasso was in Paris, right after the war, in 1946. It was cold and there was a serious food and wine shortage. My wife at the time was Paulette Goddard, and because we owned and cherished a small Picasso oil, we decided to send the artist a bottle of Château Lafite-Rothschild we'd gotten hold of, along with some black-market caviar and truffles — a present to Picasso from two admiring strangers. We found his address and sent him the goodies, artistically wrapped.

When the messenger came back, we asked, "Was Picasso there? Did you see him? What did he say?" The messenger told us that a beautiful young lady had accepted the package, whispered, *"Merci, mille fois,"* and closed the door . . . end of story.

These profound thoughts about wine and Picasso recall a song I wrote a few years ago, with the music arranged by my son Jonathon. He played the melody tenderly, and I gently sang the words:

> When all the stock markets crash
> Ripping my life-style apart,
> When my pals all split
> And my wives depart —
> And I sit around waiting
> For World War III to start —
> Then a great vintage wine
> Will comfort my poor heart
> Or a baby Beaujolais!
> Yes, a great vintage wine
> Is the state of the art:
> Or a nubile Beaujolais.

A question crosses my mind. I don't know when and how I found time to do all this. Where did the events fit in? I can't place the pieces on the chessboard. Time and space get mixed up when you are looking back. Late at night, you wonder if it really happened. This life you led and the life you are living — are they lived by the same person? Life is elastic. It stretches away when you need it close — and pulls close when you want it far away. Many of the activities I followed, I should have let go; they often brought sorrow at the time. Now, in reflection, they make me smile.

The Melancholy Tale of
The Yin and Yang of Mr. Go

THE NAME of the movie was *The Yin and Yang of Mr. Go* and it was being filmed in Hong Kong in 1970.

A Scottish-born producer had flown a group of us over there. I didn't know there were villainous Scotsmen anymore — but this man was a latter-day Macbeth.

Anyway, twelve days before completion of the film, this producer and his Canadian backers had run out of money and skipped town.

We had been given return tickets to America, but I had to bail the actors out of their hotels. James Mason said they still owed him $50,000. It was a scam I didn't think could happen in this day and age; but, as I say, the gang vanished and took the negatives with them. We could never locate the man or any of his cronies. The whole caboodle disappeared. I figured Buddha had a lot to do with it.

A year or two later we heard rumors that the film had shown up in England and somebody was trying to finish it with new actors! I could not — nor could the Screen Actors Guild — dis-cover any legal way that could be done. But it was the last we heard about it — a distant echo. The Screen Actors Guild tried to bring legal actions against "Mr. Macbeth," but he had left no hoofprints. It was a tragedy to us, because we had invested our hearts, time, and money in the venture.

I had written the script and directed the movie. A fine artist, Dong Kingman, designed the production. The only compensation I received — and still have — are a dozen beautiful colored sketches Dong created for the sets and costumes.

The rushes we saw showed that James Mason was brilliant in the leading role, as was Jeff Bridges. I still have the ragged costume and the eyelids I wore when I played the part of a tricky, devious, and wickedly funny oriental acupuncturist.

So what was the film about? Hong Kong in those days was an exotic place. Enemies and friends dealt with each other in devious ways. The English had governed the island splendidly and cyn-ically for a hundred years, with no trouble and no one in jail. They somehow maneuvered the wickedness around, like a chess game. Today, of course, the system is coming apart and Hong Kong, as we knew it, is finished. It will soon become a part of Red China — skyscrapers and all.

The plot of our film was about a half-English, half-Malaysian entrepreneur named Mr. Go, who dealt in drugs, prostitution, and deception — and that was the role Mason played. He bought and sold people and traded in illicit goods, but one day — mi-raculously — Buddha reformed him! It was based on an old Chinese legend, which said that whenever Buddha thinks it is necessary, he gazes into the eyes of a person and that person is metamorphosed; he or she is changed into the antithesis of what they had been. You might say this is the way Buddha evens things up; the Yin and the Yang!

So James Mason played the role of a beautifully wicked and very oriental villain named Mr. Go. He relished the role. In the film we saw him change his evil ways and we watched him begin to bring good into the world instead of evil.

In our story Mr. Go freed his captives and rescued a young American deserter from the army in Vietnam. That role was played by Jeff Bridges.

There was one particular speech — a speech of transformation — that James liked doing. In it he described the excitement he felt and the plans he had; and he told of his love for the Chinese all over the world. Whenever I remember how quietly effective Mason was in the role I shake my head in anguish that the damn picture was never finished.

Jeff Bridges came to see me recently and I was not only amazed at his vivid recollections of *The Yin and Yang;* I was stunned by my own ability to forget the painful details. He reminded me that ten years ago when he was looking through a video catalogue, he came upon a strange cartoon of himself. It was an ad for *The Yin and Yang of Mr. Go.* It had been released!

Jeff called the place, rented the video, and ran it for me here in Los Angeles. And I wiped it out of my mind. Jeff reminded me that until then we never knew what had happened to the damn thing. It was weird and sad watching the film, because we had all put so much heart and soul into it. First of all, there were many major scenes that we hadn't shot, and I wondered, "How could they do it without us?" Well, what they did was to hire Broderick Crawford to narrate it! And they created other scenes for him to talk about and knit the story together. Plus they had introduced animation — cartoons in the scenes! It was crazy. Nothing related to anything! And so we saw it and went on laughing and crying over what they did to our film.

What is most interesting to me is the fact that I managed to wipe it out of my mind. I never remembered having seen it until Jeff reminded me.

This was only Jeff's second film. He had finished *The Last Picture Show* but it had not yet been released. His recollections of our movie were so vivid I taped them:

> Every few weeks the producers would say they were out of money.
> So we would sit there in Hong Kong. They paid the bills — I guess

somebody paid the crew. I don't know. And we would sit there, not working, for weeks and weeks. I don't know how many weeks altogether, but I remember there was a time toward the end of it when we were "on hold."

I can't remember — but I think I got my salary. Of course, at that time it was something like $10,000 . . . maybe less. But I remember you didn't get paid. Here's another memory. You had just gotten through playing in *Batman* for all those years, on television. In one of the newspapers in Hong Kong, there were articles that went on and on about a guy who was impersonating the Penguin and raping people! And finally this man leaped off a building, opened his umbrella and that was the end of him. I heard about it when I found you pasting something up on the bedroom wall at the hotel. I said, "What the hell are you doing?" And you said, "Look at this!" You had been following the stories of this false Penguin who, umbrella in hand, had leaped off a building and smashed himself on the ground!

Now, in my mind, as I go into that hotel room of yours in Hong Kong — I remember that you were on the wagon, but you were into hash. And you, James Mason, and Jackie MacGowran and a newspaper writer would sit in a big circle and pass the opium pipe around. I'll never forget it, the sight of you and Jackie MacGowran puffing opium and reciting James Joyce. From memory! You would recite, and then pass the book around looking for forgotten passages!

I liked hanging out with you guys. And then you would get inspired and you would tell stories. It was a great feeling. It was a wonderful time for me. I was only twenty years old, and it was the first time I had been away from home, on my own, and hanging out with you and James . . . you fellows made me welcome. Also I remember the lunches we had. Usually on location you break for a half hour or an hour if you're lucky — but we had two-hour lunches! And you'd say, "Bring what you like, bring whatever is good." They would bring in giant fish — you remember that?

Something else . . . one of the great things you did for me I'll never forget. It was a very bold decision and I remember you were a bold director in your choices. You would make decisions, very large ones, quickly and [snaps fingers] bam! My character, Nero Finnegan, was a G.I. who fled from Vietnam. He went AWOL to Hong Kong, a wild young man who thought of himself as a Joycean poet. And at the time I was — and still am — into music. I would play songs, and one day your eyes lit up and I could almost see a light bulb go on over your head; ''Hey! What if you wrote rock opera? Your character in the movie?'' I said, ''What do you mean, rock opera? I've got this scene the day after to-morrow — we're going to shoot film'' — and you said, ''Yes, I know, I know. But think about it. Maybe he's not a poet, but he writes music, he writes like you do! You write music! Could you put any of this speech here to music?'' And I said, ''Well, shit! Burgess, I don't know.'' And you said, ''Here — try it!'' I said, ''But we've got to shoot this scene day after tomorrow!'' And you said, ''Go ahead — do it!'' So I went up to my room, and for the next two days and nights I worked on a tune, and I came back with two songs. One of them, I could probably sing to you right now! ''When Buddha winks his eye . . .''

And you put words to another tune that I didn't have lyrics for:

> These are the notes of a magical sadness
> A longing that floats on the thread of a song
> Oh what madness to conjure again
> What dimly was ended
> Torn is the past and mournfully mended
> On the thread of a song.

That song didn't get in the film, but I recorded it a couple of years later. Actually, I don't think you wrote the poem when we were in Hong Kong. You had written it before, but you altered it to my tune — and I ended up with a new character.

One night we went into the New Territories to shoot a weird scene. It was a fascinating place, because in China they bury their dead in one place for a while, then dig them up and put them somewhere else! We filmed in the place they put you later on. On the other side of Kowloon, in the New Territories.

It was wild. There was a full moon, and as far as we could see there were rolling hills of graves, thousands! And the graves were like big chairs, like big thrones, with porcelain photographs of the people on each one. And there was phony paper money under rocks, and there was a wind, and the paper money kept blowing, and I remember you were in the middle of a shot, and the crew didn't want to be there at all! They didn't like it — it was sacrilegious to them.

So most of them dropped out and there was only a skeleton crew (a pun!) and we were left there in the moonlight. And all of a sudden, in the middle of a scene, I hear the crew crying "Aaah, aaah," and they were staring at the moonlight hitting the porcelain pictures. Those pictures were like lights, shining in these graves! Do you remember that at all?

Jeff's memory was specific. Now I remember, very, very clearly. The whole scene. But I did not remember, until Jeff retold it, that we filmed it. I had come to believe it was some sort of a nightmare I'd had. What amazes me is that I had purposely forgotten a large part of the whole adventure. I reduced my memory, as they say, "reductio ad absurdum." I was there, and we did a few good things, but essentially, we got fucked out of the film.

But being there together, at least we established long friendships — between Jeff and me and between Jeff and James Mason — and that's worth a great deal.

Brief Sketches

OVERT SEX has given the stage and movies a financial lift in certain quarters — the lower quarters, to be exact. But to date only a few pictures have benefited artistically from the new permissiveness. Today almost anything is permitted in pictures and on stage, but not in television. Actors still have to loop a sanitized version for broadcasting usage.

"Freedom of sexpression" came into the theater abruptly. Back in 1964, I directed Le Roi Jones's *The Toilet* and *Dutchman* in Los Angeles. We shocked people. Although we received a roaring rave review from its critic, the *Los Angeles Times* refused ads quoting their own critic! For this action, the *New York Times* attacked the *L.A. Times*. Those were troubled days, as are today's, but the nature of the trouble has changed. Today the Jones plays would offend no one.

Also in 1964 I directed James Baldwin's *Blues for Mr. Charlie* on Broadway. At the previews we were picketed and booed — the play was called "angry" and "rabidly revolutionary." But the New York critics praised it and the picketing stopped. Today the language of *Blues* would not raise a saint's eyebrow.

I remember James Baldwin and I sat, all dressed up, at the ANTA Theatre ready for the New York grand opening of *Blues*. But Jimmy had a bunion, which began to hurt. So before the curtain went up, we hobbled him to a nearby saloon where we asked the bartender if he had a razor.

"What for?"

"Mr. Baldwin has a bunion," I replied.

"You going to cut his goddamn bunion off in this here bar?"

"No!" shouted Baldwin. "We are gonna slash open these goddamn golden slippers so I can move around, man."

"That makes sense," said the bartender.

He found a razor blade, and we cut away the sides of Baldwin's pumps. He felt better physically, but mentally he was angry and worried.

The day before opening we had been asked by the producers to cut out the twelve-letter word *motherfucker*, which Jimmy had laced variously into the dialogue — a word that had never been spoken in a Broadway play before.

The producers, the Actors Studio, told him the critics would walk out. I remember Lee Strasberg reluctantly brought me the news. "What do we do?" he asked.

After much soul-searching, Baldwin agreed to cut out every motherfucking one.

As director, I had to pass orders on to the cast. I half expected them to disobey — but for Baldwin's sake, the actors either cut or mumbled The Word. On opening night sounds came out like *smotherlucker* . . . and *motherfluffer!* Today motherfucker is the accepted way to begin any first-class drama — white, black, or yellow.

Blues ran well until one sad day Diana Sands — who, with Al Freeman, Jr., had the lead in the play — was asked to tell the audience that for financial reasons they were seeing the final performance. After the show a small, shy white lady went backstage and wrote a check for $10,000 to keep it running. The check

did not bounce. The shy lady was a Rockefeller, sister to Nelson —
and Winthrop and David.

Whenever I think of Baldwin's wonderful play, I think of Diana
Sands, who died much too young — three years after our show
closed. She was beautiful and black and her talent was bigger
than life — like Zero Mostel's. Both Diana and Zero, almost from
the first rehearsal, transcended their roles. He was fierce and bold,
she was quiet and subtle. A wise director sits with gentle reins
and accepts credit for the result. Diana was enchanting. I am
grateful I worked with her in the brief, beautiful time she lived.

Al Cavens, a very close friend of mine, died a few years ago. He
wasn't a famous man — but he was an important part of the
motion picture industry.

Al was a warrior, in the best sense of that invigorating word.
I am fond of Castañeda's definition of a warrior, which fits Al:
". . . a warrior takes everything as a challenge; the ordinary man
takes everything as a blessing or a curse."

I once told Al that his coat-of-arms should be a pair of crossed
sabers rampant on a field with the motto: "All challenges accepted
here."

Al was a well-known stunt man in those days. Even when he
was no longer young, he would do fearless stunt work. He was
also a brilliant swordsman — a champion fencer. He choreographed a majority of the great duels seen in films.

I was thankful for that; that's how we met. He did all my dirty
work as the dastardly Penguin in the *Batman* series. I would make
the vocal threats against Batman and Robin and then Al would
do battle for me, leaping off buildings with an umbrella as a
parachute, dueling the entire police force of Gotham City on my
behalf. He lost splendidly for me, and he did it with a foot-long
cigarette holder in his mouth. He accomplished my heroics and
I got the credit for his daring.

That wasn't unusual for Al Cavens — to do dangerous stunts
for someone else. He did that work happily all his life — as had
his father before him.

I never met his father, but I heard plenty about him: he, too,

was a great fencer — and he taught his son. Al's father choreographed most of the great sword fights in the earliest films; some
of them silent, with Douglas Fairbanks. And almost from his teens
on, Al did the same. He carried the tradition to new heights. It
was Al who choreographed and doubled for Tyrone Power, Errol
Flynn, Orson Welles, Basil Rathbone, Louis Hayward, Ronald
Coleman, and, most famously, Jose Ferrer in *Cyrano de Bergerac*.

Al Cavens became a kind of Cyrano to Ferrer's Cyrano. You
remember how, in the play, Cyrano has to speak the love poetry — in the shadows, out of sight — for Christian, who was
better-looking, but tongue-tied. So Al, and his father before him,
were the Cyranos, so to speak, behind all the great swordsmen
of the motion pictures.

I am always pleased when people see me do those very wicked,
dangerous stunts in the *Batman* reruns. And even now when kids
congratulate me for my wickedness and daring, I smile and accept
the compliment. But in my secret heart, I thank Al. He was the
one who took the risks and performed the impossible leaps. I just
appeared when it was time to quack!

Incidentally, that famous quack came by accident. I had given
up smoking years before, and whenever I put the lighted cigarette
in my mouth it would irritate my throat — so instead of spoiling
the scene by coughing, I would make a quacking noise. That
accidental solution proved memorable. When I pass kids on the
street they still "quack" me.

John Huston and
the Sea of Cortez

W HAT SHOULD HAVE HAPPENED — but never did —
was the appearance early on of a very literate friend, a
twentieth-century Boswell, who would have quietly
documented John Huston's daily doings. What he said, where he
went, whom he was with. A faithful recounting of his life, without
comment, without judgment, would have been the way to capture
John. The result would have been wondrous. Because he was an
astonishingly wondrous fellow.

I am amazed it never happened. John was tolerant of company.
Too tolerant, perhaps. People hung around him, one could say
fought for his company — he was seldom "unvisited." Also, John
was generous in his speech, in his observations. He had a worldful
of friends. But no one, at the remarkable end of each remarkable
day — for I swear, he lived through very few days that did not
have something remarkable happen in them — took pen and
paper and simply wrote down the way he was.

There have been biographies written, containing facts and figures — but they were necessarily written at a distance.

In 1985 I was on a sixty-foot boat with John, scouting the Sea of Cortez. I had, by chance, a tape recorder with me, and I would whisper notes to myself of how John and I could film a documentary of that mysterious inland sea.

After we'd been out a few days, John and I began to make plans of how to bring it about. At first I did not record much of John's voice, but as ideas developed I taped more and more of what he said.

I also wrote a proposal of how the film could be financed by the Sea World Corporation, which had provided the boat we were sailing on.

Finally, I began to record a few of John's firsthand memories of what had happened in his uproariously splendid life, to retain just a few of his long, hot memories. I'm happy I caught some of his observations of the past, present, and future — or what was left of the future.

We never made our documentary about the Sea of Cortez. But at the end of it all, I found I still had those tapes! Recently I listened to them again with John's children, Danny and Anjelica. They were fascinated to hear their father's voice again. Danny had been with us on the trip, and here are his memories.

It was March 10, 1985. I was twenty-four and my father would have been in his late seventies — and Burgess was only a little younger. I don't know exactly how old he is to this day. They were old pals.

Also, Burgess had known John Steinbeck, who wrote the book *The Log from the Sea of Cortez*, which was about this same special sea. So Dad and Burgess were "two old men and the sea." We were to be picked up at La Paz in Mexico. My father was in Puerto Vallarta and I flew in from London. Burgess was in Malibu; I met him there and drove to San Diego, and from there we took a private plane to meet Dad. There we met the captain of the boat, and a scientist, Steve Leatherwood, and another couple of ocean underwater-photography people. There was also a gorgeous girl along — almost like a mermaid, she was. Later when we got on the boat, she would slip away under the surface of the sea and we would hardly ever see her until we continued to the next stop of our voyage. And there were several other people along — a photographer, a cook, and helpers.

So we were in search of a theme for the documentary. We didn't know quite what we were going to do — we just knew that we wanted to do it! We followed Steinbeck's idea of scouting a theme as we went along — of getting our story from the elements around us — from what we saw and how we felt. The Sea of Cortez itself would dictate the theme.

Off and on we must have been at sea for about two weeks, which isn't a long span of time, but it can feel long when you're sleeping in crowded quarters and surrounded by noisy engines. I remember Burgess and I slept in the same cabin, and he used to call me his "womb mate."

The boat was a fair-sized yacht, maybe sixty feet, with two or three cabins below deck, a salon, galley, and a deck around it, so it was quite spacious. But there were too many of us and the engine noise was continuous; it rumbled and rattled with the waves. The generator on the boat had to remain on most of the time and it made a constant hum. The other noise was my poor father's continuous coughing, which was almost like an engine also; it had a sad sort of rhythm to it. You couldn't hear him when the engines were pounding — but when everything was silent, it was painful to listen to.

There was no "typical day" on this trip, but I remember the dolphins! A common event in the Sea of Cortez was like a miracle to the rest of us. At one point the whole horizon was filled with dolphins! I have never seen that many dolphins in my life — thousands and thousands of dolphins.

On other days, the mountains would turn a bright orange. And I swam with sea lions! They were quite friendly. And always Dad and Burgess and I would discuss our ideas of what this documentary was going to be about.

Our basic theme was that this sea, the Sea of Cortez, was a particular treasure in the world. It is as full of wonders as the Garden of Eden. The fish are so special and so plentiful that whales won't migrate away from this particular part of the world — they stay here, and there is a great cycle of events. That is a hint of the story we wanted to tell. The Sea of Cortez symbolized life and the earth and the universe and how they were interconnected.

One of Steinbeck's quotations from *The Log from the Sea of Cortez* said this: "Look from the stars to the tidepools and from the tidepools back to the stars again." The plankton in the sea are connected to the stars in the Milky Way. All the energy here on earth is connected with the distant energy of the universe. The connection of all things in the universe. That was the closest we ever came to a theme.

And Burgess and I had an encounter with a whale that was wonderful! We took this small dinghy out, because we wanted to get away from the noise of the boat. We brought a little microphone with us that we dropped into the water and recorded the sounds of the porpoises and whales and other noiese of the deep. The yacht sailed away and left the two of us alone in the middle of the sea.

And suddenly the head of a full-grown whale popped up right beside us, and looked at us! It was like being stared at by God. Each eye seemed the size of a basketball. With eyelashes! And she was a mother! We knew because as she came out of the water and started to arch forward, we saw that there was a little baby by her side. Then she dove back into the water and her tail made a great splash as she immersed herself in the depths of the ocean. We looked around desperately, wondering whether she would surface again and capsize us. She did reappear, but half a mile away. We waited for a while, but she did not come back. It was beautiful — a rare experience I shared with Burgess.

My father got sicker and sicker. He was preparing other feature films, I was going ahead with my career, and Burgess was hard at work on a play. Not that we all wouldn't have dropped what we were doing immediately if we had the opportunity to make this documentary, but the opportunity slipped away. The money didn't show up in time.

In a sense, it's too bad, and in another way it isn't. I mean, what's the point of the unreachable if you can reach it! And it was such a wonderful dream that we had, all of us together, and in some part of us, we still hold.

My dad and Meredith talked about everything! They talked about the war, they talked about their wives, of which they both had their share. They also talked about children, politics, and the Sea of Cortez. The sea, and the theme of the sea, laced into all these discussions. Burgess sometimes made tapes of what they said.

I remember one evening when the sun was going down and the land was turning flaming red and the blue had turned a strange purple color, and the contrast led my father and Burgess to talk about whorehouses and women wearing red dresses. And then for some reason, they talked a great deal about World War II.

There was one evening when we went to some port, Burgess and I, like sailors almost, and we got completely smashed. We really had a good drinking bout. We went to the village and ate tortillas and frijoles and drank tequila. And we were desperately hung over the next day. I remember Burgess saying, "Oh God, if you help me through this, I promise I'll never do it again!" We got into the boat, and Burgess pissed into the ocean, as one does. And he said, "Oh my God, I'm sorry! — all the fish swam away! We have poison in our bodies!"

There is a mystique about men like Dad and Burgess. That's why the quality of their work was always interesting . . . because they lived their stories. It wasn't art imitating art, or scripts imitating scripts or films imitating films. These men lived their stories.

For me the most frightening experience on the trip was my father's dying. I mean, it was a slow death, that we heard at night on the Sea of Cortez . . . his repeated coughing and gasping — the struggle to breathe. It was a sound that both Burgess and I would listen to. You couldn't avoid it. And then, sometimes, the coughing would subside and he would sleep a little. That would be during the day on the boat when everything was tranquil.

The trip affected my life — it certainly is a memory I want to hold — a precious memory. I was in my middle twenties — my "formative years." Above everything else, it was a very special time for me because I was able to spend these wonderful moments with my father, whom I loved and was full of awe and respect for. That was marvelous, and to have this buddy of his, Burgess, and now a buddy of mine, to share things with and laugh with. That made it very unique for me as a young man. . . . That and the sea, the Sea of Cortez.

I can't speak for him, but I'm sure it was also special for my father to spend that time with me and Burgess. I remember the look on his face when Burgess and I arrived there at the airport, near La Paz, to pick him up. And how happy he was to see us! He was wearing a wonderful white Mexican suit and he looked almost like some kind of a pirate, an adventurer, with all the lines on his face to prove it.

Here was my father, an old, ill, famous film director, and Burgess, with children, wives, and other responsibilities, both allowing themselves to leave all that behind and go to sea. Two mad, Irish pirates! They were rebels at heart. And I think that's the way they approached most of their lives.

What with tales of riding in the hunts with the Galway Blazers in Ireland or of the Second World War and their private lives — it was filled with color. And I think it was a very courageous act to go off to sea looking for a theme! Maybe *courageous* isn't the right word. Maybe it was a mystical quest, that came completely natural to them. They didn't need courage to make that kind of film. Two rogues.

This wasn't the last time they saw each other, because before my father came to Newport, Rhode Island, for my film *Mr. North*, he was staying at Burgess's house in Malibu. So they spent a lot of time together after that trip to the Sea of Cortez. It was a long friendship and went on until he died.

But Burgess is around — writing his autobiography. He said, "Remember the Sea of Cortez when we were looking for a theme? I'm trying to do the same thing with my lingering life!"

He needn't worry — it's all here in his book.

John Huston and Me

AS I'VE MENTIONED, John Huston and I recorded some of our conversations while we were in Mexico for preliminary work on the Sea of Cortez project, to have a record of any ideas, any concepts we came up with for the film. But many random thoughts surfaced in the process.

Old friends . . .

"What about Hemingway?" I asked. "Was he depressed?"

"He was just banged up. The depression came later. Much later."

"So it was a psychological breakdown of some kind?"

"Oh yes. He went off his head, no question about that. He thought the FBI was after him to collect back taxes. And, you know, nobody could have cared less about such things. The whole thing became . . ."

"You saw him during that last period?"

He thought for a moment before answering, "No. No, I didn't

see him. But I saw Mary [Hemingway's wife] three or four years ago. She used to stay with me in Ireland."

"By the way," I said, "I told Chartoff we were going to do this picture and he said: 'If I — ' "

"Who?"

"Bob Chartoff. The producer who did *Rocky* and *The Right Stuff* — a very charming man. He's a good friend and was fascinated by the Sea of Cortez idea. He said to let him know if we needed his help to get regular financing. I told him that we weren't going after a commercial story, but it didn't bother him. He told me that you never know."

Then my thoughts went to John Steinbeck and what he had told me just before writing his book on the Sea of Cortez. I remembered him saying, "Jesus, I'd better get down and write some fucking thing that makes sense." And then he came up with what many consider to be among the best of his work. Aloud, I said, "Steinbeck."

"What a lovely fellow Steinbeck was."

"Yes, he was," I answered, still remembering. "And very vulnerable. He lived in my house in Rockland County for several months after he ran away from his first wife and into the jaws of his second one."

Neither of us said anything for a while after that. Then, John broke the silence by asking, "Did you ever hear of Ray Scott?"

"No, I don't think so."

"Well, he got just about as bad as Hemingway. He was with me during the war in Italy. Had the courage of a lion. If it hadn't been for him, I don't think that either of the two combat films I did would have come off."

"You learned the hard way."

John seemed reluctant to leave the subject. "He'd been in China when the Japanese were there before World War II broke out. And after that, he was in a lot of other places before he came to Italy to be with me.

"After that, I caught up with Scott again when I came back to Astoria where Bill Saroyan, Gottfried Reinhardt, and all those other guys that had no business being in uniform were making these combat pictures. By then he was crazy as a fucking bedbug.

"They had made him a lieutenant once, while he was officer of the day — a job that involved patrolling various points around the place — and he decided to call some lieutenant colonel at home every hour to announce that all was well. Kept it up all through the night. Around morning, he began firing off his pistol and they had to overpower him."

Trying to square this conduct with my own army experience, I said, "So he really flipped."

"Oh no. He was just drunk. Drunk and contemptuous of his surroundings. But I got them to put him in the hospital to keep him from being court-martialed."

World War II . . .

"You were an officer, weren't you?" he asked me.

"Yeah, but first I went in as an enlisted man. It was while I was rooming with Jimmy Stewart."

"Now I remember. It was when you were both waiting to be called."

"I didn't become a lieutenant until they sent me to Intelligence School, and I was made lieutenant there. Ever hear how I made captain?"

"I don't think so."

"I was in London, standing in an elevator in the Claridge Hotel, when a four-star general — I think he was in charge of all the supplies in the European Theater — walked in with one of his aides. While we were both waiting to go up, he said to me, 'What are you doing as a lieutenant?'

"I answered, 'I'm attached to you, sir.' And, at that he told the aide, 'Make him a captain.'"

"Jesus!"

"Precisely. And there was another four-star general — he was on Eisenhower's staff — General Lee — who started me making films for the army. This also happened in London. He pulled me out of the ranks one day to ask, 'Captain Meredith, I hear you're in the movies.'

" 'Yes, sir.'

" 'Well, we want a film made to show our soldiers how to behave in England. We're guests here and I want you to do a training film about it for us. We'll get you all the facilities you need to get it done.'

"So I asked the next logical question. 'Is there any time on it?'

" 'The sooner the better. Will a month do?'

"That jolted me. 'Sir, may I have the evening to get my ideas together?'

" 'Of course. No hurry. But get started as soon as you can.'

"Next day, I told him I was sure I could do it on time, but, 'I wonder if you would help us?'

" 'How do you mean?'

" 'Would you open the film by telling me, on film, what you want me to do — just as you told me yesterday?'

"That puzzled him, so he repeated, 'What do you mean by that?'

" 'Well, would you just say on film that you want me to make a picture to show the boys how to behave. And to learn about this country. Could you say that much?'

"There wasn't much he could do about that. As he said, he couldn't ask me to do something unless he was willing to do it, too. Even so, he recruited a couple of other generals to be with him when he did his part of the film so it wasn't quite as intimate as I had wanted.

"And, so, we produced *Welcome to Britain,* which opens with these three generals saying to me, 'Meredith, go and make this picture. Get it done in two months!' I answer, 'Yes, sir,' and as they turned and walked away, I looked at the camera to say, 'I don't know why they picked me, I've only been here a week!'

"Since my approach, 'Let's discover this together,' seemed to work, I tried other things. Next I took the camera into a pub, saying, in effect, that pubs like these are all over England — 'so let's take a look inside.' After that, I did the same thing with visits into private homes — talking to the camera all the time.

"I did other things in that film, too. For example, I filmed an old lady asking a black soldier where he was from and when he answered, 'Birmingham,' she looked surprised and said, 'I'm from Birmingham, too! Won't you come over for tea?'

"Right at that point, I had the camera cut back to me where I observed, 'You know, they don't have a Negro problem over here.' And they didn't at that time. Our army was still segregated.

"I used that technique throughout. Almost every time I introduced another subject, I'd say something to the effect, 'I don't know what in the hell this place is, but let's find out.' And we'd go and find out. I got Bob Hope to explain the difference between the English pound and the dollar! His gag was he started to explain, pretended to get mixed up and said 'It can't be done — see you later.'

"The picture made a good impression on the English people as well as doing the job for the American G.I.s, so I was ordered to do another film to prepare us for the French.

"Since no one knew when the invasion of Europe would begin, I was given the highest priority for secrecy to make this film. So I went back to the States where, with Jean Renoir, Garson Kanin, and some French experts, we made a film that described what the French people could be expected to be like after their years of occupation.

"Of course, this was all supposed to be very secret, but I don't know how in hell they didn't expect the Germans to know that the only way to invade Germany was by going through France.

"It was a good picture and we were proud of it — but then it got caught up in the bureaucracy. Renoir never got over the way they took it away from us, cutting and recutting it until it was hard to recognize. In fact, it never even appeared until after the invasion had taken place."

Huston nodded his understanding of this. He said: "SNAFU and FUBAR."

"SNAFU I know, Situation Normal — All Fucked Up! But FUBAR?"

"Fucked Up Beyond All Recognition."

"Well," I told him, "not totally. You remember the actor Claude Dauphin?"

"Oh, sure."

"We used him in that film and he was furious — not because of the dirty Huns occupying his country, but because his wife was sleeping with a German general! Claude became famous in the French underground movement because in his first broadcast for them, he sent the German general a message: 'You dirty son of a bitch, I'm coming to get you! You better not leave the room with that cunt you are sleeping with because I'm going to find you and cut your balls off!'

"He was a fiery guy then. But fate made up to Claude for his marital anguish. Later when he came to America and married Antonia, happiness made him gentle.

"As a result of using Dauphin in our picture, *Salute to France*, it got a lot of attention in France even before it was released. Also, after the war, it was played everywhere, one version in English for our boys, and one in French."

Speaking of killing . . .

One day, while I was telling John of my interest in dolphins, he responded by recalling, "I saw an awful thing one time. It was while I was in Japan and they herded a whole school of porpoises into a little cove. . . . They used their boats to herd them. It was like herding cattle."

I remembered hearing about that killing. "I heard that the sea turned red."

"It happened and I actually saw them do it. It was a small cove, maybe just 100 to 150 feet across, and they closed its mouth with their boats and beat them to death with their clubs. You're right. The sea turned red with their blood."

"It still happens," I told him. "I know dolphins are intelligent, have a marvelous capacity to learn. They've even begun trying to solve the problem of the drift nets that get them — but I don't know if the dolphins ever learned to keep out of that bloody trap the Japanese set for them."

"I saw it," he said, "only because I was in Japan to do a training film. But it reminded me of another documentary I'd seen about capturing elephants in India and Burma. First they build a very strong paddock and then they get the elephants started . . .''

"My God. They stampeded them?"

He went on as if he hadn't heard me. ". . . after they get them into this trap, they bar the end. But the thing is, the first one to go in is really a Judas. The other elephants follow him in and when they realize they've been trapped, they turn on this Judas and kill him."

"In their panic?"

"No, not in panic. It's an execution. They all come around to take a crack at him. And when he's down, even the little ones — the babies — come over and stand on him. He betrayed the herd. He was the one who led them into this trap."

"It sounds like when they hung Mussolini by his heels," I told him.

Politics and such

One afternoon, I noted, "You can spot a man with real knowledge right away. Whenever he talks, whatever he says, it's precise. I wish I could say the same about some of the secretaries I've had. I'm so dependent on mine that whenever one fouls up, my whole life becomes fouled up."

"Mine, too," he agreed comfortably.

I thought about it some more. "Sometimes I think that the last really good secretary was Nixon's. Rosemary something-or-other. It's amazing how she stood up."

"Nixon probably had her put down after erasing his tapes."

We both solemnly considered this extraordinary display of loyalty until I admitted, "I often wonder why we're astonished each time by a display of iniquity in high places."

Another pause before he observed, "Oh, God, I loathe that son of a bitch — Nixon." He considered the matter further before going on. "And I don't have a very high opinion of Ronnie, if the truth be known."

"You think he's dumb?"

"He might be in some ways but he certainly knows how to

handle himself. He's clever as hell in that way. Clever as hell."

I thought back. "The first time I met him was at your house. That was way back. Then Colonel Warner — or did they make Jack Warner a general during the war? — put Ronnie and me together in some movie about a tailgunner. We were both in uniform — privates."

"I go back with him, too," he said. "I still get calls from Nancy, but she never mentions Ronnie. Her father and mother were great friends of my father, so I inherited them. Even now, every so often I run over to Phoenix to see Nancy's mother, Edith."

His words brought back some other memories for me. "Did you ever see them during their interregnum — after he went off the governorship and lost his first bid for the presidency? He didn't have any backing at all then. I remember Merle Oberon telling me that no one else was seeing him so it was up to her and her husband to see poor Ronnie. Of course, that was a long time ago — when he had that little television series. Nobody thought he'd be president."

"When I knew Ronnie," John said, "he was a very strong Roosevelt man. I mean quite liberal. Capital 'L.' So I saw it all happen — his change." He thought for a moment before adding, almost to himself, "Strange. Once, right after one of the columns reported that I'd had a few people for dinner at Chasen's, I got a call from Nancy's mother, Edith, saying that Nancy had called her in tears because I had given a party and not invited them and please do invite Nancy and Ronnie next time."

"Then what?"

"After that, I made a point of seeing them, but Ronnie certainly always bored the hell out of me. I thought he was a pain in the ass."

The yearning for peace and quiet

"John," I said, "it's not like you're a stranger here. You have really known Mexico. You like quietness — although I don't think that Ireland was exactly quiet."

"It was in its way."

"But your present place seems to be really relaxing. No phones, nothing but meditation and peace, which are about the last things you get in our business."

He thought for a moment. "When I'm doing a film, I like to seclude myself at the end of a day. I can stand only just so much social give and take."

"Me too. It struck me this morning how much I like peace and quiet and how little I get of it. And then I thought, *Jesus, I'd better hurry and do something because one day I'm going to be quiet for a long, long time!* Then another thought hit me. Of course, ever since you went to Puerto Vallarta, it became fashionable — didn't it?"

"Sure. Since *Night of the Iguana.*"

"You made it happen."

"What I did was fuck that place up. Now, just let me get my hands on the Sea of Cortez."

"I remember Tony Veiller, the screenwriter, saying that 'Since Huston discovered Puerto Vallarta, I made up my mind to buy some property there.' Poor Tony. Didn't live long enough."

John smiled. "Well, there was this piece of land near there that was owned by some local Mexican architect. He came to me, saying, 'You're going to make this picture in Mexico, so why not make it in Puerto Vallarta? I've got this little bit of land, this peninsula near there. And, John, I've got a great deal for you. You want everybody in the company living together so what I'll do is build all the places for them to stay. You can have it afterwards.' "

It didn't sound right. "You mean he was going to give the place to you?"

"Not exactly. He was going to make a stock company out of it, and if I could persuade MGM to build a dock and permanent sets, we'd have a whole little colony there afterwards. Then I'd get some stock. The whole thing certainly appealed to my sense of chicanery. But then he went on to tell me how this piece of land was going to take care of us for the rest of our lives. Later I found out that he had no rights whatsoever in the land. He was just a con man. But it was a breezy conversation."

"Burton was in that picture, wasn't he?"

"Oh, yes. He hadn't married Elizabeth then and we had Ava who, at the same time, had the writer Peter Viertel, who was married to Deborah Kerr, who was also in the picture. And Ava Gardner was feeling freewheeling and, oh yes, there was another little girl in it who played a featured role and she had her boyfriend with her. I forget her name. We had all those volatile personalities so, before the picture started, I gave them all gold-plated derringers — the kind of little pistols that the card sharps used to wear up their sleeves. Then I also gave each one five bullets with the names of the other members of the cast on them.

"I don't think there was ever a picture that was so covered by the press. They came in droves. Every boatload brought in another contingent, all of them expecting at least one murder. But I don't think that there was ever another picture that was so tranquil. Serenity was the order of the day. Everything went smooth as silk and those poor bastard reporters never had anything to write about from Puerto Vallarta except the scenery."

I said, "That's a wonderful story but you didn't even have a buck to buy your own house. You could have been a king."

He shook his head sadly. "In my whole life I've never made an investment worth a damn."

"Me too," I agreed. "If the Russians really wanted to destroy this country, they'd give me money to invest. Because then the U.S. stock exchange would crash."

"I never bought any stock."

"I did once, and it's still going down. I even bought stock in the '21' Club, the most successful restaurant in history. Nothing happened. None of us ever made a penny on it. It was only five or ten thousand, but I finally sold it for fifteen hundred."

We looked at each other, silently commiserating.

She was a Great Dame

He mentioned the elderly lady who rode her horse sidesaddle over all those huge fences surrounding her beautiful estate.

"Lady Hemphill."

"Yes. She hardly ever fell off, did she?"

"Very rarely. Just once she was dragged by a horse," he said.

"Jesus! Caught in the stirrups?"

"Yeah."

I reminded him, "Then there is Maricella. She's been important to you."

"Oh yes, very."

"She was Cici's maid, wasn't she?"

At this mention of his ex-wife, he said, "Maricella was the only good thing that came out of that relationship. . . ."

"Well, then maybe it was worth it."

"Yeah, it was worth it. It really was."

"But, my God, Cici was certainly a high price for it. I always felt that she was a shock to you. I remember once, in Ireland, you told me that you were ashamed of yourself. You couldn't believe that you had married Cici."

"I really couldn't. I stood back, aghast."

"But you weathered it, although it must have been devastating. In one of Steinbeck's books, *East of Eden*, he wrote that he never met a person who was entirely evil. Did he meet your ex-wife?"

"Hmm."

To change the subject, I said, "I guess I told you that Paulette called me for the first time in four hundred years or so. She said that her mother — who has to be ninety-five — had asked for me and wouldn't I come up and have dinner. I said that I would as soon as I was finished with shooting that Robert Frost film.

"Because I knew her mother was always fond of me, I really meant to go. But somehow, I never did. And I felt guilty. Why should I have felt guilty about it? Paulette would never have come back to me for any reason, and since I'd been away from her for twenty-five or thirty years, I didn't want to see her again. I couldn't face it. Very traumatic."

He knew what I was feeling and, I guess, to ease it, he said, "I was in the Waldorf Astoria a few years ago and she came up to me. Looked wonderful."

"Funny and fast."

"Yes and, oh yes, delightful. What was the name of that girl that played tennis?"

"Falkenberg. Jinx Falkenberg."

We remembered other girls and other times for the rest of that afternoon.

The Sea

I taped this observation while visiting the Sea of Cortez alone:

"When I contemplated coming here, I wanted to be sure I was rested and in full health. Now as I sit rolling in the gentle seas in this cove, instead of a place to prepare yourself, the Sea of Cortez becomes a place that prepares you. It's a place to get ready in.

"This is a lovely day and there are only a few people around. The sea couldn't be gentler. But then, in no time at all it will challenge us with storms. But, for this moment, the Sea of Cortez makes me healthy and happy."

Later, when we were down there together, John, in some oblique way, brought back this thought by observing, "Cactus plants contain more water than any other vegetable in the grove. You can plug into them and get a drink. All these things working — these apparent opposites — are in fact one manifestation of one principle."

"I don't know how that fits in with a statement you once made about your ex-wife Cici — 'She has all the charm of a cactus plant.' "

John laughed, and I returned to his theme by saying, "This connection with the universe needn't be heavy-handed, but it's a reappearing truth that seems to overwhelm scientists. We know that one star depends upon another and one galaxy on other galaxies. It raises hell with the Catholic Church, but we're connected with a lot of other places beside this planet Earth. That needn't be more than whispered."

He nodded. "It should only be whispered."

"But a great whisper."

"Oh yes, it should be behind everything. It should be the thing that scarcely requires a statement. Just the stars should be the audience in the making of that statement."

I answered, "Steinbeck was right on track about that in *The Sea of Cortez*."

Oh yes, The Picture

Huston said, "A documentary about the Sea of Cortez begins to sound very, very good."

"It's the appeal of Steinbeck's book," I answered.

"But you can't do Steinbeck's book, even if we wanted to. Our idea is better."

"Well," I told him, "we have a few more days to think about it as we go along."

Now the subject had his total interest. "I don't think we can assign a regular length to our picture. It has to determine its own length and you'll never be able to write a script for it. You have to go out and get the material and then rework it, like making a drawing.

"The approach is to start listing the things to be seen and the seasons when those things are available. It's a whole procedure how to go about making it — because different things occur at different times of the year . . . it's a long-distance endeavor."

He studied my face before adding, "You know what feels wonderful to me about this? Burgess, I've been listening to you for the past few days and you express your concepts just as if they were being lucidly written. Many people will never have the luck to discover these concepts for themselves, they're only going to read them and never mention them in their dealings with friends. But in this kind of a visual medium, you'll out-Faulkner Faulkner in letting the reader take time out for a while."

"This is a picture that has to be done with awe," I said.

"But not solemnly."

"Not solemnly and not with a sense of discovery, but with a kind of wonder."

"With delight. You don't have to hypothesize. You don't have to bring God into it or any of those things. It's a statement of what's going on in this moment in our lives."

I shrugged. "Let them draw their own conclusions. There's a remarkable book by Dr. Lewis Thomas called *The Lives of a Cell*. God, but it's great! He was the one who said, when they were wondering what message we could send out to read in other planets, 'I can't think of anything to send out there but the music of Bach.' "

Huston roared at this. "Bach could damn well do the score for this picture, too!"

My Schema for a Film
on the Sea of Cortez

A TWO-WEEK trip has been designed for two purposes: one main and one secondary.

The main purpose is to find a theme (a point of view) for a film about the Sea of Cortez. This theme would be expressed in a shooting script to be written and photographed at a later time.

The secondary purpose of the trip is to photograph a modest amount of still and motion pictures to be used as visual references when writing the final "shooting script" and to describe locations.

Note: In searching for a theme, an effort must be made to depart from the "Cousteau Approach," which is excellent in itself but bears Cousteau's imprint to such an extent there can be no great reward in imitating it.

Note: The purpose of the "Thema" is to unify our observations so that all pictures we take of the Sea of Cortez and everything we say about those pictures are related.

In other terms, each individual picture must be a necessary part of the total picture like brush strokes on a canvas or like notes of music in a symphony; where all notes and all series of notes are a requisite part of the final structure.

First Theme Proposed

"The Sea of Cortez is an exquisite cell in the body of planet earth."

This emergent theme resembles the concept expressed by the scientist-author Dr. Lewis Thomas in his great book *Lives of a Cell*. There he said that the planet Earth resembles nothing so much as a cell in the body of our galaxy and indeed is comparable to a cell in the human body. He also said we can see this similarity vividly if we look at the recent satellite pictures of Earth taken from space. From that distance our planet looks "uncannily like microscopic views of human cells."

This theory of the oneness of everything, the interdependence of all things everywhere, is not new but it seems to have been given fresh credence by the scientific community.

Scientists have come to believe we are more closely integrated with the universe than we ever before imagined. "We need the stars and the stars need us" is what it amounts to.

Thus, a similar view could be taken of the Sea of Cortez floating in the body of the planet Earth, integral to and inseparable from the other parts of a larger cell called the planet Earth.

This gives us a "Thema" which could perhaps unify our observations. It also suggests the use of satellite pictures from time to time, to show the Sea of Cortez in proper perspective to the North and South hemispheres, as well as its relationship to the Pacific, the Atlantic, the world — like Shakespeare's view of England "set like a jewel in the sea."

This notion is as compatible to humor as it is to wonder. It enlarges our purpose and shapes our technique.

Technically, it imposes problems . . . none of them insurmountable, but different from those which have been dealt with previously in photographing this section of the world.

Specifically, it would require air photography from time to time; and, as we said before, the occasional use of satellite pictures.

However, more important than anything else, it would necessitate the frequent use of a helicopter camera. A helicopter is the key to this approach. The reason is as follows: Just as the first pictures from the moon put the Earth in new and proper perspective (we suddenly saw ourselves floating like a small fragile cell in an immense universe), we now need to show the Sea of Cortez from a similar vantage point.

Speculation

As an example, suppose that just before we film Lauren (a well-known and beautiful deep-sea diver) riding on the back of a manta ray, we should first look down on the sea from a star; then we zoom in at a breathtaking rate to below the waves, and finally, at close-up range, photograph that extraordinary collaboration of devil fish and beautiful woman riding together in the dark shadows under the sunlit Sea of Cortez.

All part of the same universe. All related. Connected now and forever, in a timeless relationship.

The Death of Cells

Cells die and are replaced by new ones. Thus we survive. If not on one planet, then on another. If not in one galaxy, then in another. If not in this millennium, then in another. The premise is that somehow, a million light years away, LIFE WILL STILL PERSIST AND SO WILL WE.

In following this theme it is good to consider two quotations from John Steinbeck from his book *The Sea of Cortez*.

"Jesus, St. Augustine, St. Francis, Roger Bacon, Charles Darwin, Einstein . . . each in his own tempo and with his own voice discovered and reaffirmed WITH ASTONISHMENT that all things are one thing and that one thing is all things . . . plankton, a shimmering phosphorescence on the sea and the spinning planets and an expanding universe, all bound together by the elastic string of time. It is advisable to look from the tidepool to the stars and then back to the tidepool again."

Less awesomely, but with equal insight, Steinbeck also wrote: "There would seem to be only one commandment for living things: Survive! And the forms and species and units and groups are armed for survival, fanged for survival, timid for it, fierce for it, clever for it, poisonous for it, intelligent for it. This commandment decrees the death and destruction of myriads of individuals for the survival of the whole. . . . Life has one final end, to be alive; and all the tricks and mechanisms, all the successes and all the failures, are armed to that end."

Thus, we photograph the Sea of Cortez to demonstrate the twin hypotheses of the oneness of all things and the struggle for survival of all things.

A theme like this will attract writers and composers and photographers of the highest order to collaborate with us in making this film.

To all of the above projections must be added the element of TIME. John Huston has proposed that in the final film ALL EVENTS SHOULD BE HAPPENING AT THE SAME TIME. To explain this, it is easier to take a famous example:

"Where were you the hour the astronauts landed on the moon?" And we, in our film, could say: "Where was everything and everybody on the Sea of Cortez at any given moment at any future hour that we may choose?" This dimension of Time could be used dramatically to give the film form and tension.

As a parallel dimension, we could commit ourselves to the rule that ALL EVENTS in the picture should extend no longer than the length of the film.

Note: These dramatic devices have been more frequently used in the legitimate theater than in motion pictures, but in this film, they would be of high importance, not overstated but a requisite ingredient.

This obviously requires careful preparation so that each separate scene would fit within the overall time requirement.

In short, everything shown in the picture should be happening either instantaneously or concurrently.

Note: The second of these time entities (concurrently) is more commonly employed. The first (instantaneously), as far as we know, has not been attempted on film.

Alas, nothing came of this idea; and worse, John died. But if I believe in the theme of our unmade movie — and I do — somehow and somewhere in the interconnectedness of the universe our ideas for this film serve some unknown purpose.

Workshops

I N THEATER and film workshops, which I enjoy attending, students ask questions and I do my best to answer them. Most of the sessions are taped — so I put a few of them together.

Did you find that working on Rocky *was any different from working on all the other films you've done?*

Well, in show business everything is different from everything else and making comparisons isn't always helpful. I have many memories of *Rocky* — especially the training scenes. We shot them in an old Philadelphia gymnasium. It was cold and cruel and grubby, closely related to the theme of the *Rocky* films . . . which was: A poor guy wants a little touch of glory in his miserable life before he dies. He struggles for it and he gets it the hard way — against all odds. It was the old Horatio Alger theme and it worked for all the *Rocky* films, but by *Rocky V* it had lost some momentum.

Sly Stallone is made of the same rough, consequential stuff that motivated Rocky — he fights to the finish. On the first film, I sensed he was talented — that he had a kind of Marlon Brando flourish — but I had no conception the *Rocky* films would be as explosive as they were.

Can you tell us about the actual people in Rocky?

I liked the fighters we used for extras — I spent hours talking with them. Particularly the old ones like the one I played. The fight game had passed them by, so they rented a crummy gym and tried to run it. The time for them to hit it big was over before they were twenty-five. The odds are pitiful, the glory is brief — unless you are Muhammad Ali, who lasted a little longer than most. I was also fascinated by the younger fighters, minority kids mostly, from poor families. You don't get many rich youngsters to go through that grim, painful struggle.

I think the film caught the theme very well. Stallone isn't a close friend of mine, but I like him. He has a way of speaking that is terse and pointed. He always seems happy, but probably he is not — no one is. After *Rocky*, he stumbled a bit, but then he made a fortune.

Stallone's lingo reminds me of *Cannery Row* dialogue — Steinbeck loved those guys, the rough ones, and Stallone likes them too. His heart is with those characters, but personally his head is clear and his mind is sophisticated. Off camera his humor is sharp and he is a good oil painter in the modern school. In life he handles himself well, except in the realm of women. There he acts like the rest of us.

Finally, I think *Rocky* reached out and drew a new audience into films — it brought back the "identification factor," which films had somehow lost track of. *Rocky* fans said: "Hey, I'm with you, Rocky. I bet on you. I am like you. I want it to happen!" — that kind of thing. It worked.

Do you think the film was old-fashioned in that respect?

Well, does "old-fashioned" mean passé? Meaningless? I don't know. Probably the first stories were told at night, sitting around a fire. Whether the plot is old or new is not always the important factor. There's room for all kinds of plots, new and old: but there's no room for confusion. The motivations have to be clear to the listeners, the viewers, the audiences.

For instance, *Day of the Locust,* a film I was in years ago, was beautifully acted and mounted . . . but nobody went to see it. It was a box-office failure. Why? Because the audience did not, or could not, identify with the problems — it was that simple. *Day of the Locust* allowed nobody to enter the frame, and the audience were told they were animals.

I am a fan of the director, John Schlesinger, but *Locust* was puzzling. It certainly didn't do me any harm — I was nominated for an Oscar — but the public stayed away in large numbers because the story they saw on the screen said that people in general are stupid! The audience didn't feel like paying money to see themselves insulted. Like Virgil's comment, *"Odio vulgus et archeo"* ("I hate the vulgar crowd and hold them afar"), the picture had disdainful elements in it. . . . It bit the hand that fed it.

Nobody is going to stop making movies about psychotics and neurotics and odd people; but you can't insult an audience and expect them to enjoy it. It may parallel the way we are developing as a civilization, but once in a while we like to see the underdog get a piece of the action . . . and win, against the odds. That sounds simplistic, but it is the heart of the problem. The secret weapon of *Rocky* was the underdog factor.

The picture that won the Oscar in 1991 was about wolves and Indians and morality — all underdogs. Full circle. *Dances with Wolves* went back to basics . . . and the cycle will continue.

Good films, like the classic dramas, have a pivotal change. At a certain point the hero discovers his weakness, and either goes to his death or to a dramatic change or renaissance — something is different at the end from what it was at the beginning.

We used to say, "The most important thing about playwriting or screenwriting is that something or somebody has to change." But you rarely say that now — hardly anybody changes. A few years ago in *Taxi Driver,* no one changed, and it worked. In *Day of the Locust* — no one changed and it did not work.

On the other hand, I remember when I was directing *Under*

Milk Wood years ago at the Frank Lloyd Wright Theater in Dallas, someone asked that same question: "What is the secret of play-writing?" I said, "Something has to change at the end." Then I added, "Having said that, I'm about to direct a beautiful play called *Under Milk Wood* in which nothing and nobody changes — but something is revealed! An important statement is made." So there are no sacred rules.

If Rocky *was a complete film, what is gained by making* Rocky II, III, *and so on?*

Well, monetary gains ain't such a bad reward. Sometimes sequels work, and sometimes not. Something certainly was gained in *Godfather II*. There they achieved one hit and then got a bigger one the second time around. And now *Godfather III*. They are all good.

To begin as an actor you must have some kind of dream for yourself, some kind of an ideal or something you're striving for. You've been in the public's eye for a long time — what do you want now?

Well, I always have an ear cocked for the clarion call, an eye for the next role. I'm a journeyman. I'm a worker and I like to keep working. As best and as long as I am physically able.

But my life has never been entirely theater. I have other interests. It's a way of keeping sane. I can't be — or don't like to be — involved in the theater alone. It's a narrow world and you fade unless you add other things to your life.

For example, for years I was involved with Dr. John Lilly, an expert on whales and dolphins. John wrote learnedly about inter-species communication with these great-brained creatures who are being slaughtered out of existence. He and I founded the Human Dolphin Foundation with the purpose not only of saving dolphins, but of trying to establish some sort of communication with them! Lilly believed whales knew a hell of a lot more than we did about some essential matters.

I was, and still am, fascinated by such a project, such a theory. I am fascinated by the psychonauts of this world and their investigation of inner space. If you call it a far-out notion, you would be right. I believe it is edifying for an actor — or anyone else — to have other interests. It keeps your balance; it is numbing to be dependent on single subjects, single goals. In films, if you are left on the cutting room floor, or if critics kill a play you worked hard to bring in, you can say what I wrote in a poem:

> Ushers! Ushers! Bring a mop
> Wash her away drop by drop.
> Hope this won't be an estrangement
> And you'll ask me back for a longer engagement.

We need alternatives. That's how the theory of evolution works, and so do we.

What role did you like best in television?

The best part I ever had in television was as Joe Welch in *Tail Gunner Joe*. It was close to my favorite role — I don't need anything better than that in any medium. When I played Welch I was getting a splendid revenge; I had been placed on the "Red Channel" list by the McCarthy gang and this was a fine response.

Tail Gunner Joe was shown on TV not too long ago, on some obscure channel; and next day when I walked along the street in New York, various people stopped me to comment on it. I have seldom been happier than I was on that television show; and I was glad it "went well" as we say. To prepare to play him, I looked at his newsreels endless times and listened to his voice. I was fascinated by the man, and I was proud it came out well, and I was handed an Emmy.

How do you research a particular role? Was your role in Rocky *written that way, or did you go in and change it somewhat?*

Well, the role in *Rocky* was good enough so I had only to fill it out. Originally Mickey wasn't an ex-fighter, but with Stallone's permission we changed it and the change worked. My first lead part on Broadway had been in a play called *Little Ol' Boy*. In it I played a fighter who failed. I was nineteen. . . . So decades later I play an old fighter who had failed. Full cycle.

Some roles need research but others are apparent. I found a

fellow whose larynx had been broken and who worked in a creepy-looking gym. He had a voice like a frog. I couldn't imitate him, but it gave me an idea. I bought one of those instruments people use to talk after throat surgery for cancer. I tried it, but I couldn't "variate" my voice — I sounded like a one-note kazoo — so I finally forced my own voice into a growl at the back of my throat. It hurt my throat but it worked. More important, an actor's job is to find motives for the roles he or she plays. It's like the classic question, "How can I play a murderer if I've never committed a murder?" But have you killed a fly, or a chicken — killed anything? Or shot an animal? . . . Have you wanted to kill somebody? Or thought about it — in the back of your mind? John Barrymore said he easily found a touch of himself in villains — saints eluded him.

Generally not enough preparation is done for motion-picture roles; yet you need as much preparation for film roles as you do for the stage. Rehearsal is almost nonexistent on a film set. You do most of your rehearsing in your dressing room; they are always changing or lighting the set, and they often change lines a few minutes before shooting. At first I was guilty of not preparing in pictures, but I became wiser and more appreciative as the years went by. When September comes you work longer and you work harder and you grow less sure of yourself, not the other way around.

What was your most important acting experience?

It was when I learned to become the character. Not act him. Be him. It is an intricate procedure and as hard to explain as it is to accomplish. You cannot "forget" the audience; and that remains the problem to this day. You try to disregard the actual surroundings and imagine others. You deal only with the person or persons you are acting with — the key word is *relate*. And define your intentions — Why are you there? What do you want? What is your purpose? These are the major problems. That is what *relate* means — your effect on the other actors and their effect upon you.

In absolute contrast were Charles Laughton's famous "book

readings." He used quite a different technique. He talked directly to the audience . . . the "vaudevillian technique" he called it. "It's not acting," he said, "any more than I am acting now, talking to you. What I'm doing in those readings is talking to the audience, not to another actor. That's another ball game entirely."

Of course Charles was oversimplifying the problem; but, in principle, when you act a play you relate only with the persons on stage. At a party with loud music and conversation around you, you speak only to the person you like — or love or have interest in — the others are inconsequential. That is what you try to arrive at on stage.

There is an observer within the actor. I mean by that that an actor has an observer in his head. It is the famous theory of the observer observing the observed and so on. Am I clear? Of course not.

A case in point is how I came to give up smoking many years ago. There had been a big party at my house in the country back East and now I was alone. The main room had a large fireplace. I had been drinking and after everybody left I couldn't find a cigarette . . . and I found myself crawling into the fireplace looking for a butt. I remember finding a good one, and straightening it out — it had lipstick on it — and putting it in my mouth. At that moment the observer took over — the actor's observer — and the observer said, "Meredith, you are a mess. You are an unholy wreck. You are lost. . . . Here you are lighting that stinking secondhand butt and you're drunk. Take a look at yourself — you won't like what you see."

I did look, and the effect was revolting. I had become some kind of dope fiend. That moment shocked me, and still does as I recall it forty years later. From then on, until this day, I have never wanted to put a cigarette in my mouth. That "private moment" changed me, made me aware.

When you were getting started as an actor, what was the hardest obstacle?

Looking for jobs. More often than not, it is humiliating — and it is still a bad memory.

But I remember my first meeting with Eva Le Gallienne. I had been doing all kinds of jobs. She said, "You know, you don't get paid here. It's just an apprentice group." I said, "That's all right. I want to do it." I studied with her as an apprentice for two years, and entered her regular paid company for another year. After that things began to happen. Looking back, it is hard to believe how swift the change was: Maxwell Anderson wrote plays for me when I was just past twenty-one . . . playing opposite Katharine Cornell . . . five Broadway hits in a row. I never appreciated it as deeply as I do now, looking back. I will have nightmares in this life and the life to come about my early insecurities . . . but I will have smiles when I remember Eva Le Gallienne.

Is it possible to get copies of the poem you read?

Why, yes, lady! Step right up here. We're going to give you this little poem along with this little bottle and when you read this poem and drink from this bottle you'll be on top. Seriously, yes, I am happy to give you a copy and thank you for asking. Absolutely free of charge, because you're a good audience.

The poem is "The Mystic from Brooklyn" and I wrote it.

> *Stanislavsky wrote a book*
> *And I look . . . and look . . . and look.*

There is a story which a mystic from Booklyn
Told me. It has to do primarily with
The thought that possibly actors took their
Place alongside of the accepted re-creative
Artists when a certain performer (whose name
I didn't learn, but he lived fifty years
Ago — or if he didn't, listen to the story —)
Began a soliloquy and instead
Of thrusting a recitative chin out towards
The pit he retired to the center stage
Where he had rigged a kind of refectory table.
It was a speech from Shakespeare, but which play
I'm not sure. Anyway . . .

He began in a low and contemplative
Voice quite unlike anything the audience
Had heard before. His body was relaxed
And motionless; his eyes fixed
And hardly seeing; yet as the words
Came to his lips they carried a vitality
Which was thrilling to listen to. . . .
                              The audience
Became witness to the phenomenon
Of a character speaking ideas not words
And speaking them in the white heat of creation —
That is, form and content, logic and inspiration —
As though the thoughts were being written
For the first time on this earth.

Now it is for a very few
To experience the surging emotion
When there emerges from the mind a motif,
A line conception, or a stroke on a canvas
That will speak to men of all times;
Yet somehow on that night fifty years ago
A thousand unblinking eyes
A thousand singing ears
And a thousand clenched hands
Were so privileged, as when Shakespeare wrote.

Bearing them along in his imagination
And feeling a desperate need of further relaxation,
The actor felt outwards with his hand —
      still speaking —
Until he touched the table, and this somehow
Gave him strength to pursue his increasing
Task. The miracle continued, the dead experience
Was brightly fused. Then just before the end
He could no longer think to sustain his weight
So he sat on the table's edge — no one noticed
The movement though they saw him sit.
                                    They were
Ascending back through the spiraled centuries
Back through the crumbled tombs, the old habits,
Until together with him they discovered the tears

Of a forgotten sorrow. . . .
He held this grief to view for a moment
After the finished word
And then allowed it
To slip away.

This is the story's end — and the mystic's gone!
He's returned to Brooklyn, and I forgot
To have the parallel explained — the deeper
Symbols analyzed to teach us how
The trick was done!
There are cries from shadows in dressing rooms
And questions flashing from the speechless presses
(I.e. actors and critics shouting again)
"How was the line conceived, the brush drawn —?"
(*How*, you understand, not what nor when)
I never learned,
But recommend
That we
Pursue a star to where the subways end
And find the man who moves in a mystic mood
Beseeching him to scrutinize the moon
And coax along the beams what finally seems
A lunar explanation of creation —
A spell-imposing exposé of Art,
And then depart.

By the time we're much too old for laughter
By the time the subways cease to run
To take us home, we'll learn what Acting's after. . . .
But have no words to tell how it is done.

*I'd like to know how you approached your role as the Penguin
in* Batman. *I thought it was a great character.*

Ah yes, the villainous Penguin. It pursues me. It was a deliberately
overblown approach. It may have done me more harm than good,
but it made an impact. I thought it had a Dickensian quality —
or a spoof of one. It was fun to act. I was only one of many
villains, as you know. I had an elaborate makeup — a huge nose
and a great, extended stomach. It was as complete a disguise as

you could get — but people recognized me in it. The interesting thing about the Penguin was that I made only a few episodes, maybe nine or ten. And one feature film.

It's amazing how many people equate me with that one brief role. I still receive hundreds of requests for pictures. The recent feature picture *Batman* ignited reruns of the series. It never stops. Recently a newspaper qualified me as "best known as the Penguin." It's really an idiot's corner to get yourself into.

Why did you take the part in the first place?

Well, everybody was taking parts in *Batman* — from Frank Sinatra to Otto Preminger, everyone. It was the trendy thing to do back then. The Penguin stuck to me because the character was vivid. There were probably twenty-five "lead villains": the Joker, the Cat Woman, and so on.

When Eva Le Gallienne was presented with an award and I was one of the speakers, I told her the first part she had given me was that of the Duck in *Alice in Wonderland,* in which I had to strap roller skates on my knees, and I said I wanted to thank her because "it defined my career: I went from a Duck to a Penguin."

Soliloquies have always mystified me — do you have anything to say about those?

Soliloquies are a challenge. They work absolutely for an audience, but they pose problems for the actor. Who is the actor talking to? Only crazy people talk to themselves at such length. (All of us mutter occasionally.) Just last week I was rehearsing some lines to myself in a New York taxi and the driver said, "What? What's that?" I said, "I was just talking to myself," and he said, "Well, as long as you don't answer yourself you're all right." You try to find what I call "consciousness without an object." You let the audience overhear.

You need an audience, even if you're talking to yourself. Somewhere along the line comes this question: How do you say a speech like this out loud? "Oh, God, God, how weary, stale, flat and unprofitable seem to me all the uses of this world." That is about as pessimistic as you can get — so how do you convey such misery? What is the key?

I thought Nicol Williamson was a successful actor in soliloquies. I don't know why precisely, but he evidently relished talking to himself.

Laughton and I worked out a theory along these lines:

A soliloquy is a dialogue made to yourself when you are alone. The audience overhears it — but the speaker pretends they do not. Shakespeare may have had something else in mind:

> Is it not monstrous that this player here,
> But in a fiction, in a dream of passion,
> Could force his soul so to his own conceit
> That from her working all his visage wan'd;
> Tears in his eyes, distraction in's aspect,
> A broken voice, and his whole function suiting
> With forms to his conceit? And all for nothing!
> For Hecuba!
> What's Hecuba to him, or he to Hecuba,
> That he should weep for her? What would he do,
> Had he the motive and the cue for passion
> That I have? He would drown the stage with tears,
> And cleave the general ear with horrid speech;
> Make mad the guilty, and appal the free;
> Confound the ignorant, and amaze indeed
> The very faculties of eyes and ears.
> Yet I,
> A dull and muddy-mettled rascal, peak,
> Like John-a-dreams, unpregnant of my cause,
> And can say nothing; no, not for a king,
> Upon whose property and most dear life
> A damn'd defeat was made.
> — *Hamlet* (Act II, scene ii)

Hamlet was not talking to an audience as I am talking to you; he was thinking out loud — thinking private thoughts. That's the only hint I can give and when it works, it works well. You yourself may experience it once in a while in life when you are alone and your emotions are running high. You will speak out loud — to no audience except yourself.

Let's say you finally get a theater job but you're already working fifteen hours a day five days a week; how do you escape from it?

That's a problem. The first year or so when I studied with Eva, I waited on tables and so on. You have to make yourself a living. And keep in mind there are people worse off than yourself. Let me tell you a fable-like story.

A picture I did was called *The Sentinel.* I don't remember whether it played to much success, but I mention it because it concerned freaks — people born severely misshapen. I worked every day with these people and they taught me an unforgettable lesson — a lesson in gratitude. They were wonderful folks and delighted to be in a film. I hope they weren't disappointed in the result, because they were very touching and sensitive — all of them. We worked closely during those weeks, and I was reminded that there are problems in this world more complicated than my own.

If you have an emotional scene to do and the temptation is to really act the hell out of it, to be visibly shaken or to cry, even, do you have a better chance of making the audience cry if you don't?

That's a complex question, to know at what point you hold back. It's a question of taste, really. If an actor gets too convulsed, the audience watches him or her clinically, and loses emotional involvement. Certain actors emote their way through a big scene and you find yourself saying, "Look how good he's dying!" It's quite different from feeling you're dying with him . . . we are all guilty of swimming in those waters. It is the essence of the problem. The number of tears does not matter — that is purely technical. The essence of sorrow is invisible. It is the color of air . . . and the texture of wind.

I'm on the board of the Actors Studio and we discuss this often . . . how do you "teach" it? Some actors think if they raise their emotions by some sort of manifest weeping that's the answer.

But more probably the answer is closer to speaking truthfully . . . if the emotions come, they are not seen but felt.

Do any of you read G. Spencer Brown or the other new philosophers about the observer and the observed? The observer tells you, "This is what I like. This is how I want to be presented to an audience, just this much and no more."

What does Shakespeare say? "Speak the speech, I pray you, as I pronounced it to you, trippingly on the tongue: but if you mouth it, as many of your players do . . ." And then he says, "Nor do not saw the air too much . . . but use all gently; for in the very torrent, tempest . . . the whirlwind of passion, you must acquire and beget a temperance that may give it smoothness." Shakespeare must have gotten tired of actors emoting and gesturing and shedding meaningless tears.

When you find the right balance and know that you're on the right track, it's a fine feeling. Here is a good notion: "Pay attention to your intention!" In other words, what are you up there for? You're there to get a point across. If it's difficult for you to get the point across because of an emotion that fires up under you, wait. You are not there to suffer. Hold back a little. Hold your cries. That is what happens to all of us when we are faced with grief or despair, or when we try to tell someone we miss them. Or hate them. An emotion sometimes leaps up like a panther and takes over. When that happens, you do your best to stifle it. Bring it under control. So it is on the stage.

My only sister was close to me. A few years ago at her funeral in Bermuda, I thought I was in control. But as I started to read the Scriptures, at the church service, I was suddenly hit. I couldn't read, or see, or hardly stand. From nowhere a river of memories welled up. I struggled to read the Scriptures, but I couldn't. As the Bible said: "By the waters of Babylon, I sat down and wept."

They are secret things, emotions. Too much time is spent in many acting schools concentrating on bringing those feelings up to the surface. You must be able to feel things, but you must also be able to tame them. So there again I have no words to tell how it is done, except what I call instinctive wisdom.

Would a good example along those lines be the performance of the late Peter Finch in Network? *He was on a very high key, but if he had scaled it down perhaps it wouldn't have been as effective.*

Or if he'd overdone it, it wouldn't have been effective. That's really the magic. To be able to give a bravura performance, as he did, is both difficult and fulfilling. It was a superb achievement, not only in light of the fact that it was his last, but because the impact was vivid and immediate. The stirring words by Chayefsky were a key element. Peter could have acted as well as he did with a lesser text and failed. But the author's words were significant. They had blazing power. When the message is limpid, it is better to speak quietly. That's the one rule you can be sure of.

There is a very, very moving moment in Rocky *when you go to ask him to take you on as his manager, and at the end of the scene when he turns his back and goes into the bathroom, you leave. Then we see the two of you talking on the street, but we never hear what you say — we just see it from a distance — and that said more than any words. Who made the decision to do that?*

John Avildsen, the director, shot it two ways, close and far, but I think he was wise to use the long shot. The average cutter is crazy about close-ups. Except for chase scenes, there are hardly any scenes with movement and space anymore. We will return to it, though. Witness *Dances with Wolves*.

You played so much on the stage in your early career and then came to the motion-picture business — did you at that time or do you at this time make any conscious adjustment?

Oh, yes, I know what you mean. Yes, you have to. Film requires a smaller projection, but equal energy. It's quite different. You don't need to project with a microphone, for example. Although all ''live'' stages are miked now, because actors are not used to projecting and audiences are not used to listening. They are accustomed to TV, where you can turn the volume up or down, or motion pictures where the volume is always loud. (They have to be, with all the popcorn-eating and the talking.) There is no difference in the quality, but there is in technique.

Certain actors can focus their feelings better than others. Their relaxation is so complete, their concentration so intense, they are like a magnifying glass that starts a fire from the sun, concentrating the beams. Some actors on stage need to talk no louder than a whisper, yet you hear them perfectly in the last row.

It is also true in motion pictures. The concentration, the whole mental commitment. Redford is excellent at this. He's finely tuned in to each idea. He doesn't take big chances, but what he does he does with total concentration. Stallone also. And Marlon Brando is the best of all. Even today, mostly retired, he can still do it, if he wants to. And if he gets the right material. There was nothing like his intensity in *Streetcar* and in *Waterfront*. Also, in *Last Tango in Paris*, the seething moments over the corpse. And, finally, *The Godfather*.

A Final Story:
The Girl with the Golden Eyes

S OME TIME ago a college offered me an honorary doctor's degree and asked me to make a speech. I went blank.

This sudden blockage of the creative process has happened to me many times before and I've never understood it. So I decided to talk about the blockage.

I began like this:

"It Will Happen to Most of Us." The Bible says it happened to Noah. When the rains started, Noah was confused and said:

"Lord! Lord! What shall I do? Shall I build a rudder?"

The Lord couldn't hear him because of the thunder, so Noah had to repeat it louder:

"A *rudder*, Lord. 'R' as in Robert, 'U' as in uncle — yes, Lord, a rudder."

But the Lord still couldn't hear or wouldn't hear, so Noah herded the animals onto the ark and sailed straight to Ararat. Without a rudder. Sheer luck.

It happens to everyone, big or little, saint or sinner, old or young, again and again and again. It's a hard problem to handle — when your brain stops working!

Here I was, giving an address at a college, and all I could think of to say at that melancholy moment was that I had absolutely nothing to say — no news, no advice, no ideas. I was in a dry spell. To quote the great playwright Samuel Beckett, I was "Waiting for Godot." I was empty-handed and empty-headed. Have any of the rest of you ever felt that way? If you haven't, you will.

Personally, the only hope I had was this:

I had been at this impasse many times before, and each time the crisis passed.

I have faced it when I was young and now that I'm older I'm still coming face-to-face with it. I have found, over the years, that if I am quiet and patient, it will pass.

I faced it when I left college many years ago. I was in utter despair then. I hope none of you is as despairing as I was. But you may be in the future.

I worked my way out of it somehow — and I'm sure you have done the same thing. And will again.

It comes and it goes, like the turning of the wheel.

Maybe I am developing a theme here. Maybe I have something to say to you after all.

Maybe what all of us are seeking is what Robert Frost called "a momentary stay against confusion."

I don't know what this particular day means to you — but for me it is a moment when I'm trying to make plans for the tail end of my life. I'm not saying my end is coming quickly; I'm simply saying that from here on in — my future is a hell of a lot shorter than my past.

This is somewhat different from your situation, of course.

You are full of futures.

The only thing that's finished with you is your childhood. And your home. In the strict sense you can never go home again, as Thomas Wolfe said.

As for me, what I've come to realize is that when you get older the future can be just as uncertain as it was when you left college at twenty-one or twenty-two. How's that for a comforting word? But it's part of the theme that's emerging as I talk.

As I've mentioned, my son and daughter are grown, with lives of their own, Jonathon as a musician and Tala as a painter. We all move about the globe. I notice my children and my wife have crises just as severe and just as often as I do. We try to help each other — except, of course, when we are all besieged at the same time. In that case, nobody's much help to anybody, even themselves.

So my theme is — like the seasons of the year, life changes frequently and drastically. You enjoy it or endure it as it comes and goes, as it ebbs and flows.

A few years ago, I was in New York City wandering around Central Park with Carroll O'Connor, more widely known as Archie Bunker. It was a beautiful day and the park was full of activity — break-dancing, marathon bicyclers, joggers, young girls and old men walking. It looked like a Breughel painting come to life. We stopped and watched for a long time — the sound of the merry-go-round in the background. Finally he said:

"Let's go home and find something to worry about."

We did. His television show had dominated the airways for many years. Now suddenly it was over! He felt lost. He had to begin all over. Strange situation. Like Churchill after World War II, when they threw him out of office.

Even Archie Bunker felt depressed, as all of us feel from time to time. Of course he went on to even greater glories. Contentment is a perishable commodity. That's what makes it precious. Some people call it "divine discontent."

And that is all the wisdom I've learned in all my years. Maybe that's all I'm supposed to learn.

To conclude, I've written a short, short story for you.

There once was a man who made such a success of his life and was so beloved that on his eightieth birthday important news reporters from all over the world gathered around him and begged him to reveal the secret of his splendid life. Here is what he said:

"The secret of a good life is the knowledge that all your problems will disappear and worse ones will take their place."

The reporters were unhappy with this downbeat statement and told the old man that an idea like that would not sell newspapers.

The wise old man smiled and said, "I see your point. Try this one; it is a riddle I learned from Don Juan; write it down correctly, please: The root of human distress is a sense of alienation from the natural order of the universe."

The reporters laughed nervously, not knowing what to make of that one. They didn't even bother to write it down. They thought he was stalling . . . and he was!

Then, a beautiful girl reporter with golden eyes (the old man had never seen golden eyes before) asked him: "Sir, what are the top priorities in the world today for young people?"

He replied, "There is but one priority for *all* people, young or old; you must know what the priority is, don't you?"

The beautiful girl with golden eyes said, "To bring peace and prosperity to the world?"

"That's the easy part, my dear."

She looked surprised. "And what is the hard part, please, sir?"

"To get rid of the war and poverty we have, to dispose of them. It will be as difficult to dispense with them as it was to build them."

"And in the meantime?" asked the beautiful golden-eyed girl. "What should we do?"

He looked at her a long time and then he said, "We need more people with golden eyes!"

"Thank you all very much," he told the reporters. "I am greatly honored."

Then he beckoned the lovely girl with the golden eyes, and very quietly whispered, "Would you like to have dinner with me tonight?"

My desk has just shifted beneath my pen as I write — the second aftershock this morning! Nineteen ninety-three was a challenging year. We survived the Malibu flood, fires, and now earthquakes. In between, I managed to complete work in two films (*Grumpy Old Men* with my friends Walter Matthau and Jack Lemmon, and *Tall Tales* for Disney). I don't know what tomorrow will bring — but so far, so good.

Index